NORTH ISLAND

TASMAN

SEA

SOUTH ISLAND

STEWART ISLAND

The Snares

Auckland Islands

Chatham Islands

Bounty Islands

Antipodes Islands

Campbell Islands

SOUTH PACIFIC OCEAN

TASMAN SEA

C. Farewell

Golden Bay
Collingwood

Takaka

D'Urville I.

TASMAN
BAY

Karamea

TASMAN
MTS.

Motueka

NELSON Picton

Richmond

Wairau

BLENHEIM

COOK STR

WELLINGTON

Awatere

L. Grassmere

C Campbell

Westport

C. Foulwind

Buller

R.

Murchison

KAIKOURA RANGES

Clarence R.

PAPAROA RA.

Reefton

SPENSER MTS.

Lewis
Pass

Kaikoura

Runanga

GREYMOUTH

Taramakau

Brunner

Hanmer

Waiau

Conway R

Parnassus

Hokitika

Waiau

Ross

Arthur's
Pass

Waipara

Hurunui

Franz Joseph Glacier
Fox Glacier

MT COOK

Oxford

L.
Coleridge

Kaiapoi

PEGASUS

Rangiora

Waimakariri

BAY

CHCH

Lyttelton Hb

Methven

Lincoln

BANKS
PENINSULA

Akaroa Hb

Haast
Jackson
Jackson Head Bay

SOUTHERN ALPS

L.
Tekapo

L. Fairlie

ASHBURTON

Geraldine

Ellesmere

CANTERBURY

Awarua Pt
Awarua Bay

Haast Pass

L.
Pukaki

Temuka

Rakaia

Rangitata

Milford Sound

Mt Aspiring

L.
Ohau

L.
Benmore

TIMARU

BIGHT

Bligh Sd.
George Sd.

Milford
Sound

Te Wanaka

L.
Hawea

Otematata

Waimate

Caswell Sd.

Queenstown

Cromwell

Ranfurly

Waitaki

...pson Sd.
...retary I.

L.
Wakatipu

The
Remarkables

Alexandra

OAMARU

...ul Sd.
...g Sd.

Kingston

Roxburgh

...sea
...Sd.

Manapouri

Lumsden

Palmerston

FIORDLAND

SOUTHLAND

Mosgiel

Otago Peninsula

L.
Monowai

Makarewa

Milton

DUNEDIN

L.
Hauroko

Winton

Gore

Balclutha

Taieri

Tuatapere
Riverton

Mataura

Wyndham

Kaitangata

Otatara

Clutha

Waiau

Oreti Beach

INVERCARGILL

Tokanui

FOVEAUX STR

Bluff

Mataura

Ruapuke

Paterson
Inlet

STEWART ISLAND

Port Pegasus

Southwest Cape

0   50   100
MILES

MEN
of the
MILFORD
ROAD

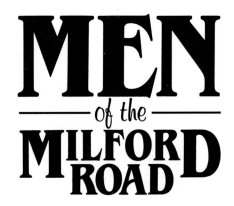

MEN
of the
MILFORD ROAD

Harold J. Anderson

Published by Craig Printing Co. Ltd, P.O. Box 99, Invercargill.

First Impression 1975 A. H. & A. W. Reed Ltd
Second Impression 1985 (ISBN 0 908629 17 6) Craig Printing Co. Ltd
Third revised and enlarged edition 1990 (ISBN 0-908629-27-3) Craig Printing Co. Ltd
Fourth revised and enlarged edition 1994 Craig Printing Co. Ltd

ISBN 0 908629 41 9

Printed and distributed by Craig Printing Co. Ltd,
67 Tay Street, Invercargill, New Zealand. 1994 106105

*Dedicated to my wife Lola
whose substantial contribution
made this book possible*

CONTENTS

LIST OF ILLUSTRATIONS

PREFACE

WHEN I RETIRED I realised I would need something to keep me occupied. What better than to think back on the many projects shelved in the past working years just on account of lack of time?

There were many of these, and some still remain as dreams for the future. One of the dreams ever with me was to write of that band of people who lived and worked in the wild and beautiful Eglinton, Hollyford and Cleddau Valleys.

On looking back I see these people as what might fairly be termed the last pioneer community in New Zealand. The very isolation of these valleys and the necessity of one person having to rely on another formed a bond between them which exists to this day.

It was this maintenance of contacts and friendships that enabled me to assemble much of the material for this book. And, what is more, it has again put me in closer contact with many of my old friends in the Valley.

I have had assistance from a very large number of people in writing this book and I wish to thank them all. In particular I must refer to Jim and Beryl Sutherland, Jack and Nell Dawson, John Christie, Duncan White, Mrs Jack Hodge, and the Ministry of Works and Development.

Again, with photos I have been very fortunate, and must in particular thank George Jones, John Christie, Kurt Suter, Jim Sutherland, Wilson & Horton Ltd., the staff of the Alexander Turnbull Library, and Bill Beattie.

Harold J. Anderson

18 Tremewan Street,
Linden, Tawa,
Wellington.

xi

NOTE

For sake of convenience the Hollyford Valley has been referred to as "The Upper Hollyford" (*Marian Corner to the Homer Tunnel*) and "The Lower Hollyford" (*Marian Corner to Martins Bay*)

INTRODUCTION TO SOUTHLAND

"GOOD-DAY MATE – how's she goin'?"

The speaker was a little man, muffled up in a long and very shabby overcoat, an overcoat which looked as if had been hanging in a stable or an old washhouse till its original black, grey or blue had faded into that indeterminate shade of green which modern colour consultants would probably describe as "antique" or perhaps "moss" green. This colour, nevertheless, was a very common one at that particular time – the mid 1930s – when the ownership of a warm coat was much more important than its colour, age or style.

I told the little man I was feeling pretty good, but in fact I was far from feeling good: I was right down in the dumps.

In the first place I'd been promised a job in Auckland – a city which I knew and liked, and where I had a number of friends. But then I'd been told it was on a relief scheme somewhere down in Southland, somewhere high up in the Southern Alps. With the winter approaching fast the prospects didn't seem too bright, but these were depression days and one took a job where it was offered and asked few questions.

The fact that winter was approaching was all too evident on this particular evening. Dunedin was experiencing a crackling frost and although I had just consumed a hot pie and a cup of coffee at the Railway refreshment room I was shivering like a half-set jelly.

Another reason for despondency was that, as far as I was aware, I didn't know a single soul in Southland. All in all I was cold, lonely, and somewhat homesick.

But I wasn't the only one with troubles: the little chap who had spoken to me also had something on his mind. He asked whether I was "on this train", and I gathered that he wanted to know whether I would be reboarding the train and going beyond Dunedin. On telling him that this was my intention he said "Yer wouldn't be goin' right through to Invercargill would yer?"

I assured him that this was exactly what I would be doing and with this his face lit up. "You'll do me, boy!" he said, and in the next breath he asked "Could yer do us a favour?"

Here it comes was my first thought, as in those days of depression a "touch for a bob" (one shilling) was not uncommon, and because of this and my own shortage of cash, I left this question unanswered.

The next thing the little fellow did was to shove a letter into my hand and in an appealing manner he said, "Then will yer post this as soon as yer get to Invercargill? My missus told me to post it before I left but I forgot. This letter's important, and she'll give me hell if she finds out."

"No trouble at all," I said, and I took the letter from him and shoved it in my pocket. At this stage it struck me that this was an opportunity to get a bit of first-hand information about Southland and the Hollyford Valley relief camp where I thought my job might be, so I told my little friend that I was going to a job in the Public Works Department (PWD) in Southland and asked him to tell me a bit about the area.

For the next ten minutes or so I was given a detailed list of the virtues of the province, with special emphasis on its wonderful climate. He must have used the expression "Sunny Southland" at least six times. His tone was so convincing that I felt that what he said must surely be correct, and when he went on to tell me about the warm sea current which runs along Oreti Beach, a few miles from Invercargill, I was even more encouraged.

I asked him about the Eglinton and Hollyford Valleys where I understood the PWD had established relief camps for the un-employed. He assured me that these valleys contained "the finest scenery in the whole world". After a bit of further questioning however, I was somewhat deflated to find that he had never visited either spot, but he assured me that many of his friends had visited or worked in these places and that what he said was true.

The fact that I was to be employed by the PWD seemed to please him greatly. "Good on yer, boy," was his comment. "I used to work for the old PWD on the Duck Creek job near Invercargill. Up to our bloody knees in mud most of the time – but I've been on worse jobs," he hastened to add. "We had a pretty good co-op contract gang on that job and we always made more than the ordinary relief rates."

He then wanted to know what sort of work I would be doing, but I had to confess that I was not sure, but it would be in the store or the office.

On hearing this he said he had heard that a number of new relief jobs were to be started by the PWD in Southland and that several new offices and camps were to be set up in various areas around the district. "Good opportunities there, boy," and then he leaned over in a confidential sort of way and said, "Do you know the very best job in the whole of the PWD?" I had to confess ignorance, so he proceeded to answer his own question. "It's the paymaster – he's the most important man in the whole outfit." He then told me of a few PWD paymasters he had known during his term with the Department and what good chaps they were.

"That's the job ·yer want to get," was his final summing-up. He then went on to say, "You'll like Sunny Southland, especially if yer like trampin' in the bush, it's the best bush in the whole world." To add a bit further to Southland's praises he said, "If yer like shootin' there's millions of rabbits, deer and pigs." At this I pricked up my ears as I had always been keen on shooting, though in the areas of the North Island where I had lived most of our pleasure on shooting trips came from the tramping, as there were generally more hunters than game in the areas we were able to visit.

"What about fishing?" I asked him.

"Tons!" was his reply.

He then went on to detail rivers – the Mataura, the Aparima, the Waiau, the Oreti, the Otapiri and so on, and it soon became apparent that on this subject he was at home and spoke with authority. For quite a time he poured out a wealth of information on fishing but all too soon it was time for me to board the train, and as

---

[U.B.—132.

UNEMPLOYMENT BOARD, NEW ZEALAND.

Registration Card for Unemployment and other Relief.

Issued from **PETONE** *Bureau.*

YOU ARE REQUIRED TO PRESENT THIS CARD WHEN APPLYING FOR RELIEF.

These Unemployment Board cards were common in the 1930's. Interesting extracts from the back of this card are:–

5–7–34 Unemployment Board boots type A/5 issued.
24–12–34 Xmas grant
2–2–35 Weekly work ration 21 hours. Weekly earnings 28/–
20–3–35 On No. 5 Scheme – P.W. Dept. Wainui Hill.

Mr E.H. King

3

I did so my little friend again remembered his letter, and his final words were, "Don't forget that letter, boy – post it as soon as yer reach Invercargill." At this stage the guard blew his whistle and my companion waved and was lost in the crowd as the train moved off.

I returned to the warmth of the carriage and began to think about the little man in his long faded coat. What was his wife like? I felt sure she would be big and fat, as more often than not little men seem to have large plump wives. Would she really give him hell if she found out he hadn't posted the letter? What was so important about it? Who was it addressed to? Why did it have to be posted in Invercargill? At this point my hand automatically slid into my pocket and I drew out the crumpled envelope, which was addressed in large scrawling handwriting to a Mr Fishbonder, and at this point I began to wonder whether I had done an improper thing in looking at the name and address, and I pondered on this for quite a time.

Then I fell to thinking over the things the little fellow had told me, and as I did so my spirits began to rise. Perhaps this "Sunny Southland" mightn't be so bad after all? Instead of going to some dreary relief job perhaps I was starting a new and exciting period in my life? I liked this thought and kept turning it over and over in my mind. My whole mood had now changed and these happier thoughts, the warmth of the carriage, and the monotonous clicking of the rails finally began to have their effect and I dozed off.

At the Invercargill station I collected my bags and stepped out on to the platform. The hard frost at Dunedin had nothing on that at Invercargill, and my first few breaths seemed to freeze my lungs. Nevertheless I remembered that I had promised to post that letter, and I had just shoved it into a post box when a voice said "Hullo, Harold – what are you doing in this part of the world?"

I looked up to see a tall rangy young chap in his mid twenties.

"Good day, Stan," was the only reply I could manage for a few moments. It was Stan Scott, an old rowing clubmate I hadn't seen for some time past, and I still remember the thrill of meeting him so unexpectedly.

In a few seconds we got ourselves sorted out and I told him how I happened to be in Invercargill that evening. He told me he'd been moving around the country working at his trade and shifting jobs from time to time. Fortunately he had not so far been out of a job. "You know me, Harold – I settle down for a while and then I get itchy feet and move on."

After a few minutes in filling in the essential gaps in our history Stan told me that he'd met the most wonderful girl in the town and had become engaged. I said this might be a cure for his itchy feet, and he didn't disagree.

4

He then wanted to know where I was staying for the night. I told him the address of the private hotel and he helped me carry my bags to this place which was quite handy to the station.

I wasted no time in booking in at the hotel and getting into bed and was greatly surprised and pleased to find that there was a large stone hot-water bottle tucked in at the foot of my bed. In the modern era of electric blankets this may not sound much of a luxury, but on that particular evening this small thing added to my feeling of wellbeing, and it wasn't long before I was sound asleep.

2

A FROSTY MORNING

I WOKE EARLY next morning to find that there had been an exceptionally heavy frost, and after a good breakfast I decided to have a quick walk around to familiarise myself with the town. After walking around for quite a while I decided that it was getting near time to show up at the Public Works office, so I headed down Tay Street in the general direction of the Government Buildings. As I neared the intersection of Tay and Dee Streets I could see that quite a fair crowd had assembled there. Every now and then there was a roar of laughter and at this early hour, on such a freezing morning, this intrigued me, so off I went for a "look-see".

These two streets are at right angles to each other and they meet at a War Memorial so placed that traffic proceeding down Tay Street had to go round behind it to turn the right angle into Dee Street. It was at this point that the crowd had assembled and I was soon to find out what they were laughing at.

The street on the far side of the Memorial sloped away from it rather than towards it, and this necessitated a slow turn at the best of times. On this particular morning however the frost had resulted in very extensive icing of the sloping corner and this was having a devastating effect on cyclists.

As I arrived I could see all eyes turned up Tay Street, and when I looked that way I could see a young chap coming towards us on a racing bike with those long, curly low-slung handlebars. He had a scarf around his neck and his hands were well covered by leather gloves, but even these gloves were apparently insufficient to keep his hands warm as he was riding "no hands" and had his arms folded for extra warmth. The excitement of the crowd could almost be felt as he approached the corner and – what the spectators no doubt hoped for – the sudden skid.

This young chap however, had not been born yesterday and must have sensed that something was amiss, as he very slowly unfolded his arms and leant forward and took a firm grasp of the handlebars. At the same time he slowly reduced speed as he approached the corner. The disappointment of the onlookers was intense and even to this day I feel ashamed to think that I shared these sentiments with them. The world likes a trier however, and

6

there was a bit of handclapping and cheering. The lad smiled and raised his hand to wave to those applauding his sagacity – and before he realised it he and his bike were skidding over the icy patch in different directions. Once more the crowd were convulsed with laughter. The young rider also appreciated the joke and as he picked himself up he joined in the laughter, and, after parking his bike, mingled with the group of onlookers to await the next victim.

The next to come down the road were several young women. Whether or not Southland young ladies had an extra in-built sense I don't know, but all were pedalling very slowly and managed to dismount before reaching the turn. Nevertheless the crowd showed its appreciation by giving them a cheer, and once again all eyes turned up the street looking for the next victim.

They didn't have long to wait for the next cyclist, and he proved to be a butcher's boy.

As I write this it strikes me that I haven't seen a real live butcher's boy for many many years past so I digress for a word or two of explanation. In years past every butcher's shop had a butcher's "boy". These boys had two distinguishing badges of office: first was the familiar dark blue-and-white striped butcher's apron, generally half a dozen sizes too large; and second was the bicycle, fitted with a massive iron frame over the front wheel. Into this frame went a huge split-cane basket with an enormous handle on it. Inside the basket were the customers' orders, all neatly wrapped up in off-white paper. On each parcel was the recipient's name and address, always written in indelible pencil, together with a list of the prices of each article and a final total of the amount due.

It was one of the duties of the butcher's boy to make deliveries to customers, as in those days few went shopping in their own cars, and few retailers had delivery vans. For some reason or another the wages of a butcher's boy seemed to remain static at something like ten shillings a week. As time went on the butcher's boy was absorbed into the shop staff and took over more important duties such as sweeping the sawdust off the floor or scrubbing the massive section of a tree trunk which acted as the butcher's chopping block.

As this particular butcher's boy approached the corner he appeared to sense that a spill was expected of him so he accelerated and was apparently going to do a well-controlled broadside, thus fooling the onlookers. But fate was against him. In fact he didn't even get as far as the corner, as the effort put into speeding up was enough to throw him off balance. Over he went, bike, bag, apron, meat, butcher's paper and all.

Unlike the lad on the racing bike, the butcher's boy could not have been in the happiest of moods and he found little joy in the situation. He propped his bike up against the gutter and started to pick up his parcels, and as he did so some of the meat started to fall out of its flimsy paper wrapping. This annoyed him even further but it added greatly to the amusement of the crowd. The final package retrieved was a huge bundle of sausages and instead of coming up as a single unit the various strings started to slide out of his hands. By this time the boy was seething with rage and he virtually wrapped his arms round all the sausages and flung them into the basket as hard as he could. With this he pushed his bike down the street and the crowd settled down again.

As time went on there were a few more casualties and passers-by kept joining and leaving the crowd. Things now took a somewhat serious turn, as the next person cycling along the road was a youth with a sizeable pane of glass under his arm. The crowd grew quiet and several attempted to warn the lad, but it was of no use however, and over he went. The pane of glass broke into hundreds of pieces but fortunately the boy was not hurt. This was the signal for the crowd to disperse, and an onlooker said he would phone the Council and ask for sand to be spread on the road. He explained to me that this was the usual procedure on this corner on a frosty morning but apparently on this particular day there had been an omission on somebody's part.

As I headed off down the street I struck up a conversation with one of the onlookers who had been standing near me for some time, and we had a further laugh over one or two of the spills.

On my way down the street after leaving the hotel I had located the Government Buildings but as yet did not know exactly where the Public Works office was situated. In the circumstances I asked my companion and he said he was himself going into the Government Buildings and would show me the office. As we reached the building he indicated a door and I was rather surprised to find that he accompanied me into the PWD office. In fact he did more than this; he went into another door and after a second or so he appeared behind the counter and with a large grin on his face he put out his hand and said "Welcome to the PWD!"

I had met my future boss.

For a while he enquired about my past experience and then went on to tell me of the various construction works being carried out by the PWD in the area.

The story told me by my little friend on the Dunedin station to the effect that a number of new relief jobs were being opened was substantially correct, and extra staff were being assembled to cope with this increase of activities. At the time I arrived the jobs which the various recruits would occupy had not been settled.

The main job under way was the completion of the "Milford Road", which at that time the Department called the Lumsden –

8

Invercargill Government Buildings of the 1930's. "Welcome to the PWD!" grinned the author's new boss.

Free Lance Collection, Alexander Turnbull Library

Te Anau – Milford Sound Main Highway. This had been completed through the Eglinton Valley and the main job still to be done was the section in the Hollyford Valley – about eight miles. The Homer Tunnel had to be driven and the balance of the road from the tunnel to Milford Sound – about eleven miles – had to be constructed. The tunnel itself had just been started.

Construction camps had been set up in the Hollyford Valley and at Milford Sound. The tunnel was to be driven from the Hollyford Valley end and the idea was that the road and bridges on the Milford side would be completed to more or less coincide with the completion of the tunnel. The roadwork on the West Coast side was commenced at Milford Sound and was proceeding inland towards the tunnel site eleven miles up the Cleddau Valley.

My new boss went to no end of trouble to show me through bundles of departmental photos and maps, and what I saw convinced me that Southland was, without a doubt, a scenic wonderland – a conclusion which was substantiated on hundreds of occasions as I got to know the district in the years ahead.

Following a description of the PWD jobs in Southland and the general geography of the province, my new boss surprised me by asking if I had any preference as to the job I would like to work on

9

and he again ran over the various existing and projected jobs, particularly mentioning the Marian Camp in the Hollyford Valley and the Milford Sound Camp. As I have already said, the tunnel at that time had only just been begun, and Milford Sound must have been the most isolated spot in New Zealand. The only access in the winter time was by boat and the trip was made from Bluff. One has only to read of Captain Cook's exploits in this area to know of the perils of these seas.

I take my hat off to the departmental employees who braved those hazardous trips. The boats chartered by the Department to do these trips were the *Tamatea* (Captain Hamilton) – well known on the Stewart Island run – the *Kekeno* (Captain Roderique) and the *Ranui* (Captain Thompson). The fact that a life was never lost on these trips is a credit to the discipline and seamanship of these Bluff mariners and their crews.

But I am jumping ahead of events and must return to the point where my boss was sounding me out as to where I would like to work. Jobs in those days were hard to get and I was somewhat loath to make a choice, so I said I'd prefer him to make the decision. He didn't press the matter; and later in the morning he made a point of introducing me to the various people who make up a Public Works office – engineers, architects, overseers, storemen, survey staff, foremen, draughtsmen, and so on.

On this day my new boss had planned to visit a number of jobs around Invercargill itself, and he said it would be a good idea for me to go with him so that I could see what was going on in the area. He also wanted me to meet the staff men in charge of the various works.

When we set out on this trip my immediate boss, who was the chief clerk, said I was to call him by his christian name. This was unheard of in my previous jobs, as in those days of depression the man in charge was always looked up to with the greatest respect and, in offices particularly, was invariably referred to as "Mr" So-and-so. In fact many people addressed senior staff as "Sir".

I soon found out however, that the use of christian names in the PWD resulted in no loss of respect for senior staff, nor did it lessen their ability to control staff under them. In telling me to use christian names the boss went on to say: "The discipline in this Department is mainly self-discipline. We treat you like a man and expect you to act as one. We don't breathe down your neck. What we do is to give you a maximum amount of responsibility and plenty of work and ample scope for initiative. If you're any good you come up with the answers".

I thought this to be as fair a proposition as one could ever hope for and my spirits, which had been boosted on the previous evening, continued to rise. I stress again that these were depression days, and in many jobs staffs were treated more or less as mere chattels.

I met a large number of staff that day and there was a friendly attitude everywhere I went. There was a warmth of welcome in that southern town. I failed to find the gloomy depression attitude so common elsewhere throughout the country and this first day's impressions were confirmed in the months ahead. It was as if a new world had opened to me and as time went on I found this to be exactly what had happened. For me the gloom and fear of the depression years were over.

By the time we got home that evening the boss had decided that for some months he would keep me employed in the Invercargill office and that the question of my going out to one of the construction jobs would be left over.

As I had met up with Stan, who was working in Invercargill, this suited me down to the ground and when I met him that evening he arranged for me to get accommodation at the house where he was boarding. He also took me around and introduced me to his fiancée, a lovely red head, and to her mother and father and other members of the family. Here again I was given the warmest welcome, and by the time the evening was over I had good friends, good accommodation, a promising job, and a growing regard for "Sunny Southland".

In bed that evening my thoughts went back to the little fellow I had met at Dunedin on the previous night and all the good things he had had to say about Southland. Over the years I have often recalled this meeting and the change of heart which it triggered off, and the exciting and happy days spent in New Zealand's "deep south" – halcyon days – nostalgic memories!

3

GETTING BROKEN IN

FOR SOME WEEKS I had a variety of jobs. I filed vouchers away, entered details of hours worked on a system of cards, helped the storeman to take a physical count of his stock and then to reconcile this physical count with the stores shown on his cards. This seemed a never-ending job and many and devious were the methods used to adjust surpluses and deficiencies.

Another job I helped on was the ordering of materials. The storeman used to phone firms for quotes for various items and, when received, these quotes were set out on long lists and a decision made on which quote would be accepted.

I well remember the first letter I had to deal with on this job. I opened it up and it was handwritten and went something like this –

> Hollyford Valley
> Date................
> Snowing like Hell.

It then went on to detail various requirements and finished up "Please do this pronto."

Such profanity and levity in official correspondence was quite new to me. I had previously worked in a starchy semi-legal office, simply loaded with red tape. Every letter was beautifully typed, then vetted by the man next up in the "pecking-order". He would invariably have it redrafted, retyped and submitted to the next up in the pecking-order, and so on. Finally the letter would be despatched, and it was odds on that the ultimate product would be near enough to the first effort submitted by the office boy. Perfection in everything was all that was required and one can just imagine what a strained working atmosphere this created.

In contrast, I found that the PWD staff had an enormous volume of work to attend to, and down-to-earth practical methods were the only way of getting results.

I found that all branches of the Department had to work with each other and despite busy days there was a friendly attitude throughout. And, what's more, there was always time for a bit of fun or a practical joke.

I well remember an early experience of this. I had been working in the stores section for only a few days and had to take a great bundle of quotations into the storekeeper for approval. He took the quotes from me and while he was studying them I noticed a very highly polished circular brass grease-cap lying on his table, of the type used on bearings of older kinds of machinery. The idea was to unscrew the top off the cap and remove it from the cylindrical body, fill the cap with grease, and then lightly screw the top back on. In practice the whole thing would be mounted adjacent to a bearing and all that was necessary to inject grease into the bearing was to screw the top of the cap down a couple of threads, and this would force grease through a small aperture into the bearing.

Having nothing to do while the storekeeper was looking at the quotations, I picked up the object in my left hand, and with my right hand I screwed the top of the cap down a couple of turns. It was a beautifully made article and could well have been off an old Rolls Royce. There was practically no friction in the thread at all, so I screwed it down a bit further and all of a sudden there was a distinctly squelchy noise and there, neatly in the palm of my left hand, was a curly blob of grease about the size of a five-cent piece. Not only did that grease cap look to be a very well made article, but it had proved itself to be fully operational. This was due to the fact that Joe, the storekeeper, had skilfully loaded it with the finest grease. All then that was necessary was for some mug to come along and start fiddling with it, and he paid the penalty. I was just another mug.

I was somewhat shamefaced as I looked at the blob of grease in my palm, but Joe merely looked up and said, "Don't worry, you are only the sixty-seventh who has done that," and he opened his drawer and pulled out a "tell-tale sheet" numbered 1–100 and put a line through number 67. At the same time he pulled out a roll of toilet tissue, tore off a strip, and handed it to me to wipe my hand on. As I took it he pointed to his wastepaper basket to indicate where the used tissue should be deposited.

He then spent a few seconds very carefully reloading and resetting the grease cap and placed it on his table. At this point he said that this trick had recently backfired on him, as one of the local MPs had been in his office and, like me, had fallen for the trick. Joe said that the MP., like the late Queen Victoria, was "not amused".

It was only a few days after this that word was received from Head Office that the main relief jobs in the district were to be stepped up to take more men and that a number of new works were to be started up. This in turn meant that the pay section, in particular, would have an immediate large increase in work. Because of this my boss told me that I was to remain at the Invercargill office and would be put on to the pay section. In due course I would be expected to be fully responsible for this section of the work.

In most concerns, in those days, pays were quite a simple procedure. A man worked perhaps for 40 hours per week at say 1s 6d per hour, which would be 60s, and from this his tax would be deducted and he was paid the balance.

On the PWD relief jobs things were different. In the first case a workman would be sent to the job by the Labour Department, which would pay his fare – say £2. This amount would have to be deducted from the man's wages and refunded to the Labour Department. On jobs such as the Hollyford Valley works there would be a canteen, a cookhouse, a store etc., and if the workman dealt with these, his purchases would all have to be deducted from his wages.

To give an idea of the complexity of the pays, here is a list of the various items that were deductible from workmen's day wages on the Hollyford Valley (Homer Tunnel) job:

Unemployment tax and quarterly levy of 7s 6d
Fares advanced
Canteen purchases
Half-pay allotments to wife
Court order deductions for dependants
Union dues
Cookhouse dues
Repayment of wage advances made by Department
Deductions to private shopkeepers etc. authorised by the workman
Departmental charges for electricity, coal, wood and other stores
Deductions for stores lost, e.g. gumboots
Hollyford Valley Medical Association deductions

On the Hollyford Valley job and at Milford Sound all the men lived on the job and were totally reliant on the Department to supply all their wants. They bought their stores at the canteen on credit, and most of them had quite a number of the deductions referred to above taken off each payday.

It was a Departmental rule that the pays were to be made not later than eight working days after the end of a pay period. This meant that when a pay period closed on a Friday night, the time-books would have to be filled in and totalled, and all the deductions would have to be calculated and tabulated after the end of the period. This usually involved the staff on the construction job working the whole of the weekend. The idea was to get all of their timebooks and lists of deductions ready for despatch to Invercargill by a special delivery, which would probably reach Invercargill about Wednesday evening. Three working days were thus gone already, and not a jot yet done at the Invercargill office. Assuming the paysheets were available first thing on Thursday morning,

A typical co-op gang of the 1930's, near The Divide. Bill Flanagan (*left*) and Ginger Krause (*bottom centre*)

Weekly News, Bill Beattie photo

which often was not the case, this left five working days in which the Invercargill pay staff had to check the additions and calculations in the timebooks, check the thousands of canteen and other dockets, write out wages sheets for several hundred men, make the multitude of deductions I have spoken of above, and balance the sheets. Then there were the envelopes to be made out, the money had to be drawn from the bank and put in these envelopes, and they had to balance out at the end.

All of this was done with a shoestring staff, and the general rule was that when a big pay came in, the whole of the Invercargill office accounts staff would be co-opted if necessary. The usual thing was for overtime to be worked every night from when the paysheets came in to the office till the pay left for the job on the following Wednesday.

If there were holdups, and these were not infrequent, staff often worked overtime on the Saturday and Sunday. These were depression days and we were not paid for overtime.

In briefly trying to give an idea of the pay procedures, I have referred only to day-wages men. This was just for the sake of simplicity. However, the PWD had a system of incentive payments termed "co-operative contracts", or "co-op" contracts for short. This involved the formation of a workmen's co-op gang which elected a "headman". This gang would then take on work on a piecework basis. For example, they might take a contract for the excavation of 1,000 cubic yards of rock at so much per cubic yard. The idea of course, was that a good gang, working well, could then earn at a rate considerably above day wages. There were a host of variations and rules involving such things as payment for extras, and what should happen if the Department took a man off his contract etc. Other items were special allowances for the headman etc. These were many and varied and do not really matter, but the co-op contracts were also subject to the many deductions I have referred to above.

The general way in which a co-op contract was dealt with was for the engineer, at the end of the pay period, to have a "measure-up". This meant that he physically measured up the amount of rock excavated in the period, to take the example I have quoted above. If it was 300 cubic yards, he would work out the gross amount payable to the gang at so much a yard, and off this amount would be taken the cost of explosives supplied etc. and the resultant amount would then be apportioned between the gang according to the hours each man had worked. From each man's share would be taken his personal deductions for canteen, coal etc., and the balance, if any, would then be paid to him. I say "if any", because it was not uncommon for a new man coming on to the job to have so much owing to the Department for fares, canteen purchases to stock the larder etc., that he might not have any surplus to draw in cash for a month or two.

When the co-op contract men were being paid the headman received a copy of the co-op sheets which detailed the work they had done and the amount due to them. It also showed every item deducted and the final amounts payable to each man. This sheet also showed one very important figure, which was *the amount per hour* the contract gang had made for the period. This of course, was the yardstick. If the day wages rate for labouring was 1s 6d per hour, and the gang made 2s 1½d per hour there could be great joy in the gang. As the rate per hour increased or decreased, so did the degree of joy experienced.

In making up pays in those days, we had no calculating machines. Our only mechanical aids were adding machines and the books of tables to calculate day wages. All the intricate split-up of co-op contracts was done with a stub of a red Royal Sovereign pencil – plainly marked "New Zealand Government".

For the next few weeks I was the busiest young man in Invercargill and, not having worked with figures since I left school, I had plenty of leeway to make up. In due course I got the hang of things and started taking out the pays on the small jobs around Invercargill.

During this period, my room-mate Stan had introduced me to a number of his friends and their hospitality was overwhelming. One long weekend his fiancée's family took us for a trip through Central Otago and the experiences we had – seven of us in a large old-fashioned Buick – are still spoken of when we happen to meet up again.

4

MY FIRST HOLLYFORD PAY

MY BOSS CALLED me into his office one morning and told me that in future I would take over full control of the pay section and make all the large pays personally. This would involve my travelling to the Hollyford Valley by car or runabout once every two weeks and making shorter trips to places within an eighty-mile radius of Invercargill.

The return trip to the Hollyford Valley, with side runs to Lumsden and Lake Manapouri and later down the Lower Hollyford road, was about 380 miles, and the time taken on the trip varied from about twenty-two hours to four days depending on a variety of circumstances, the most important being the weather.

The roads were metalled for practically the whole distance, and generally the surface was of about six to eight inches of loose shingle.

For a start it was a frightening experience to be driven over this shingle at about 60 mph, as one gained the impression that the car was not fully under control – particularly when cornering. After a while however one's confidence returned as this shingle was quite negotiable to experienced drivers. One feature that was impossible to get used to was the dust which plagued us in dry weather.

The timebooks and all the other paraphernalia for my first pay duly arrived in Invercargill and naturally I was a bit anxious that everything should go ahead on schedule. I was still quite in-experienced and slow on the job but the lads in the office rallied round, and by the middle of the following week the pay was finished and ready to take away. Early in the week I made enquiries about who would drive the pay car and I was told that the resident engineer who was in charge of the Invercargill office would be going with me and I should arrange matters with him. I had only spoken to him on a few occasions and was certainly a bit nervous when I went in to see him. I said I understood he would be going with me and I wanted to know when he wished to leave. He then said to me, "Mr Anderson, you're running the pay trip and I'll be ready at any time that will suit you."

I was taken aback somewhat at this, coming from the senior man in the district, but said I would be ready to leave the office on Wednesday morning at 8 am.

I was there at 6.30 am and twiddled the combination lock on the safe, mumbling to myself something like, "36 left, 28 right, 34 left, flick her over and open she comes."

I then checked over everything that I required – paybag, paysheets, spare copies of co-op contract sheets, timebooks for the new pay, a supply of sharpened copying pencils etc. All-important was a hard-covered surveyor's field notebook as in this I had noted about fifty things to be done on the trip as well as a standard checklist of all things to be taken up with me.

I had been warned that in the past the pay cars had sometimes left Invercargill and done the 100 miles to Te Anau and, when the first man was to be paid, it had been discovered that the folder of paysheets or some other vital item had been left behind. This of course involved a return trip, and there was no joy in that.

Fortunately nothing like this happened and we got away on time. The resident engineer was W.G. Pearce, or Big Bill as the men on the job called him when talking among themselves. The staff generally referred to him as "W.G."

As I was loading up the pay car he was sitting there rolling innumerable cigarettes and carefully packing them in a tobacco tin which he placed beside him on the front seat of the car.

We had a Ford V8 sedan which even in those days was a very good performer, and I soon had it loaded and off we went. Nothing was said until we got out of the town and then "W.G." said, "You know, Mr Anderson, there's quite a chance on long pay trips like this that we could be held up and robbed. If we are, my own private view is that a live civil servant is better than a dead hero." He did not elaborate or say any more; he just lapsed into a silence which was broken only when I spoke to him. Naturally I found this one-way communication a bit difficult to cope with and I too kept quiet. I noticed however that he was very bright and affable when talking to Tom Plato the overseer at our first stop, which was Te Anau, and he introduced me to Tom saying, "This is Mr Anderson, the new paymaster."

I was surprised at his using the term paymaster as I had not heard this used since I was spoken to by my chance acquaintance at Dunedin on my way to Invercargill. In the Public Works office the term pay clerk was used, but in the field I learned that it was invariably "the paymaster" and I was to find that on isolated jobs such as we were visiting, the paymaster was a man of high status who had a quite unique relationship with workmen on the job. He was a go-between the men and the "Establishment". He was not reckoned as one of the staff men out on the job who came in daily contact with the workmen and had to exercise control and discipline. This, combined with the isolation, could engender frictions and the workmen were at times not on the best of terms with some of the staff. I think this particularly applied to staff engineers who were responsible for measuring-up co-op contracts and setting rates for co-op contract work. Naturally the men wanted the rates to be high and the engineers had to keep them at least to a reasonable figure: here was a fertile ground for disagreement.

The New Zealand Workers' Union was also a force on these jobs and sometimes it would agree with the Department against a worker and on other occasions it would support his case. This also could engender a bit of friction between the men and the union. Here again the paymaster was not closely involved with the local union and a workman felt he could discuss any point with the paymaster and expect to get an unbiassed answer. The above of course is written with hindsight, and on that particular morning at Te Anau I was certainly not so equipped.

I quickly paid the half dozen or so men at Te Anau and as soon as I was finished the boss started up the car and we set off around the edge of Lake Te Anau on the eighteen-mile trip to Te Anau Downs station. Again there was a long period of silence, and every now and then the tin of pre-rolled cigarettes would be opened with one hand and one extracted. This was lit from an electric lighter in the V8 – quite a novelty in those days.

I was not aware of the names of the surfacemen whom we would encounter in the next thirty miles or so, but these were "old trusties" and well known to my companion. He would break the silence by saying something like "Gus McGregor will be the next," and I would extract Gus's envelope from the 800 or 900 others packed in alphabetical order in slots in the suitcase used as a paybag. Some workmen would have a number of envelopes as they might have had a spell on day wages and been in one or more co-op contracts in the pay period.

The paysheets on which the workmen signed were numbered from 1 to about 150 and each envelope had the paysheet number written on it. What I had to do on meeting a man was to ascertain his name. I then picked out the envelopes with his name on them. The first envelope would show say number 16 on the top left corner and another, say number 48. This meant that the workmen had to sign two paysheets – numbers 16 and 48. The sheets were in a springback folder and I would flip them over to page 16 and would hand him the first envelope, but only after he had signed. I then flipped the sheets over to page 48 and the same procedure applied.

It will thus be realised that even a delay of a minute or less on each stop would multiply as hundreds of men were paid, and it was my aim – particularly when we knew who we were approaching – to have the envelopes in my hand, the paysheets open at the

The road enters the Hollyford Valley. Part of the Marian camp is visible below the car. Date *circa* 1936.

"Making NZ" Collection, Alexander Turnbull Library

correct spot, the side window down, and a pencil ready to hand to the payee. It was still hard, however, not to spare time for a few words to a surfaceman who rarely had any contact with the outside world.

As we left Te Anau Downs station, we struck inland, crossed the Retford Stream and proceeded up the famous Eglinton Valley, paying surfacemen as we went. At Knobs Flat we met surfaceman Alf Alcock, who was almost as well known as the wild and beautiful valley in which he lived. I well remember this occasion. As he was talking to us he was holding his shovel out at arm's length, when a bush robin perched on the end of it and sat there for quite a while – completely unworried by our presence.

Leaving Alf we went on a bit further and came to the sawmill, which was under the control of head sawyer Nick Ward. From then on we started to meet up with various gangs and at Cascade Creek, which was a sizeable camp, we spent some time paying the men.

After leaving Cascade Creek we paid small gangs as we went. I had still failed to break through the silence when we were on our own but was introduced to quite a number of the gangers and foremen who were well known to "Big Bill".

Finally we came to the Marian camp in the Hollyford Valley which at that time was the headquarters for the whole construction job. It was about eight miles from the Marian camp, by the most precipitous access track to the upper end of the Hollyford Valley, which was the point where the Homer Tunnel was ultimately pierced.

When we reached the Marian camp I was introduced to the local engineer-in-charge, and also to the other staff members including timekeeper Dan Campbell who afterwards invariably accompanied me when I paid the men in the Hollyford Valley. Dan took me round the camp and we paid as many men as possible. By this time work had finished and we got ready for the evening meal which we were to have at the staff mess.

Mr Pearce and I were accommodated in the 10ft. × 8ft. guest hut, which had two bunks – one above the other. He said, "We'll toss for positions," and he flipped a coin. I called "heads" and he said without batting an eyelid, "You're right – you get the top bunk." I sensed then that this tall rangy quiet man might be something of a humourist.

It was a fine but very cold evening and we had enjoyed clear weather all the way up. Judging by this first trip, one would never have suspected the vagaries of climate which could be encountered in this area.

We lined up for dinner and, as ever on these trips, I had to lug the paybags with me wherever I went as there was no safe in which they could be stored.

We had a discussion after dinner and decided it would be pointless trying to make any further pays up the road as the men would all be in their huts. It was for this reason that on most future occasions, I left Invercargill at 4 am so that we virtually started our day's work at 8 am at Te Anau, which was about 100 miles on our journey. This left us a full day to catch the men while they were working.

It was usual for the Hollyford staff to gather in the staff mess of an evening and there were a few diversions. Some played cards or chess but generally they chatted, and I was to learn that many and varied were the stories that were told of an evening.

There was generally a considerable amount of lighthearted leg-pulling, and this particular evening I could see that something was going on, but I couldn't quite make out what it was. A couple of the chaps said to Dan Campbell the timekeeper, "You look a bit tired tonight, Dan, you should get to bed early." Dan assured them that he was OK and no more was said. A bit later Dan said to me, "There are a few things I'd like to talk to you about. I wonder if you'd come over to my hut?" This was apparently what the crowd

22

Problems are discussed at Marian camp. *Left to right*: plant overseer Harry Morgan, engineer-in-charge John Christie, resident engineer W.G. ("Big Bill") Pearce.

Hazledine, Invercargill

Dan Campbell, ever proud of his "Men of the Road", with Valerie Walker at the *de luxe* post office, Marian camp.

Weekly News, Bill Beattie photo

had been waiting for and I could see a few sly winks. I was to learn later that Dan, who was a perfectionist in everything relating to his job, invariably got newcomers aside and gave them a thorough briefing so that there would be no room for any misunderstandings. It was the prediction by the men that Dan would do this that had amused them earlier.

When we got to Dan's hut he asked me what my christian name was. I said "Harold." "O, that won't do," was his reply. "That's a bit too fancy – like Clarence or Cuthbert. We'll call you Harry," and from that date on I was Harry out on that job.

The next thing he wanted to know was whether I had a good oilskin coat and I told him I had a butterfly cape. "Not good enough," he said. "The weather here can be cruel. We've just got some very high quality full length Le Roy oilskins in the store and in the morning I'll get them to issue you with one." This he did, and he also arranged for me to be issued with new thigh and knee gumboots and a powerful five-cell torch.

Dan was a short, thickset man of middle age who had "been around" and held good jobs. He was fanatically attached to the job and to "The Valley" and given any choice of jobs I doubt whether he would have ever left the Hollyford. I was to find out that he was a most indefatigable worker, and a perfectionist. It was nothing for him to work all night at the end of a pay period, getting his day-wages and contract timebooks ready for despatch to the Invercargill office. Dan was known and respected by the men on the job and the large numbers of tourists who visited this valley.

For several hours that evening he briefed me on every possible facet of the job. He told me of the way in which the workmen regarded him, the engineers, the union, the paymaster etc. He said that in the eyes of the men, I, as paymaster, would be the most important staff man on the job and that they would often come to me as an intermediary. He also said that they would rely heavily on me, as they did on him, for contacts with their relatives away from the job. He stressed that on each trip I would be asked to do many things beyond what might reasonably be expected of me. "You just can't avoid it," was how he summed it up, and I found he was right.

He recommended that I should interpret the New Zealand Workers' Agreement fairly and said that he adopted the attitude that if a point could reasonably be construed to be in the worker's favour it should be granted. If not, he was equally emphatic that it should be stoutly refused.

He then went on to tell of the types of people who were employed on the job. There was a complete cross-section – accountants, bank officials, labourers, carpenters, tunnellers – many of them victims of the depression – though some were there by choice. Many were happy to have quit a job to which they were unsuited, and quite a number found the outside life both pleasing and peaceful. Dan said that by and large these people, despite all their difficulties, were reasonably happy and my experience over a number of years was that there was a lot of truth in this. Perhaps it is that the human animal can show great fortitude in the face of want and adversity, whereas in a state where things come easy, he tends to appreciate them less?

Dan then went on to tell me of many incidents – some funny, some fantastic, some tragic. He told me of the qualities of some of the men, and forecast that many would leave the job when times improved, much the better for the experience they had gained.

He finished by saying, "History is being made by what I call the 'Men of the Road'. There are future leaders in the men passing through this job, and some will achieve fame. Children are being reared here, and men will die here."

I was to find on future trips that these get-togethers of an evening in the staff mess were part and parcel of the job.

During the period when we were paying out it was a constant rush to endeavour to reach key points at the most appropriate time. This would generally be when men would be assembled in gangs rather than spread out over a section of the job. An example of this would be when all men were withdrawn to the tunnel mouth so that a round of shots could be fired.

If I could be there when this happened, valuable time would be saved, and such savings often avoided the necessity of staggering round on a cold and stormy evening with a heavy paybag, paying individual men in the single huts or married quarters.

It was often necessary to discuss matters with the engineers, overseers, storekeepers and other staff men, but during the day they were spread out over the job and for one reason or another they could rarely be contacted.

Of an evening however, the single men would have their meal at the staff mess and afterwards some of the married staff would drop in from time to time. These men were living in a narrow glacial valley high in the mountains, and were denied the simple pleasures available to a town dweller. They were sixty miles from a licensed hotel and officially liquor was allowed on the job only on special occasions and in restricted amounts. The nearest doctor was at Lumsden, 100 miles away, and the nearest hospital was at Gore, forty miles further on.

Their social life, therefore, consisted largely of their contacts with workmates, and much of this occurred in their evening get-togethers. A visit from outsiders was welcomed, and in many cases the visitors brought in parcels from relatives, or helped in many ways to maintain contact with the outside world.

As I was a regular visitor and always had my own transport I was able to do much to assist, and the appreciation shown by my many friends in the Valley, amply rewarded me for the effort involved.

It was in the early hours of that morning that I left Dan's hut and crawled into my bunk.

Next morning Big Bill asked me to get another driver for his car as he wished to discuss job matters with the local engineer-in-charge.

A driver was obtained and Dan and I set off up the tortuous access track to the point at the head of the Valley where work had been begun on the Homer Tunnel.

Dan introduced me to every man we paid. "Hullo, Jack – meet Harry Anderson the new paymaster." And then, if time permitted, he would give me a brief bit of information about each man. If we came to a big co-op gang all assembled together, my introduction would be to the whole gang. Dan, ever a diplomat, however, would always have a word to say – "This is the best rock gang on the road." And for the next gang, "Their contract rate goes up every pay." And so on.

What amazed me about this man was the multitude of requests made to him. "Dan, will you send me up a Tatt's ticket?" "Dan, here's ten bob to give so and so." "Dan, here's a quid, will you send a postal note out to my wife and a letter saying I'm OK?" On and on it went. With each request Dan just poked the money in his back pocket or tucked the information away in his photographic mind. He made no notes but at the end of the day it was a revelation to see him sit down and mentally go through the men he had seen and then attend to their innumerable requirements.

On this first day I had a large number of requests of every variety, many of which were to attend to matters in Invercargill, and I carefully noted them in my red notebook. The weather remained calm but very cold and dry, and it was late in the afternoon when we got back to the Marian camp. We decided we would stay the night and leave for Invercargill next day.

In the morning I was lying in my bunk when a hand slowly came up from below and grabbed my blankets and steadily pulled them off the bed. "Come on Andy, time to get up." No more "Mr Anderson", no more long silences. I had apparently come up to requirements and was to find that I had made a very good friend. To Mr Pearce I was always Andy; in the office it was Harold, and out on the job it was Harry.

26

On the formation line: Jim Sutherland (*seated*) talks to George Auld with the steep-sided Mt Christina as a backdrop.

Weekly News, Bill Beattie photo

After breakfast we sat around for an hour or so tidying up various matters and then started off for home.

On the way back Big Bill gave me a lot of background information about the job.

He told me that the section of the road from Te Anau to the Te Anau Downs Station – about eighteen miles – was constructed as a relief work in 1929–30 and that by about 1934 it had been extended as far as The Divide, which was about fifty-three miles from Te Anau. There were mile posts on this road and a very convenient form of indicating any location had been devised. It was "the 4-mile peg" or "the 18-mile peg" and so on.

At the time of my first trip with Mr Pearce the road had been more or less completed to the Marian camp in the Hollyford Valley. This was the Department's headquarters camp. From this point, construction gangs were spread over the remaining eight miles of rough access track to a point where work had been begun on the tunnel. Work was also proceeding on the eleven miles of road from Milford Sound to the tunnel site. About 150 men were on this job and were camped at Milford Sound.

Mr Pearce talked about the various physical features and the main points of interest on this trip. Here is what he told me.

The road skirts Lake Te Anau for the first eighteen miles and it then strikes inland over the Retford Stream and enters the spectacular Eglinton Valley. It passes a point known as The Bluffs at the 31-mile peg and I was told that one of the overseers, who was a keen fisherman, invariably spent a few minutes with a baitcasting rod on one of these bluffs. It was rarely that he did not get a nice Atlantic salmon or rainbow trout. In this area was Mt Eglinton, 6085 ft., and along the road at the 40-mile peg was Knobs Flat, so called because it was flat and had a lot of knobs on it. These knobs were small symmetrical hillocks and from the description I was given, one couldn't miss the place.

The thirty-mile run up the Eglinton Valley provides a magnificent view of lakes, bush and mountain scenery, particularly around Lakes Gunn, Fergus, and Lochie. On this particular trip we stood on the edge of Lake Gunn in perfectly still conditions and gazed at a mountain peak rising above it. The top of the peak was covered in snow and this gradually merged into purple rock. Lower down was the green of the beech forest, which extended right down to the water level. About halfway up the mountain there was a very thin horizontal band of blue mist. The whole picture was perfectly mirrored in the flat calm of the lake. Big Bill and I both agreed that we had never seen anything to compare with it. This scene was indelibly photographed on my memory and I can clearly visualise it to this day. As we feasted our eyes we were privileged to see another unusual sight for just below us, perched on a log, was a crested grebe, nowadays not too plentiful a species.

Coming through the beech forest in the Eglinton, the traveller should keep his eyes open for what is known as the Disappearing Mountain at 36½ miles. This is an unusual illusion. Going north one first sees a high mountain peak through the tops of the beech trees. As the car proceeds, the gradient on the road is such that the peak looks as if it is disappearing like a ship sinking below the waves. This is a sight well worth seeing.

At this time the road had been finally completed beyond Cascade Creek to the head of the Eglinton Valley to a spot beyond the Divide, where there was a very steep drop down into the Hollyford Valley. As one starts to descend steeply from the Divide there is a beautiful view of the Lower Hollyford Valley – and what an opportunity for the man with a colour film – particularly if the rata is in bloom.

The drop from the Divide is about 700 feet into the Hollyford Valley below, and at the foot of this gradient was the Marian headquarters camp. At this spot a plaque was later erected com-

Marian camp staff, 1936. *Back row, left to right*: Bruce Wilson, Norman Nisbett, Bill Hall, Duncan White, George Jones, Doug Stewart, Roy Hunter, Jack Whitmore, Watty Tattersfield. *Front row*: Dan Campbell, Mossy Boord, Joe Lloyd, Tom Smith, John Christie, Don Hulse, Harry Morgan, Jack Dawson, Harry Double.

J. H. Christie

memorating the rescue dash carried out by Dave Gunn in December 1936. (This is mentioned in a later chapter.)

Near by on Falls Creek at 56 miles are the Christie Falls named after John Christie, engineer-in-charge on the Hollyford job in 1935–36. These spectacular falls were discovered by Mr Christie and are a short distance upstream from the Falls Creek bridge.

The Hollyford River runs down the main valley, having its source at the site of the inland portal of the Homer Tunnel.

The Hollyford flows past the Marian camp site in a southerly direction and then turns inland and flows on in a more or less northerly direction until it reaches Lake McKerrow, finally reaching its mouth in the Martins Bay area on the West Coast at a point north of Milford Sound.

In contrast, the Eglinton River, which also has its source a mile or two from the Marian camp site – over the saddle in the Lake Fergus area – flows due south into Lake Te Anau and then, known as the Waiau, enters Lake Manapouri, ultimately reaching the sea at Tuatapere on the southern coast of the South Island.

The Hollyford Valley has aptly been described as a canyon carved out of rock by the ice of the ages, and it is skirted by some of the highest peaks in the Fiordland area. The cliffs of the mighty Mt Christina, 8210 ft., tower above the Marian camp site, and further up the same side of the valley are the several peaks of the Crosscut Range, 7600 ft. Proceeding up the eight miles of the valley beyond Marian, one sees straight ahead the uniform shape of Mt Talbot, 6945 ft., while on the left is Mt Belle, 6850 ft. At the foot of Mt Talbot the valley forks (hence the name The Forks). On the right is the Gertrude Valley which leads up past Black Lake to the Gertrude Saddle, 4870 ft. The fork on the left rises fairly steeply to the Homer Tunnel mouth, 3023 ft. Right above the tunnel is the Homer Saddle, 4480 ft., on the other side of which is the Cleddau Valley leading to Milford Sound about eleven miles further on.

I have heard it said that at the Marian camp site the cliffs on either side are so steep that in midwinter the sun is seen for only twenty minutes at midday – that is if it happens to be shining. How correct this is I cannot say, but from my observations it would not be far wrong.

The average annual rainfall in the Hollyford and Milford area is about 300 inches but on occasions daily falls between 10 and 20 inches have been recorded.

On giving me this last piece of information Mr Pearce said "Just try and imagine it – over a foot and a half of rain in one day!"

On this return trip we had quite an uneventful run and reached Invercargill in mid-afternoon. Thus ended the first of about fifty pay trips I was to make as paymaster to the famous Hollyford Valley and Homer Tunnel.

Harking back to that first evening with Dan Campbell, I well remember him stating that the story of these "Men of the Road" should be recorded and written. It would be a most human document.

He even suggested that I should think of writing the story. He knew and loved that Valley as a mother loves her child, and he longed for its story to be written. Little did I ever think that years later I would be endeavouring to capture just a few of the very human day-to-day events and, that in doing so, I would be rewarded by re-living those memorable days and enjoying once more the company of the "Men of the Road".

5

PAYS AND RABBITS

THINGS WERE SO HECTIC in the office that it seemed no time before the next Hollyford Valley pay was due. On this occasion I decided to get away at 4 am so that I could pay right through the job and reach men at the extreme head of the Hollyford Valley before they knocked off work. This would then give me time on the following day to pay the few I had missed on the way up, attend to the various incidental jobs necessary, and get back to Invercargill in daylight. This also minimised the chance of breaking into the third day and, as we were so busy with the stepped-up programme, any economies of time were worth while.

On this particular pay we had a bad start. We drew the cash from the bank about 2.15 pm and had hoped to get it all made up by about 6 pm and it was then my intention to have the evening off.

No sooner had we got the money from the bank than a contingent of men arrived in from Milford Sound. They had come round by boat and had had a bit of a session at the Bluff hotels and then headed by the quickest means to get a "draw" on their pay from the Invercargill office.

This was the procedure we had to adopt with men coming from Milford Sound as some of them would probably have been on the job for months without coming out. It therefore took some time to make up the day wages sheets, calculate the co-op contract earnings and generally settle their accounts with the Department.

By the time we made these pay advances there wasn't much left of the afternoon so I decided we would have to finish the Hollyford pay in the evening. Three of us came back and by about 10 o'clock we had just about finished putting the money in the envelopes. In fact there were only about three more to go and in a big pay this was always a moment of excitement. Would the pay balance? In other words, when we came to the last envelope would the money left on the counting table be correct?

This evening our luck was out. The amount of money left for the last envelope was £5 over and this meant that we had to check through every envelope – and there were upwards of a thousand of them – to find the error. This involved a critical decision – where should we start? Should we open the envelopes from A to Z or Z to A, or some other way?

The usual procedure was to toss up, and this we did. On this occasion the toss was in favour of starting at A. We were lucky, as the error was soon picked up in the envelope of a man whose surname began with D. We put the £5 note into his envelope and soon sealed them all up and into the safe they went.

My driver on this trip was called Mac and he said he would be at the place where I boarded at 4 am. I did not like to set an alarm as it would wake the whole house so I gave him a key and told him to come into my room and wake me if I was not already up. As it happened I woke in time and went out into the kitchen. The coal range had been stoked up the night before and then dampered down, and my landlady told me just to turn up the dampers, open up the front and give the coal a jab with the poker and it would be away in flames. Sure enough this was right and in a few minutes I had boiled two eggs and made a couple of pieces of toast. By this time the top of the range was glowing and the kettle boiling. I filled the teapot and poured myself a cup of tea. Mac arrived at this moment and he also had a cup of tea and in no time we were on our way to the office.

All the gear was ready in the strongroom and soon we were heading along Dee Street for the open country. We were only a few miles on our way when there was a blurred shape in the beam of the headlight and then that sudden thump so well known to South-landers in those days. We had run over a rabbit.

"That reminds me," said Mac, "the cook at the Marian asked me to bring up some rabbits. We'll stop at Castle Rock and I'll knock a few over."

All went quietly for a while and then there was a thump on the windscreen. "A German owl," Mac explained. "We hit them occasionally."

Up to this stage we had been travelling quite steadily as we had ample time to get to Lake Te Anau by 8 am. Mac however, must have had further thoughts about the time it would take us to get the rabbits as he said, "I think I'll have to tread on the exhilarator a bit," and he did just that.

I thought he was having a little joke in referring to the "exhilarator", but as I got to know him I found that this was his version of the word accelerator. Mac had one or two other unusual expressions that I remember. One was that he "stood on the brakes and stopped like a shot out of a gun". Another was to refer to snow conditions as "jet white".

He had a total disregard for rear-vision mirrors. If he wanted to see what was behind, he half stood up, turned completely round

Horses of the Milford Road–with *(left to right)* packman Dusty Miller, butcher Tommy Jones and storekeeper Jim Sutherland.

Weekly News, Bill Beattie photo

and stared out the rear window for an extended period. When we were travelling along a dusty stretch of deeply shingled road at around 60 mph or more and Mac did his about-turn act, I was really scared.

With the increase in speed we soon reached Castle Rock, which is at a right-angle turn in the road before it reaches Mossburn. Mac slowed down and stopped and then switched off the headlights. He got out and went round to the back of the runabout and took out his .22 rifle. I had my five-cell torch and he asked me to shine it on the side of the road. I did this and saw that there were literally dozens of rabbits sitting beside a gorse hedge which served the purpose of a fence.

Mac shot six in a few minutes from the same spot and put them in a sugarbag. He cleaned and skinned them at a stream further up country when the light was better. Depression days they were, but with the millions of rabbits running round Southland there was no shortage of meat as long as you liked "underground mutton".

We got to Te Anau on time and paid the whole maintenance gang before they set out on the day's work. We set off around Lake Te Anau and had not gone far before it started to rain and it was such a deluge we just had to crawl along. We paid the odd surfaceman here and there as we passed. When we got to Walker Creek it was so high that it looked as though the bridge was in danger. We crossed it smartly and further up the road we met a surfaceman who told us that the abutment of MacKay Creek had washed out and that we could not go on. He was hoping to meet somebody who could get a message back to Te Anau. We agreed to do this so he hopped in the cab with us. Fortunately we had only gone a short distance back when we met the truck from Te Anau loaded with men and gear and expecting trouble. When we got to MacKay Creek there was about an eight feet gap but by this time the water had subsided somewhat and the overseer decided that he would lash some of the loose bridge decking across the gap to enable us to get our runabout across.

It looked reasonably safe as each track was about three feet wide, but the overseer would not agree to our driving the vehicle across. He rigged up a block and tackle system and his men towed it over empty in about ten minutes. We followed on foot and were soon on our way again.

At the Marian camp we were met by Dan Campbell, and started up the Hollyford Valley, paying as we went. Dan, who was also the postmaster at Hollyford, told me that he had a letter from one of the hard cases on the job who was out on leave. This character, known as Tim, had been saving hard for a long time and had decided to go out for a while and do a round of the race meetings. Apparently he hadn't been doing at all well and in his letter he had put the nips into Dan for a loan of five pounds. "He's as safe as a bank," said Dan, "and I'll have no hesitation in sending the money away. I'll give you the letter to post when you get back to Invercargill."

As we humped the paybags from gang to gang Dan was getting his usual run of requests to "Bank £3" – "Send me two bobs' worth of stamps" – "Write and ask the wife if the baby has arrived. I am OK," etc. All of these he recorded in his computer like brain but on this trip there was another request which was repeated about half a dozen times. It went something like this. "Dan, here's two quid. Will you get a postal note and send it to Tim at (such and such an address). He's running short but I don't mind sending it to him as he's as safe as a bank."

Sometimes the amount asked for was £3 but in no case did it go to the extent of the £5 that Dan had been asked to send.

After a while Dan had quite a wad of notes to be sent to Tim and as we were sitting in the runabout he said, "I don't think I'll bother to send that five quid to Tim. If I send this other money he should be OK till he gets back. Anyway, if he really gets short he knows he has only to get in touch with me and I'll send it immediately." After a short pause he said, "Tim's a man you could trust with anything – safe as a bank."

34

All this was said without a smile and if anybody asked me to describe Dan I could not do better than relate the above incident. He was a character right out of a Dickens novel – a bit of Micawber with a touch of Pickwick and Sam Weller.

While speaking of this Tim I remember another incident in which he was involved at a later date. We were paying out and it had been snowing heavily and was bitterly cold. Everybody was wrapped up in all sorts of warm clothing with an oilskin or butterfly cape on top. Dan and Tim chatted for a while and, just as we were about to go, Tim said, "Where's me envelope?"

I didn't have it in my hand so I said "I've given it to you." This was logical, as my first move on getting to a man was to find out his name and then get out his envelope. On the envelope would be the number of the paysheet, say number 66. I would then flip over the paysheets to page 66 and the man would sign. As I had found the sheet and Tim had signed, it was logical that I had already handed him the envelope.

To satisfy myself, however, I had a look in the paybag in alphabetical order but Tim's envelope wasn't there. Then the comedy started. It was snowing lightly and it was so cold that my hands were frozen and I had difficulty in using them. I couldn't use gloves, as this made it impossible to handle envelopes, pencil and paysheets.

I told Tim I couldn't find his envelope and that he must have it. I must admit however, that I wondered whether I had dropped it or put it in my pocket. I started to fumble through all my pockets and Dan and Tim did the same, but to no avail. The other chaps in the gang were highly amused. One reckoned Tim had palmed it off to someone else, while another enquired whether he had swallowed it. Someone else offered an unprintable suggestion as to what he had done with it, and this caused another roar of laughter.

Finally I had to lay the paybag open on the back of the runabout and go through every envelope to see whether it was out of alphabetical order or whether it had slipped down and was lying flat under the other envelopes. With my hands so cold this checking was a slow process, but the envelope couldn't be found and by this time I had a bag of soggy envelopes due to the wet snow.

As Tim, Dan and I were getting more and more perturbed the gang were becoming more and more hilarious. One of them asked Tim if he could search him. Tim agreed and his mate said, "All right, drop your tweeds." At the thought of this happening in the snow even Dan and I had to laugh. Someone referred to a brass monkey and there were further laughs.

We were still puzzling over what could have happened. Tim had a final search and all of a sudden he yelled out, "Wait on!" He put his hand into his trousers pocket and shoved it well down, and the

The Tunnel, early 1936. The snowfalls came later in the year.
"Making NZ" Collection, Alexander Turnbull Library

In compressor room are overseer N.J. Dawson (*in hat*), attendant Harry Matheson, and tunnel shift boss George Annesley.

N.J. Dawson

further he shoved the further his hand went. "Got it!" he yelled at last, and out came his hand with the envelope in it. What had happened was that he had put the envelope in his trousers pocket and, like lots of trousers pockets in those days, it had a big hole in it. The envelope had slid down the leg of his trousers till it reached the point where he had tucked his trousers into his socks. He was wearing knee gumboots and when the envelope finished its downward slide it was about six or eight inches below the top of the gumboot and securely held.

On all previous searches Tim had just patted his side pocket and it was obviously empty.

After we left Tim and his mates and were approaching the Homer Tunnel portal, Dan said he had a very important piece of news for one of the men working there. An advertisement had appeared in a national weekly newspaper requesting a certain Mr X (whom I will not name) to get in touch with a firm of English solicitors as he had been named as a beneficiary in a substantial estate. This man had a most unusual christian name which was known to Dan and me, and this left us in no doubt that he was the man sought.

When we reached this man Dan gave him the copy of the advertisement and he just glanced at it and confirmed that he was the man sought. He said he would write to the solicitors and thanked Dan for his trouble.

This advertisement continued to appear in the paper at intervals for some months and once or twice Dan enquired whether a reply had been sent.

"No, not yet Dan, I just haven't got round to it – I must do it though," was the reply.

Twelve months later Dan enquired again, and the answer was the same. Dan said that he was convinced that this man, along with a number of others, had found peace in this wild valley and was prepared to leave the outside world to its own troubles. As far as Dan Campbell was concerned, I am certain this applied to him too. He had been a man of the world and held good positions, but after a long association with him I had no doubt that the highlight of his life was the period when he was postmaster and PWD timekeeper in the Hollyford Valley. Hundreds of men relied on him for a multitude of tasks, many of which were of a private nature, and Dan was always there to do what he could. It was his way of life.

I remember him on one occasion giving us a rundown on his various activities and he finished up with the statement, "I'm also the official Tatt's agent and the postmaster, and as such I have power to marry people." I don't know whether he had this power or not but if he did he would have made a thorough job of it. He was a purist in everything he did and had a prodigious capacity for work. He was always ready at any time to help his "Men of the Road".

I have digressed somewhat and will return to that particular pay day. After paying all the men on shift in the tunnel we called in at one of the married quarters for a plate of hot soup and then set off back to the Marian camp for the evening meal.

After dinner it was the usual cards, letter writing, chess, draughts and a series of discussions on events of the day which continued for quite a while.

One man was getting a bit of a rough time this evening. It was overseer Jack Dawson, who was the owner of a fiery horse called Darky. In those days departmental vehicles were not over-plentiful, so Jack decided to provide his own transport and purchased this horse.

Actually a good horse was the best means of travel at that stage of the road, as the access tracks were often not negotiable by motor vehicle. It was also a good method of crossing the river. Jack Dawson, being well over six feet in height and of rangy build, made a fine picture on his steed, and in a way represented the pioneering spirit so necessary on that job.

One particular characteristic was that Jack always wore a felt hat, which in those days had much wider brims than they have today. These hats he wore were not flamboyant sombrero types but just ordinary everyday felt hats, but Jack, being such a big man, stood above others and these hats he wore always pinpointed him – particularly in a group.

It appeared that earlier in the day he had gone along to the Cinques camp and met up with overseer George Auld, and they were proceeding up the valley looking at the various jobs as they went. Jack was leading Darky by the rein and they came to a temporary access bridge. The spacing of the decking timbers on this bridge was so wide that Jack decided that the horse would not be able to negotiate it, so he told George Auld he would ride the horse through the water while George crossed the bridge on foot.

The river was running fairly full and about halfway across Darky stopped. Jack had his feet well up to keep them dry, and not wanting to delay too long in midstream, he gave Darky a good jab with his heels.

Jack did not know exactly what caused the trouble, but somehow or other his long legs must have upset Darky, as the horse suddenly bucked. The riverbed was stony and the horse lost his footing and over he went and Jack with him. From then on it was a rolling mass of Jack and Darky for half a chain downstream, but finally both managed to scramble out of the water.

The portal completed, 1936, but the notice reads "Tourists Not Allowed". *Left to right*: Don Nicholson, Tom Maher, ? , Joff Ramsay, Bob Carter, Finn Farquhar, ? , Frank McCash, ? , George Clark, Danny McLaren, Euan McDonald, Hughie Neely, Alec Duncan, Bob Wassell, Bert McKnight, Watty McDonough, Max Bocock, Oscar Cattaruzo, Tom Montagu.

Kent Collection, Alexander Turnbull Library

Jack was of course wet through, and this was no joke on a freezing morning. Worse still was the fact that he was unable to see anything at all, but fortunately it turned out that this was not due to any physical injury. Somehow or other in the roll downstream, Jack's hat had got jammed hard down over his eyes and, having been thoroughly soaked, it was virtually shrunk on to his head and he could neither see nor get his hat off. Ultimately George Auld with the assistance of men working nearby managed to cut slits in the felt and finally removed the hat.

Jack then decided to go back to the Cinques camp and get a change of clothes. George Auld lent him a pair of pants and Mrs Brotherston handed over a pullover belonging to her husband Lex. The pants were about halfway up his calves and the pullover reached down about as far as his navel. Thus did big Jack Dawson walk from the Cinques camp to his own hut in the main camp, and it goes without saying that the men in the various gangs along the road made the most of such a glorious opportunity of "poking the borax" at the boss.

When Jack got to the staff mess that evening he found that his mates were also laughing at his misfortunes. In a goodnatured way he said he hoped he might have found at least one or two friends there who would have been sympathetic. Sympathy however, was not the order of the day as someone then disclosed that after the

39

spill in the river, Darky had taken off down the Lower Hollyford Valley and had not been seen since.

After a time there was a lull in the conversation and then someone said "Have you noticed that the rabbits are moving further up the Eglinton Valley? I saw two near Cascade Creek yesterday."

Several others confirmed this and general opinion was that they were thriving in the bush.

Suddenly I remembered a story about rabbiting told to me some years before and it occurred to me that it might be worth relating. I enquired whether anybody was interested and soon found that I had the floor so I began my story.

Some years ago I was at a friend's place in Palmerston North, along with a number of other guests and the conversation gradually got round to rabbit shooting. One of the party, Arthur, was apparently a keen shooter and he came out with the following yarn.

In the long summer evenings he and a mate used to head off a few miles out of town to an isolated spot near the coast where there were miles of sandhills. The procedure then was for one to go north and the other south so that they would not be shooting each other.

The car was always parked by a large macrocarpa tree on the roadside, and a standing arrangement was that they would return to the car before darkness fell as otherwise they would have difficulty in finding it.

Arthur explained that there were plenty of rabbits but it was not easy shooting as the sandhills, although not high, were quite steep in spots and the rabbits soon popped out of sight.

While out one evening he had been wandering round for quite a time and had only shot one rabbit, so he decided he would have to concentrate a bit more. He crawled up to the top of a sandhill and there, sure enough, was a sitting shot. He let drive and hit the rabbit and decided that he would pick it up and head back for the car. He put his rifle down and ran down a slope to where the rabbit was lying, but unfortunately he caught his foot in a tuft of grass and came a terrific cropper, and off shot his glasses. At this point Arthur, with a bit of a sheepish grin said, "You chaps who don't wear specs won't really appreciate this, but I'm so shortsighted that without my glasses I'm useless – everything is just a complete blur."

He then went on to say that he knew the rabbit was somewhere in the hollow at the bottom of the slope, and without worrying about his glasses he went on and groped around with his hand till he located it. He started crawling back, at the same time feeling around for his glasses, and much to his dismay, he got back as far as his gun without finding them.

By this time the light was failing a bit and he really panicked as he knew he would have no show of finding his way back over the sandhills without his glasses. He left the two rabbits and, picking up his gun, walked back in the general direction of where he thought his glasses were, hoping that the last rays of the sun might shine on them and give him a clue to their whereabouts. He had no luck so he tucked his gun under his arm and got down on his hands and knees and started to feel round for them. Still he couldn't find them, and now he really panicked. He kept hold of the gun as he knew that if he put it down it would be lost. In the finish he was crawling flat out backwards and forwards with his eyes about two inches above the ground, the gun held in one hand and the other hand patting the sandy ground trying to locate his glasses.

At last he felt something – it was his glasses, and fortunately they were still intact – so he thankfully put them on and set out for the car. As he was going back later than usual he fired a couple of shots to let his mate know he was on his way. He soon reached the car and the pair of shooters returned home.

Next morning he went to work at his shop, and after a while in came the local constable, who was a great friend of Arthur's. His visits were generally of a very leisurely nature, but this morning he was all of a bustle and obviously full of business. He had no time for the usual pleasantries and the first thing he said to Arthur was –

"Were you down the Foxton Line last night shooting rabbits?"

"Yes, why?"

"Did you see anybody with a gun acting a bit funny?"

"No," said Arthur and then asked the obvious question. "Why, what's wrong?"

The policeman then went on to explain that a local Maori had been walking over the sandhills about dusk, and on coming over a ridge had been confronted by a man with a gun in his hand. This man had a wild vacant look in his eye and on seeing the Maori he pointed the gun at him and rushed in his direction. The Maori turned and ran and a number of shots were fired at him but fortunately he was not ·hit. He was pursued for about half a mile but managed to get home absolutely exhausted and put a phone call through to the police.

By this time Arthur had got the message. It was obvious that the Maori had appeared over the sandhill just as he was doing his mad scramble after his glasses, with the rifle under his arm and, no doubt, pointing in the direction of the Maori. He must have looked a fearsome sight. He had then fired two shots to let his mate know he was coming, and the Maori thought that these were for him. The bit about having been chased for half a mile was imaginary, but in Arthur's mind it was a justifiable addition to make the story well worth telling. After all, that Maori had to tell that story in the local

41

pub for years ahead and unless he could spin it out a bit the barman would hardly have time to shout more than two or three times.

When the policeman had finished his version of the story, Arthur burst out laughing and gave the policeman his side of the tale. They had a good laugh together and the policemen lost no time in phoning up the local watch house and letting them know what had happened. Funny and all as it was, the policeman was much relieved, as he could see no fun in stalking over those sandhills looking for a madman with a gun. . . .

After this story was finished we left for bed. We had a number of things to attend to on our way back to Invercargill and wanted to get an early start next morning.

6

FROSTY WEATHER

INVERCARGILL HAD BEEN having a spell of exceptional frosts, evidenced by about six or eight permanent holes in the vegetable garden where I boarded. These holes remained where parsnips had been growing. The method of getting them out was to drive a pick into the ground beside the parsnip and then lever it out – something like a tooth extraction. The ground was frozen so hard that the hole just stayed put, and all of this despite that "hot" or was it "warm" current that runs along Invercargill's Oreti Beach.

One morning my landlady was doing the washing and she hung out some long bath towels. A bit later she went out to put a few more on the line and the number one lot were frozen hard as a biscuit. She held them horizontally in front of her and there was not an inch of deflection.

If this was the picture in Invercargill, what would it be like in the Hollyford Valley? The pay trip was due and I was soon to find out.

We got away about 7 am as it just seemed too cold to get out of the sheets any earlier. I had to call in at Gordon Macauley's store at Mossburn, and what we saw there didn't help us any. The tap was frozen solid and beside it was a lemonade bottle which someone had filled with water. It had frozen and the expansion had resulted in a five or six inch blob of ice poking out of the top of the bottle. I won't tell the story about the ducks sitting on the ground and not being able to get up – that only happens in Central Otago.

It was cold, however, so we went over to Crosbie's Hotel and had a couple of rums.

On our way again and we were soon at Te Anau. We came in rather fast on an icy patch behind a truck, put on the brake a bit too suddenly, and we had a bit of a crunch. It took several hours to fix and from that time on we were running late. We had to visit men in their huts instead of catching them on the road, and everything had got out of kilter.

It was dark early and foggy through the Eglinton Valley, although the fog was often just above the car and not too troublesome. It was cold, however. We experienced no major difficulties till we got past Cascade Creek, and then we were in real strife. A thick pea-soup fog was the trouble and it was right down to ground level. We switched on the windscreen wiper and what we had was "instant" ice. One wipe of the blade and there was a smear of white ice right in front of the driver's eyes. We soon found out that there was only one way we could make any progress: I had to stand on the left-hand running board, with my long torch shining in front and tell Charlie, the driver, whether to steer left or right. Even this involved a bit of guesswork on my part and obviously our pace was about as slow as it was possible to go in low gear. Never was I colder.

We got to headquarters well after midnight and found that one of the two guest huts had an occupant in it. There was a note from Dan Campbell however, saying that one of us should go into the other guest hut, which also had one occupant in it. Charlie took the first hut and I headed for the other and went to open the door. It was locked, and I hammered on the door to no avail. I could have wakened Dan Campbell or some of the others but I just didn't have the heart to do so. The New Zealand Railways bus was parked nearby and I opened the door and in I hopped, paybag and all. I lay on the seat and froze and I doubt whether I slept at all. I remember sleeping in a shed at the Picton rowing regatta years before, and waking up in the morning to find myself curled up on a set line complete with hooks. That was just child's play compared with that night at the Hollyford.

As soon as the cook was up and around I sidled over to the cook-house and had a warm drink and some toast and asked him why the guest hut was locked. He didn't know but I found out later that some official from the Post Office had slept there. He must have been scared of ghosts or very security-minded. I could see no point in even asking him what it was all about as that would not alleviate my night's sufferings.

Dan, of course, wanted to know what was wrong and I told him the sad tale. He then told me they had been having record frosts up the Homer end of the Valley and had to attack 44-gallon drums of solid ice with a pick to get water to boil the billy.

To add to all the delays, I had a number of things I had to discuss with several of the staff members and it was late before we set off up the valley and later still by the time all the men were paid. "I've had it" was my summing up, and I decided to stay that night in the Valley.

I spent the first hour or so after dinner over at Dan's hut as he had a few jobs to do and a few things to discuss with me. Then we went over to the mess for the usual evening get-together.

On this particular evening there were a number of shorter stories told and I remember two about Maoris and one about a Yugoslav or

Upper Hollyford Valley, looking north. The road follows the riverline.

J.H. Christie

Dalmatian, as they were then termed, told by a foreman who had come from a North Island job.

The first was about a gang of Maoris who were making really good progress on a contract. The engineer-in-charge was very keen to keep the gang together, but every now and then there would be a request for leave to return home and the reasons given generally covered such things as harvesting the kumara crop or planting corn etc. Leave was invariably granted, so the need for ingenuity in concocting reasons diminished and in the finish it was generally "to attend the tangi for my grandmother who has just died".

One day a chap came along with his application for leave, beautifully handwritten, as only a Maori can write. The excuse as usual was to attend the tangi for a grandmother. The timekeeper, who himself was a bit of a character, said, "I'm sorry to hear the sad news about your poor old grandmother. There must have been a lot of them dying lately on the East Coast."

The Maori boy, looking very sad, almost with a tear in his eye, solemnly agreed and said, "That right Jack – very true – I only got three left."

Needless to say, the leave was promptly granted.

The other tale concerned a Maori landowner on whose property a road was being constructed. This owner was very helpful to the Department and was highly regarded. One day his wife asked him to lend his new car to her favourite nephew. His ideas about the nephew differed greatly from those of his wife but he reluctantly agreed, on the stipulation that the car was to be driven at a reasonable speed. As often happens, the car got out of control on a corner and was badly smashed. The nephew was seriously injured and the local engineer felt'that he should call on the landowner and express his sorrow about the nephew.

When he got to the farm he found the Maori ruefully surveying the wrecked car, so he went up to him and said he was very sorry to hear the bad news that had struck him and his family.

"It certainly is bad news," said the Maori. "The crankcase is split from one end to the other."

The nephew in due course recovered and I hope the car was covered by insurance. As the engineer said afterwards "It's just a matter of priorities and I got them wrong".

The story about the Dalmatian concerned a truckload of bags of oysters which was derailed near a PWD camp. By the time the débris was cleared away, the oysters were definitely "off" and this Dalmatian was telling the foreman all about it. He said it was "The biggest stink you ever saw – you could hear him two hundred yards away."

The next story started in the following manner "These events happened when I was on the West Coast" – familiar words in any town in New Zealand, and often heard at the Hollyford staff mess. This is how the story went:

A late session was in progress in one of those West Coast hotels and all and sundry were there. Most police raids were made after the publican had been duly warned and had time to clear out the bar. But ever on the basis that "Justice should not only be done but be seen to be done", it was the practice of the police to put on an unscheduled raid every now and then, and names would be taken. These would in due course be called out in court and the usual procedure was a response of "No appearance, Your Honour" and the penalty "Fined five shillings." On this particular occasion the bar contained the visiting magistrate and the local solicitor, who were drinking together. The police arrived all unannounced and names were taken. Later, when the cases came up for hearing, there was a string of "No appearance, Your Honour," and the usual five shilling fine.

The name of the visiting magistrate was not mentioned and it may have been that he was exempt, being a guest at the hotel-or for some other good reason. Towards the end of the proceedings the name of the local solicitor was called. When this occurred there was the usual "No appearance, Your Honour," but the magistrate looked up sharply from the papers on his desk and peered over the top of his glasses.

"Is this Mr So-and-So the local solicitor?" enquired the magistrate sternly. On being assured that it was, he said, "He should know better than this. He should set an example in the district. Fined two pounds."

The next story was about a raid on a West Coast hotel, but in this case the usual warning had been issued to the proprietor. When the police arrived the bar had been cleared and the sergeant was shown through. He was new to the district and had never met the publican before and, wanting to be affable and make a bit of conversation about the weather, he said "It's a bit murky tonight isn't it?"

The publican, ever on his guard, thought the sergeant referred to the heavy smoke-filled air of the bar and said "Fair go, Sarge – you don't expect us to clean the smoke out as well? The last man wasn't as fussy as all that!"

The next story was about a new engineer on an East Coast job. This chap was young and keen – a new graduate from the university. At heart he wasn't a bad sort, but he had that new graduate's contempt for the foreman type – you know the sort of thing. He recognised that foremen were a part of the engineering setup but he was also aware that they did not hold his high academic qualifications. Later on he would, of course, learn that those beautiful U-shaped footings for concrete walls to be built on rock, so neatly drawn on his plans, would in practice be any old shape. He would also find that these foremen he looked down on would often be called on to adapt those very beautiful plans to meet practical difficulties not expected by the designer.

One point this engineer was very keen on was sanitation, and he arranged for the long row of earth closets to have a special kind of seat cover which ensured that the flies would be unable to get in. All other cracks and openings were also sealed. The men on the job called the final product "insulated thunderboxes".

One day on this job it was very warm, and one of the men felt the need to visit the toilet. While sitting there he thought he would have a quiet smoke and pulled out his pipe and matches. He lit his pipe, and being a man of careful habits he did not throw the match away, but opened the lid of the privy next to him and dropped in the lighted match. As he did so there was a terrific explosion and

A chilly payday. *Left to right*: Dan Campbell, the author, engineer Duncan White on formation line, Lower Hollyford Road

Author

he suffered considerable injury to his nether parts. But, as he told his mates later, "My injuries were very serious but they could have been twice as bad."

On subsequent enquiry it turned out that the long hot spell, combined with the very tight lids on the toilets, had resulted in a high concentration of inflammable sewer gas. As one of the foremen said later "These new university types are all right in theory. Ask them to multiply 10 by 10 and they will get out that 'swizzle stick' (slide rule) and tell you the answer is 99.9 approximately. Sometimes however they are a wee bit light on the practical side."

With this story supper was served and the party broke up.

After breakfast next morning we were just ready to leave for Invercargill when Dan Campbell came hurrying over to us with a message. It appeared that one of the men had returned by railway bus from Dunedin the previous evening and had an urgent problem. He had lost his false teeth and wanted me to order a new set from his dentist in Invercargill.

This man had a habit of making a trip to town about every few months, and while there he tried to catch up on his arrears of drinking. At times he would overdo it a bit and his mates would then bundle him into a taxi and take him to wherever he happened to be staying.

It was about this stage that his false teeth seemed to cause him some annoyance and, according to his story, he would sometimes take them out and put them in his pocket for safe keeping. From this point on, his account of subsequent events would vary considerably, but one fairly common conclusion was the loss of his teeth. This event was a standing joke among his mates on the job and someone suggested he should order an extra set which would always be available on his return. This suggestion was only made in fun but it was taken seriously and the emergency set was duly ordered, and I got the job of picking them up from the Invercargill dentist and delivering them on one of my pay trips.

In the circumstances I couldn't see what was the urgency in this particular case and I asked Dan Campbell what all the fuss was about. At this point even Dan had to grin. It seemed that on this particular trip out the man had to attend a wedding in Dunedin, and just to make sure that all would be well, he took *both* sets of teeth with him.

Habit dies hard however, and he managed to lose both sets of teeth on the one trip, though he explained to Dan that things could have been worse as he had managed to attend the wedding complete with teeth.

In the circumstances I said I would help him out, so before going into the office in Invercargill I stopped outside the dentist's surgery and placed the order for a set of teeth. "Not again!" was the dentist's only reaction.

Working on the fullsized tunnel. Overseer Tom Smith (*in hat, centre*) and below him (*with pipe*) tunneller Frank McCash.

MOW Collection

7

IT SNOWED!

ANOTHER HOMER TUNNEL TRIP was due and from all accounts Fiordland was in a savage mood. Somehow or other over the months I had begun to think of Fiordland as a supreme female in charge of the area – much in the way that yachtsmen think of Hughie as the man who sends down the breezes. When this "Lady of Fiordland" decreed really fierce weather, our trip could be tough and of several days duration.

On this occasion there had been an exceptionally heavy snowfall, with extremely cold temperatures and heavy winds. In some places the snowdrifts were feet thick and it was impossible for vehicles to travel unless preceded by a snow plough. There had been a number of avalanches which came down to road level.

As communications from the tunnel area were cut off, the Invercargill office engineers were not aware of the extent of the trouble, and they decided on an immediate inspection. All the best vehicles were requisitioned and when we came to look around for a pay car, all that was left was a Model A Ford tourer fitted with those oldfashioned detachable side-curtains with celluloid windows – apparently to let in some light. These curtains may have had some use in keeping out the rain, but they fairly nurtured draughts.

We left at 7 am and it was still dark. There was a light flutter of snow as we left Invercargill and this got worse as we went on. At Winton, about twenty miles north, it was snowing heavily and Joe, who was one of the regular drivers from the workshop, said it would be wise to fit chains. He stopped outside the Winton Cemetery and in no time the chains were on. Joe mentioned that the famous (or infamous) Minnie Dean was buried in this cemetery, and went on to tell us how she used to dispose of unwanted babies for a fee.

On one occasion, however, she made a train trip and an observant guard noticed that she had a baby in her arms. At the end of the trip he noticed that she now had no baby, and had apparently dumped it into a river as the train passed over. Enquiries following this incident led to Minnie's arrest. She was later found guilty of charges of murder and had the doubtful honour of being the first woman to be hanged in New Zealand.

Joe had a sequel to all this. He said that there was a blood-red mark on her tombstone and that on the anniversary of her death this mark became much more "bloody" as he put it. He recommended that we have a look at the tombstone and I said I would sometime do so. I must have made about forty further trips to the Homer and on each one it was my intention to visit this "bloody" tombstone. Perhaps I was always in too much of a bloody hurry to spare the time, and my subsequent visits to Invercargill have not been through Winton. This desire to have a peek at Minnie's tombstone is with me to this day, and I hope in the not too distant future to satisfy this long cherished whim.

We had a passenger on this trip – one of the chaps from the office who was being transferred to the Homer job and he had his gear stowed on the back seat with the paybags. This meant that the three of us sat in the front seat and there was not too much room.

After we had done a few miles, a clanking noise developed; one of the chains had came adrift and with every revolution of the left front wheel was smacking against the mudguard. We tied it with string, which lasted about five minutes, so we just had to put up with it.

As we got further north the snow deepened, and as cars in those days did not have heaters, we were almost frozen stiff. We called in at the hotel at Mossburn and had two or three rums, which certainly warmed us up. In fact the treatment was so beneficial that Joe suggested we buy a bottle of rum – "just in case we get snowbound between here and Te Anau".

As it happened we didn't get snowbound, but we did get stuck on several occasions and the two of us had to push while Joe steered out of the drifts. By this time we were again suffering from the extreme cold and had a few more swigs from the rum bottle. In fact, by the time we arrived at Te Anau we had drunk the lot, but this didn't seem to have any marked effect on us other than to warm us up a bit. When we arrived at the Te Anau Hotel, we were met by the proprietor, Ernie Govan, who was having a quick peek out of the front door at the weather.

"What are you doing with that old jalopy?" were his first words, and after we had told him the story he said, "Come in and have a quick one – you look frozen."

We trooped into the bar and Ernie shouted for the three of us. We all had a rum, still believing this to be the best thing to keep out the cold. In true style we then, in turn, shouted for Ernie. At this stage he asked if we would be staying for lunch and we said we would. He then left us and went into the kitchen to tell the chef.

From then on things happened at remarkable speed. The cumulative effects of the rum and possibly the change of temperature took their toll, and in a few minutes we were about half-silly. To this day

Entering Marian Camp in rather cool weather.

George Jones

I truly don't know which of us it was who initiated the move, but I will take the blame. I picked up the rum bottle off the counter and poured each of us a "Jimmy Woodser" which we downed very quickly.

Ernie then came back to the bar and said, "I don't ordinarily leave a bottle of spirits on the bar when I'm away, but I know you boys so well that I don't even bother to check on the level of the bottle when I leave." The grin on his face left no doubt that he was awake to us and I am sure that at the next evening session he enjoyed with the local PWD employees, he would have related what happened, and that his story would be embellished to make it worthy of such a well known raconteur. Ernie certainly told a good story and was also an avid listener to travellers' tales, which were all added to his repertoire. Although he regarded the whole matter as a good joke, his remarks on that occasion provided me with one of the most subtle rebukes I have ever had and I remember it to this day.

By this time lunch was ready and we trooped into the diningroom, where we found that we were the only occupants. I dumped the paybag beside me and managed to collect my thoughts sufficiently to order something to eat. The room was stifling hot, and this did not help us any. We had just about struggled through our meal when I looked around and through the haze I saw our local resident engineer and two of the top-brass engineers from Head Office. They had just returned from the inspection at the Homer Tunnel. I was flabbergasted. I told my two mates, and the state of our thinking was such that one of them even suggested that we should open up a big double-hung window beside us and leave by that route. I saw no fun in that suggestion however, and was still wondering what to do when in came Ernie, who told me that he had some parcels to be delivered at points up the valley. These parcels were at the rear of the premises and he suggested we go out the back door and pick them up. This was a bright move and we promptly took the cue and went that way. Imagine my horror however, when I looked back and saw Joe the driver with his arm half round the neck of one of those top-brass engineers and talking to him in a very animated manner.

This episode is painful to me even to this day, and I will hurry through it. We collected the parcels and moved round the building till we got to the car, which we loaded up. By this time Joe had put in appearance.

"What the hell was your idea in going and breathing booze all over them?" was my query.

"It's all OK," was his reply. "I went to school with his boys and know him well. He'd have been very hurt if I hadn't gone over for a chat."

This may have convinced Joe but it did nothing for me. It was too late to worry however, so we set off up the road to the music of the clanking chain. By this time the haze was wearing off a bit, but we told Joe to drive quietly. He did this for about four miles and then out on to the road shot a half-grown black-and-ginger wild pig.

The light of battle gleamed in Joe's eyes and off we went along the road after that pig. The pig stuck to the road for a while, although he ran a zigzag path at times. The road could not clearly be seen as it was covered in snow, and finally the pig went *zig* and Joe went *zig* after him. Unfortunately the road at this point went *zag*, and that is where we left it, and the Model A slid sideways into a ditch – or "borrow-pit" to use the correct roading term.

We stopped without any appreciable damage, got out and decided to have a smoke. The pig by that time was out of sight. Although the ditch was not very deep, we found when we tried to back out that the wheels would not grip, so somehow or other we would have to get someone to tow us out. Our luck was in, because not long after, along came a PWD road maintenance truck, and towed us out none the worse for our experience.

At this point I have to relate something that happened on the next Homer pay trip that I made with the resident engineer. He was telling me of various happenings on the job over the years and of the trouble and adventures that had taken place.

"At one stage, Andy," he said, "we had trouble with the pay people drinking too much at the hotels on the way up." Then he added: "Fortunately we don't have that trouble now."

He made his point and I got the message, loud and clear.

After the pig incident, we had a slow and uneventful trip for about twenty-five or thirty miles, but were still suffering severely with the cold. Fortunately we met another road maintenance truck and the surfaceman had the billy on. We had several cups of hot tea and got on our way again. We arrived at the Marian camp at about 4 pm and I picked up Dan Campbell, and the pair of us ploughed around in the snow and paid the men at the camp. They were all in their huts and it was slow going.

At one hut we found a man doing very fine needlework, and Dan told me that he knew of five men on the job doing crochet, knitting and embroidery. Others he said did carving, wood inlays and landscape paintings. One man, a keen trout fisherman, made fly rods, and I was very much taken aback on one of my visits when he called me over to his hut and presented me with a beautiful rod and some flies which he had tied himself. This rod was equal in workmanship to anything I could buy at any sports dealer. In addition it had a unique feature – at a point just above where the reel would be attached was my actual signature. I found later from Dan Campbell that he had been asked to get a copy of my signature which was then traced on to the cane of the rod and gone over with Indian ink. The whole rod was then varnished. I've caught many fine fish on that rod.

We had dinner at the staff mess and afterwards played cards. It was the usual poker game with chips at ten for a penny, with limit rises of five chips, so nobody really got fleeced.

At the end of the evening someone suggested we finish up with a "freeze out" and this was agreed to. The rules of this form of sport were simple. Each player had to have three threepenny pieces and on the first round all put in one threepence. An ordinary poker hand was then dealt and cards were bought as required. There was no betting as all hands were tabled face up and the man with the worst hand was "frozen out". All he had to do however, was to put in his second threepence and he was in again. After losing three threepences, however, he was frozen out for good. This went on until only two players remained and on the final game the winner took the whole kitty.

Next day the weather was still bad and we had to travel the full distance from Marian to the Homer Tunnel behind a tractor fitted

Paying out in cold cash. Dan Campbell and a bridge carpenter are signing paysheets, author is holding pay bag, Jack Dawson looks on, and the Model A is wearing chains.

Author

"We travelled behind a snowplough". Driver Jack Hodge (*peaked hat*) sits with driver Ron Topping (*goggles*). Big Bill Pearce and John Christie are walking up behind.

Ray Wilson

up as a snowplough. Jack Hodge, well known around Riversdale, was the snowplough driver, and on a few easy stretches he handed over the controls to me.

Dan and I paid the men along the route and my fingers were so cold that I could not lift the envelopes out of the bag. I held a pencil in the palm of my hand and stuck it into the envelopes and prised them out.

At one hut there was a chap who had a nasal accent and claimed to be a Yank. He had a broadcast-band battery radio and told Dan he could get Chicago on it. He invited Dan to his hut one night and apparently all that Dan could hear was a conglomeration of whistles and crackling noises, plus what Dan thought were bits and pieces of Australian professional wrestling. This sort of reception and the Australian wrestling matches were about the limit of the sets in those days. The Yank was quite confident that he was getting Chicago, however, and when Dan asked him how he knew what it was, he had the simple answer "Bud," he said, "can't you hear them police whistles?"

A bit further up the valley we came to a hut and Dan told me that the occupant had installed what was the only inside toilet in the whole area. Actually it was not a full-scale job – just a urinal, and he was very proud of it. When we knocked at the door, the occupant came out and signed for his pay, and Dan asked him how the convenience was going. "Scone-hot," was his description, and Dan with that puckish humour of his asked if I could view the installation. This was agreed to with a certain amount of almost girlish giggles and there it was in its glory. Not exactly a Clochemerle version but nevertheless very efficient. It consisted of a conical petrol filler jammed into a piece of steel tubing. The other end of this tubing had then been poked through a knot-hole in the wall and the petrol filler wired into position. The steel tube used was a pair of bicycle handlebars which had been sawn in half. This, the proud owner claimed, avoided the necessity of making tricky bends in the pipe – they were already there.

We ploughed our way steadily on and soon gave up any thought of getting back to Invercargill or Te Anau that day. We would have to put in a second night at the Valley.

One of our calls was on a chap who had recently had a good win in the Art Union, and Dan took the opportunity to congratulate him. The result had appeared in the Invercargill paper and the nom-de-plume published was "Tinburn". Dan of course wanted to know what prompted him to use such a curious nom-de-plume, and the proud winner said that he hadn't used that nom-de-plume at all.

"Well what did you use?" asked Dan.

"Tinbum."

Obviously the press in those days was a little more prudish than it is today.

The rest of the day passed without any unusual incidents and we were back at the mess for dinner – cold and hungry.

That evening we all congregated after dinner and the usual round of chaffing went on. This seemed to be the way of relieving the tensions and on this particular evening it was poor old Dan Campbell who was in the gun. It seemed that on the previous pay one of the men had asked Dan to place £3 on a horse called Rocks Ahead. Dan, like most of the men on the job, was interested in racing and thought that Rocks Ahead was such a poor bet that he wouldn't send the money to the bookmaker but would carry the bet himself. "I'll sit on it," was the term he used when he told his mates. Unfortunately for Dan the horse won and paid £3 odd, and Dan had to pay the £9 or £10 to the original punter.

"It's 'rocks ahead' for me for the next few months," said Dan, to the great amusement of his mates. £10 in those days was a lot of money in anybody's language – so rocks ahead it was for poor old Dan.

Talk then went from racing to mice and I learned of the terrific plague of mice that there had been in the Eglinton Valley at an early stage of the road construction. Photos were produced showing the floors of huts and stores to be almost covered with them and we were told of the various methods of catching them.

Apparently the most popular was to half-fill a 4-gallon kerosene tin with water and build a wooden platform round the top about three inches wide. A series of little see-saws was then fitted up on this platform with one end overhanging the water, and on this overhanging end a piece of bacon or cheese was tied. A few sticks connected the wooden platform to the ground and the stage was set. The mouse climbed up the sticks on to the platform, walked out on the see-saw and down into the water he went. The see-saw was balanced so as to return to its original position after the mouse had left it. The main fun came from making and improving the mousetraps, which goes to support the old adage that "The pleasure is in the hunt – not in the kill."

Later on, one of the foremen who had been on the South Island Main Trunk railway told a story and as it involved the paymaster I found it very interesting. It seems that on a section of railway under construction north of Parnassus, the track ran beside the Conway River, and when the paymaster arrived a small locomotive was standing waiting for him. Loco drivers in those days worked long hours and earned good money, and after his pay packet had been handed over this loco driver opened it up, counted the money and

Aftermath of an avalanche. Men of the road are attending to injured mates.

Bob Taylor

then extracted a £5 note. He then took out a round tin of Riverhead Gold tobacco, which at that time was wrapped in a greaseproof packing which lined the tin. The driver very carefully lifted out this packing and put the £5 note at the bottom of the tin. He then replaced the paper package and the small amount of tobacco it contained, and put the tin back in his pocket.

The paymaster thought that this was a bit unusual but made no comment, and was soon on his way paying the rest of the men.

On his next trip however, he heard the sequel to this story. It appears that next day the small amount of tobacco was finished and the loco driver, after making up his final smoke, slowly pressed the lid back on the tin, leaned out of the cab of the little loco and heaved the tin into the Conway River. He lightheartedly watched the tin hit the water and then saw it start off downstream. Suddenly the awful truth hit him. There, floating down the Conway, was his tin still with the greaseproof paper lining in it and under the paper was that precious £5 note that he had extracted before handing his pay over to Mum.

At this point the Conway ran parallel with the railway for a considerable distance and the river was not particularly fast-running. There was a chance of getting the tin, so the driver yelled to the fireman to hop in the cab and the chase was on. In a minute or two

It Snowed!

the train was away and the tin was soon in view. The driver kept
pace with it for a while, hoping it would run ashore or into a
backwater, but with no luck.

He then decided on a bold move – flat out for a while, slam on
the brakes, down the bank with a shovel, and fish out the tin.

Action kept pace with theory for a while, and when the stop was
made they headed off the tin and were waiting with the shovel when
it floated into view. The final act of retrieving the tin did not run to
plan however. As the tin came floating down towards the two men,
they could see victory in sight, but at the last moment it took an
outward swerve and it passed them.

Off again in the loco, pass the tin, and down the bank was the
order of events. This time the tin floated near enough to enable the
driver to get the shovel under it. He was a bit over-anxious, however,
and in stepping back he stood on a slippery rock and the tin fell off
his shovel. There was one pleasing feature, however – the tin was
riding high and dry and it seemed that there was little chance that
it would sink.

The same routine continued – start the engine, pass the tin,
down the bank and this time there was no trouble. The tin just floated
into a backwater and it wasn't even necessary to use the shovel.

Avalanche damage seen from inside the tunnel.

Jim Sutherland

The driver just picked up the tin and climbed up the bank. He opened the tin, pulled out the greaseproof paper lining and there, in all its pristine glory, was the crisp £5 note.

Naturally the rail gang he had left behind wanted to know why the loco had suddenly taken off, and the story was told to the amusement of all. Unfortunately this tale was related in the pub and went the round of the camp until it reached the ears of the loco driver's wife. She failed to see anything funny in her husband "nicking" £5 out of the pay packet, and by the time she had finished her tirade he couldn't see the funny side either.

After this story had been told it was getting late so we had supper and turned in for the night. We were away early next morning and on the return trip we found that the weather improved as we got down country and all in all we had a reasonably pleasant trip home although it was still bitterly cold.

8

PAYS, PIGS AND CRAYS

I WOKE JUST as we arrived at Te Anau at about 7.30 am. Mac was driving and I realised I had been asleep most of the journey. "You're a beaut," he said. "You promised to drive part of the way."

I asked him why he hadn't wakened me and he said, "I hadn't the heart – you looked so peaceful." I didn't argue further as I felt so peaceful. That extra sleep was what I had wanted.

All the road maintenance gang hadn't arrived at the Te Anau Depot so we waited around for a while and had a chat. One of the men said they had found a wonderful new bait for trout – a small live mouse with a hook lightly nicked into his belly. Highly illegal no doubt, but we were assured it was very effective.

One of the chaps had a bike which he intended to use on the job and he asked me to arrange for him to be paid a cycle allowance. I agreed to do so and he told me of a job that he had previously worked on where all the men but one had bikes. This man's mates were often at him to get one but he steadily refused, and one day they asked him *why* he wouldn't get a bike. In a broad Irish accent he said, "Begorra – I have no time for them – bike riding is a lazy man's job. It's only walking sitting down."

Just at this moment the rest of the gang arrived by truck and I paid them. One of them remarked that they had got a couple of new pig dogs and suggested that we work late that evening and get away early next morning and have a go at some pigs. As an extra incentive he remarked that these dogs were excellent holders, and then added, "They're bloody beauts – got a bit of bulldog in them."

He was preaching to the converted so I said to Mac, "What about it?"

"OK," he said, and we arranged to meet at 7 am next day.

It may seem strange for us to arrange shooting trips like this during working hours, but under the conditions we encountered we were virtually free agents and never worked by the clock.

As usual we were in a hurry and soon headed off. In view of our projected trip we were travelling fast and cutting stops to a minimum time, but at about the next four or five places I collected some sort of a job to do – either up the road or in town. Out came the red notebook and I made the necessary notes.

61

The Te Anau maintenance truck. Overseer Tom Plato smokes a cigarette, J. Hogan holds the bumper down while Digger Scully folds his arms.

H.J. Gawith

We soon reached the sawmill and were just in time to strike a cup of tea, which was very welcome. I paid the men and just as I was getting ready to leave, Nick Ward the head sawyer, called me over and said, "I've got a beech burr for you. It'll make a lovely clock for your bedroom." He went over to his hut and came back with a very nicely shaped beech burr somewhat larger than a soccer ball. A burr is a form of external growth found on beech trees. It is generally attached to the trunk of the tree by a very small connecting branch and can usually be removed from the fallen tree quite easily. In appearance it is something like a pumpkin, covered over with round knobs of bark about as big as marbles. The inside of the burr is really one large mass of knots — or rather one large knot — and the grain when polished can be very spectacular.

"I've had this drying out for some time," said Nick, "and if you'll come over to the mill I'll put it through the saw and see if it's any good." We walked over to the mill and he switched on the circular saw and once more I had it brought forcibly to my notice that these men earned their money the hard way: instead of ten good fingers there were about five complete, and the balance consisted of stumps of varying lengths. Nevertheless it was an adept pair of hands that put that burr through the saw. About two-thirds of the side of the burr was sliced off and the same then done on the other side. This left a roughly circular piece of timber about two inches thick and sixteen inches in diameter, with the outside edge of the circle covered with rough nobbly bark.

"It's a beauty, Harry," he said, and with a further deft movement, he sliced the piece of timber in half, and after examining it carefully he handed me one piece and said, "Here's a memento of the Eglinton Valley."

He then suggested that I should dry the burr out further and get it smoothed off and french-polished and have a clock inserted. I did this and I still have that clock today. It has been admired by many people and is a very appropriate reminder of happy days spent in the Eglinton and Hollyford Valleys.

The beech-burr clock – Nick Ward's "memento of the Eglinton Valley".

Author

I thanked Nick for the burr and we were soon on our way again, and as we got up the valley a bit further Mac pointed out some poles supporting a wire. He said that this was the phone wire to the Marian camp and that in some places the top wire of a fence was used. I don't know whether this was correct, but I do know that sometimes it took half an hour to say a few words when phoning from Invercargill and the usual joke of the office was that it would be clearer if you just poked your head out of the window and shouted. In bad weather there was no chance of getting a message through at all.

While we were paying a gang a bit further up the road, a PWD truck pulled up beside us so I told the driver to tell Dan Campbell that with any luck we would be arriving a bit earlier than usual. As it happened we did arrive early, and picking up Dan, we continued on paying right through to the tunnel. We had missed half a dozen or so men back at the Marian and we managed to get back and pay them before the evening meal. I was certainly tired and hungry that evening. We had left Invercargill at 4 am which meant getting up at 3.30 am. I had certainly had a bit of sleep when I left Invercargill, but the only refreshment we had on the way up were the cups of tea at the sawmill.

After the meal there was a bit of a singsong and later a discussion about half a dozen points raised by the union. I was affected by this so I joined in. Later on there was the usual tale-telling and I'll tell this one in the narrator's own words:

This story is about three very wellknown PWD characters. The first was the clerk-in-charge on the South Island Main Trunk railway construction job – the second was called Bev and the third was known as Nip. The clerk fellow, of course, was a fixture on the job, but the other two didn't belong to the South Island Main Trunk but operated from Wellington, moving around the country quite a lot.

It came about, that at one stage Nip and Bev happened to be down at the South Island Main Trunk job together and they suggested to this clerk-in-charge fellow that he should arrange a crayfishing expedition. This was no sooner said than done, and that evening this trio and three other chaps made their way over the rocks to a favourite "possie" where crayfish abounded. The method of catching them was so simple that it had to be seen to be believed. The only equipment required was a crayfish "pot" and a piece of old fish or paua for bait.

The so-called pot was really a circular net strung on to a ring made of $\frac{3}{8}''$ round steel. The net was made so that it hung down about eighteen inches in the middle, similar to the landing nets used by trout fishermen. A piece of cord was tied tightly from one side of the ring to the other and in the middle of this cord the bait was tied. This pot was suspended on a system of ropes so that it could be lowered off the rocks into the water and pulled up in a horizontal position.

When our little party arrived at the right spot Mr Clerk-in-Charge and Nip and Bev clambered out on a projecting rock, baited up, and heaved in the pot. The rest of us had caught so many crayfish in our time that it was old hat to us, so we sat on the rocks and enjoyed a quiet smoke and started to demolish a few bottles of beer. We had one job only, and that was to shine our torches when called upon.

About twenty minutes later the clerk-in-charge chap yelled out that he was going to have his first "haul-up" and that he wanted us to switch on the lights. We did this and he started pulling up the pot. It was in about six feet of water and he gave a hefty heave for a start and then slowly pulled in the rope. When the pot got to the top of the water it was full of crayfish and they were hanging on to the sides. This was quite a usual catch in those days and the technique was just to wait until the surplus either crawled or dropped off. If this was not done the pot was too heavy to lift on to the rocks.

In due course the surplus crays fell off and the three fishermen hauled up the pot and loaded the catch into sugarbags. They kept on fishing and made several hauls and soon all the bags were full.

Bev and Nip were reluctant to stop fishing but there was no point in continuing. Nip was staying at the hotel for a week or so more and had no use for the crays, and the four South Island Main Trunk employees didn't want any as crayfish were so plentiful in that district that the residents were tired of them and they couldn't be given away. This just left Bev. He had brought a tramper's pack with him from Wellington and was returning from Christchurch on the ferry next evening. He loaded this pack with the crayfish and wanted one of us to take the crays home and cook them in the copper. This didn't appeal as we had all decided to go and have a few quiet drinks at the hotel up the coast at Kaikoura. Someone suggested that Bev should get a load of crays on his next trip, but he definitely wasn't having any of that.

In the finish Mr Clerk-in-Charge had a bright idea. We would take Bev's pack to a spot nearby where a friend had a wirenetting cage in a rocky pool which he used for holding live crays for bait. We could put the crays in there till next afternoon, when Bev would leave by car for Christchurch to catch the ferry. It was explained to Bev that this was the ideal arrangement as he would arrive in Wellington with the crays still alive and kicking, and they couldn't be any fresher than that. He was delighted and so was everybody else – nobody wanted to be cooking crays at midnight.

After Bev's pack had been filled we had a couple of sugarbags of crays left over so we tipped them on the rocks and left them to crawl back into the water. One recollection I have is of someone shining a torch on to an old-man cray which was just about to drop over a ledge into the water. This silhouetted him for a moment and one of the non-fishermen, exhilarated by the beer, fired half a fish at the cray and registered a direct hit. The cray and the fish went over the edge together. It was rumoured afterwards that the clerk-in-charge fellow had had a shot at the cray with a empty beerbottle.

Having dumped Bev's crays in the trap and cleaned ourselves up a bit, we set off up the coast to the hotel. It was about nine o'clock or a bit later when we got there, but business was still brisk. We had a round or two of drinks and the talk came round to fishing. We mentioned that we had caught some crays, and the hotel proprietor's wife said her husband had been out in his boat and had caught some very nice fish. We showed the right amount of interest, and a couple of rounds of drinks later she brought out two plates. One had a big blue cod on it and on the other was a butterfish (greenbone). These were duly admired, and Bev asked that the plates be pushed over his way so that he could have a real good look.

This Bev was a very tall, wellbuilt man with a very neatly trimmed moustache, and all in all had a very distinguished look. He dressed particularly well and was very well spoken. As the plates were pushed over in his direction, he stood up to full height, slowly poked his fingers into his fob pocket and took out a very elegant little penknife. He opened this slowly and then, picking up the blue cod, he poked the blade through the base of its tail, and drawing it backwards he split the tail. He then held the split tail in front of the electric lamp and peered at it for quite a time.

"It's in beautiful condition," he said. He then did the same with the butterfish and pronounced it too to be a very fine fish.

By this time everybody was watching this bit of by-play but not a word was said, although there were several commercial fishermen present. Bev put the fish back on the plate, and the proprietor handed him a towel and he wiped his hands. Nothing more was said about the fish and in due course we had a few more drinks and left for home.

Next day I was talking to the clerk-in-charge and asked him what was Bev's idea in splitting the fishes' tails. He said he hadn't a clue, so he had asked Bev that morning why he did this. Bev said, "No reason at all. But it really looked good, didn't it?".

This was Bev – he was a born humorist – known in the PWD from one end of New Zealand to the other. There were others of his ilk – Knocker, Mick and Cocky, Gormy, Gilbert, Pritch, Kassler, Farach, and so on. What a shame their exploits have not been fully chronicled.

This tale did not finish here however, but it was months after before the South Island Main Trunk people heard the sequel. Bev left for Christchurch that afternoon with his live crayfish in the pack and caught the ferry for Wellington. When he arrived back at the Government Buildings next morning he had a further adventure to relate.

He had got on the ferry all right and put his bag and his pack of crayfish in his cabin. He then wandered around the deck and when the bar opened he dropped in for a drink or two. He had been there for quite a while when suddenly, to use his own words, "I was grabbed from behind, and in no time they had clapped me into irons." He was then told that a man sharing his cabin had gone into it and heard a loud ticking noise which he thought must be a time bomb. He reported it immediately to the purser. Nobody was game to go into the cabin, but a steward identified Bev as the other occupant of the cabin and Bev was immediately arrested and "clapped into irons".

Bev then vowed to his captors that he was innocent of the charge but did mention that he had the pack full of live crayfish. To prove his point he asked to be escorted back to the cabin and got out the tramper's pack. Sure enough, those crays were making quite a noise as they ground their jaws together as crayfish are wont to do. As Bev said, "It could well have been taken for the noise of a time bomb, and it says something for the ship's crew that they acted so efficiently and promptly."

That was Bev's story when he got to Wellington, and whether it was believed or not he wouldn't have cared. His comment would no doubt have been, "Well, it sounded all right, didn't it?"

Author and Harry Double. The Model A's side-curtains were efficient ventilators on a freezing day, and car-heaters were unheard of.

Author

The decision-makers. PWD engineer-in-chief John Wood (*with stick*), resident engineer W.G. Pearce, district engineer T. Ball of Dunedin, are on the Gertrude Saddle deciding on the route for the proposed road and tunnel.

J.H. Christie

Next morning we were up too early for a meal at the cookhouse, so Mac said, "It'll have to be a rabbiter's breakfast for us today— a trip to the toilet and a cigarette."

We were soon on our way and had a forty-mile drive to the pig country. On these trips we always carried guns, as there was often a chance of a shot at a deer on the road or grazing just out of the bush on the edge of the Eglinton River. The chance of getting a shot at a pig was more remote, but on one occasion we hit and injured a pig while rounding a corner in the runabout. This slowed the pig down considerably and I was able to shoot it before it got into the bush. On another occasion we came on to a herd of about thirty deer on the road at Knobs Flat, and they were not greatly concerned at our presence. We slowed down and they trotted in front of us for two hundred yards or so before they broke away and entered the bush. On this trip we had a passenger and did not attempt a shot.

When we arrived at the agreed place the other two chaps and the dogs were waiting. These dogs looked as though they could be very useful, and we were hopeful of a good day's sport.

I must admit that after we had tramped about half a mile or so I began to doubt the value of these dogs. They were tearing all over the place and making enough noise to wake the dead. I mentioned this to one of the owners and he said that all they wanted was "a bit of training", so he immediately administered this – with his boot. Of one thing I was sure, these dogs had been claimed to be good holders, and they certainly looked it. They were some degree of bulldog and had jaws like a hippopotamus.

By this time we were coming on to signs of recent pig rooting and suddenly one of the dogs set off through the scrub with the other soon after him. They headed up a steep face and over a ridge while we followed as fast as we could, and from the noise ahead it was clear that something was happening.

By this time we were really keen, and finally came up with the dogs – and what a sight! One dog had his jaws clamped over the nose and mouth of a sheep, and the other was running round and worrying it. The not-so-proud owner of the dog let fly with his boot, but the dog hung on. By this time the sheep was in a bad way and one of the dog owners cut its throat. Two sheep and two cut throats later we decided to call it a day. We were told that these were wild sheep but, wild or not, none of us was prepared to keep going so we turned back.

About halfway back we saw a pig running flat out across a bare patch about two hundred yards ahead and I had a shot but missed. The only members of the party who didn't see the pig were the dogs but, as Mac said, it was a new experience and a nice day so we could have done a lot worse. We got back to Invercargill earlier than usual.

9

AN UNFORGETTABLE STORM

I REMEMBER one particular pay trip very well, even to the extent of being able to quote the day, month and year from memory. In the first place I was running against time and had to work day and night to get the pay up to the job a bit earlier than usual. This was because I had some leave due and wanted to use it to go to the North Island to visit my fiancée, whom I had not seen for a long time.

For this reason I was keen to have all pays well up to date so that when I asked for leave it would not be refused on account of pressure of work. I remember one evening getting a young engineer to assist me by doing a host of co-op contract calculations on his sliderule while I made out paysheets. Such a help was he, that in a fit of generosity I offered to shout him a meal of fried filleted sole – a famous Southland dish, especially when one went to Son Tall's restaurant in Dee Street and tried out Mr Tall's own variety of worcester sauce.

We did just this and the meal was so good that I thought of ordering a second helping. Money being tight in those days I thought better of this, but did offer to shout my mate another helping. He accepted with alacrity and soon polished off another sole. I don't quite remember why I did this, but when the second fish had been demolished I asked him if he would like another return. To my horror he accepted.

I did not renew the offer, but next day I told one of the chaps in the office about it. "That b . . . 's got hollow legs," he said. "I was on survey with him once and he ate us out of house and home."

In due course I managed to prepare the pay two days earlier than usual and got away to a very early start on the actual payday. Jack, who was a head chainman in the Invercargill office, agreed to come as my driver and we had the resident engineer's maroon V8 Ford sedan. I always liked doing the pay in this vehicle as it had a sort of ridged velvet cover on the seats, which made it warm – a great consideration in that climate. It was also possible to leave the paybags open on the back seat and all I had to do was to turn round and dip out the envelopes as I required them. In the 10 or 15-cwt runabouts there was just the single front seat and it was

Single men's 10′ x 8′ huts at Homer camp.

Kurt Suter

necessary to have the paybag sitting on one's knee all the time and to open and shut it as required. Just as a point of interest, none of the cars we used was equipped with a heater in those days and the nearest we got to luxury on odd vehicles was a strip of glass on the windshield carrying electric wires which were supposed to stop fogging. They did not provide any heat. Considering we operated in sub-freezing temperatures at times and, more often than not, the snow in the Hollyford in the winter was feet deep, we seemed to manage reasonably well. Perhaps I was a bit younger than I am now.

At the start of this trip the rain was steady but not torrential. There was a nasty wind however, and altogether we had a most unpleasant time. It was one of those days which was sufficiently wet to be classed officially as a "wet day". Only essential workers such as road surfacemen and repair gangs actually had to work.

For this reason I had to go into the single huts and the married quarters to find the men, and this was time-consuming. First of all I had to have a look at the new babies, and then the wives produced lists of things they wanted me to get and bring up next pay. Some just gave me a sealed note with instructions that I was to pay what the shopkeeper asked and deliver the parcel back on the next trip.

If ever medals should have been dished out on any job for loyal and patient companions, it would have been to those Hollyford Valley wives. There were virtually no pictures, kindergartens, shops, women's clubs, television, or in fact any social amenities at all. In the winter it was practically impossible to venture outside with

71

Mt Talbot, at whose base The Forks camp was situated. Homer Saddle to the left, the Gertrude Saddle to the right.

J.H. Christie

children on many days. Washing and drying children's clothes must have been a nightmare as the only laundry facility was a kerosene tin on a coal range. They were even denied the joy of a summer garden as the ground was all rocks.

By the time I had got round with the pays on that trip, my red notebook was loaded with things to be done. This is just what I did not want on this particular pay, but that was how it seemed to go.

At this stage of the job, the headquarters camp had, in part, been shifted to The Forks which was situated at the foot of the steep slope leading to the Homer Tunnel portal. The Forks is so named because the valley at that point forks two ways – one leading to the Gertrude Saddle, the other to the Homer Saddle.

At the time there was no guest hut at The Forks camp so all visitors were boarded out. I stayed with Harry Double in his 10 ft x 8 ft hut, and as this was his home he naturally occupied the bottom bunk.

I had my evening meal with Don Hulse, the engineer-in-charge and his wife Grace, who, with their two children, had staff married quarters at The Forks camp.

After dinner it really started to blow and I took my leave of Don and his wife and headed for Harry's hut. He had left the cookhouse and was at his hut when I got there. This hut had a large open fireplace with a galvanised iron chimney about five feet wide at the base and tapering away at the top. When I got there Harry had a lively fire going and a reserve pile of split beech logs about two feet high. The fire was really roaring, and we sat and smoked for a while. The wind then began to get stronger and stronger and, as it blew, the flames started to lick out into the hut just like a forge.

It would have been the safest thing to have doused the fire, but we were frozen stiff as it was and did not want things to get any colder. As we couldn't dodge the flames very well we both got into bed and Harry, being in the bottom bunk, got the benefit and the danger of the naked flames while I was literally smothered in ashes.

Our beds were palliasses filled with straw supported by wire mattresses made of hurricane wire. The wind by this time was terrifying and the rain was torrential. After a while the hut shook so much that I lay face down, clasped my arms around the palliasse and took a good grip of the hurricane wire mattress and hung on like grim death.

There was more to come however. The river became bank high and then overflowed, and we had quite a depth of running water under the hut. There is a song I remember that has a recurrent phrase "And that's not all", and that certainly applied this evening. Things went from bad to worse. The lightning flashed almost continuously and the thunder in this valley fairly shook the ground like an earthquake.

I was still hanging on like grim death and having what I thought might be my last puff of a cigarette, when a further complication arose. With each terrific gust of wind, the gable roof started to move up from the top plate till there was a gap in one spot of about eight inches. I thanked the Lord for the law of gravity as every now and then when there was a lull, the roof dropped back into place and I breathed a sigh of relief, but this would only be for a spell and the gap would open up again.

In the finish I felt sure we were going to lose that roof, so I slid down and stood on the floor as I had visions of being chopped about if the roof did go.

The fire by this time had just about burned out as we hadn't stoked it, and I was able to move about a bit. I moved over to the window and looked out, and in the flashes of lightning I could see Don Hulse moving around outside his house but could not make out what he was doing.

The rain cleared for a short spell and in the dark periods between flashes of lightning I could see the showers of sparks from massive rockfalls thousands of feet above on the slopes of mighty Mt Crosscut. Added to all of this was the continuous roar of avalanches high up on Mt Talbot, 6945 feet, Mt Belle, 6850 feet, and Mt Crosscut, 7600 feet, which encircle and tower sheer above the Forks Camp.

View from Homer Saddle. Mt Crosscut dominates the scene and dwarfs Homer
Camp (bottom left centre). Farther along the road five huts of the Forks Camp
are just visible. Scene of the author's "unforgettable storm".

Weekly News, Bill Beattie photo

This mighty turmoil of the elements continued for long hours after midnight and sleep was impossible.

At last however the wind abated, and the fearsome lifting of the roof became less frightening. I warily climbed back into the top bunk and ultimately fell asleep through sheer exhaustion. Next morning the wind had dropped quite a bit and the river had gone down. Someone facetiously remarked that everything seemed to have returned to "subnormal".

I later asked Don Hulse what he was doing outside in the storm and he told me that his roof too was in danger of lifting and he was trying to get a few strands of number 8 wire over it to hold it down. He said he ultimately gave it up, but I did notice on my next trip to the Homer, that all huts and houses at The Forks camp were securely wired down.

After breakfast we finished off the pay fairly quickly and set off for Invercargill. We had only got as far as Monkey Flat, which is about two miles down the valley, when we came to a ford. The water was deeper than it looked and it may be that Jack took it too fast, but before we knew what had happened the water was level with the floor and the engine stalled. Jack made one or two attempts to start it but without any success. I yelled to him to put it in reverse and put his foot on the starter. He did this and the starter motor gently wound us back on to dry land. We waited for a while for things to dry out a bit and Jack then put his foot on the starter button and, much to my surprise, the motor started. I waded across to cut down the weight and he had another attempt to cross, and miraculously he got through without any trouble.

The weather on the return trip was cold but reasonably fine, and we made good time. We were both dog-tired and shared the driving. While Jack drove I slept, and vice versa. On returning to the office I cleaned up all the odds and ends, working till after midnight. I left notes of the dozens of errands to be done for the men and wives, and early next morning I left by the express for what I considered to be a well-earned holiday.

10

TE ANAU TALES

WHAT A DAY! Everything seemed to be going wrong, and at five o'clock in the afternoon we had just made the 100 miles to Te Anau. We called in at the hotel and the genial proprietor suggested that we should stay the night. He said that things were a bit quiet at the moment and that he would look forward to a pleasant evening. "I always enjoy it when you boys come in with your wild and woolly stories," was the way he put it.

As I have said, the proprietor himself was a wonderful storyteller and many and varied were his anecdotes. If at any time he suggested that we should stay the night we did so as his personal guests, and were treated with the greatest hospitality. I think I'm safe in saying that at that time the Te Anau Hotel rated as high as any in New Zealand, and it was very pleasant to add a touch of real luxury to what were sometimes pretty rough-and-ready trips.

We had a very fine dinner and afterwards were introduced to the only other visitor. He was the representative of a large zoo in Berlin and was very keen on getting permission to take some keas. He asked us about these birds and the only advice we could give him was to mind out that they didn't pick his pocket. The proprietor explained to him that they picked everything else in sight.

We were told that a few of the locals would probably be in for a drink later in the evening, including Gus, and Tom Plato. The latter I always regarded as "the mayor" of Te Anau, as he was so well known in the district.

While we were waiting around we went for a stroll along the road and came to the PWD depot, where we stood chatting. Suddenly an outsize bumblebee flew in and headed straight for the window-pane, where there was an array of spider webs. As the bee hit the webs out shot a very large spider and the battle was on.

Someone called out, "Come and have a look at this scrap," and we all moved over smartly to view what turned out to be a primeval struggle. The spider was about the same size as the bee, and despite the terrific whirring of wings it deftly spun a web around the bee and started to tie things up nicely. The bee then made a prodigious effort and almost broke free, but that spider was no sluggard and he soon had the bee wrapped up again. Once again it started to

Horsedrawn ancestor of the mighty 'dozers'. Standing at this old grader's controls is overseer Tom Plato.

Hazeldines, Invercargill

break away and we felt ourselves almost cheering it on, but the spider had to be contended with, and on each apparent breakaway it would make a quick recovery and start spinning a shroud for the bee.

The battle had been going for about ten minutes and on a number of occasions we were almost tempted to release the bee as the odds were so heavily loaded against it. It was already tiring fast, but in a flash there was a dramatic end to the struggle. The spider suddenly seemed to fling out all his legs except the back two, which remained firmly attached to the web. He shot backwards and finished by hanging upside down from the web – as dead a spider as there ever was. It reminded me of the last act of a cowboy movie where the goody shoots the baddy. It was as dramatic as watching a boxing match in which a boxer being carved to bits by his opponent suddenly lands a lucky straight left and wins by a knockout.

The rest of the story can soon be told. We all looked at each other and smiled with sheer pleasure at this unexpected result. The bee, just to prove that it still had a bit of fight left in it, gave a lusty whirr of its wings, broke free from the web, and quickly headed out the door through which it had come.

The method of despatch of the spider was beyond my knowledge but whether its demise resulted from a series of injuries or from one fatal wound did not matter. The result was dramatic, unexpected and final.

We returned to the hotel, gravitated to the bar and on this evening the first main point of discussion was the bane of all

77

Not a West Coast "Panner" but Charlie Reynolds in the Eglinton Valley peeling spuds for tea in the early days of the road.

Weekly News, Bill Beattie photo

construction camps – camp cooks. It was generally agreed that if a cook was the sort who would remain on a job for a long time and not get on drinking bouts etc., he would be found to have some other outstanding weak point. Generally this was the inability to boil hot water without burning it. Rightly or wrongly, the male cook was always maligned.

Then came a number of stories of the wonderful dishes turned out by various cooks, followed always by the tale of how the cook had fallen from grace and had to be dispensed with.

A variety of methods used by disgruntled cooks to get their own back on their employers was trundled out, but most just wouldn't be printed if I disclosed them. One very potent form of reprisal was mentioned however. The cook that was mentioned would go along for a while and then it would be necessary for him to be reprimanded for something. As soon as this happened he would become sulky and start honing his knives, then testing them out by shaving the hairs on his arm. In the finish it was decided that he must be sacked but no one was game to tell him so, in case he should decide to start cutting a few pieces of throat before he went. The problem solved itself as he went on leave and never returned to the camp.

The talk then turned to local characters and the tales they told, and one chap was criticised as "a bit of a blowhard". I remember the proprietor jumping in to defend him and saying, "Don't criticise him – he just embellishes the truth. There's nothing better than a good story, and what a dull world it would be if we didn't have our share of raconteurs and humorists and other characters." This remark has stayed with me, as it showed a degree of tolerance which I feel we should all try to exercise. I learned quite a few useful lessons from the proprietor of that hotel.

We then moved on to a variety of tales and I remember one fellow named Fred telling a tale about someone he boarded with in Dunedin. This chap never worked consistently, and his father used to pay his board and give him a few shillings a week for pocketmoney. He had casual jobs from time to time but one regular way he had of getting the odd shilling was to borrow off every new boarder who came to the house. As he never paid the money back this source soon dried up. This particular fellow was known to have gone to bed with riding boots and spurs on, and it was generally considered that he was "barmy".

Fred, who was telling this story, went on to relate something that happened to him one day. He was in a great hurry to get down town, and seeing the barmy bloke hanging round he said, "I'm in a hurry to get to town – what about a loan of your bike?"

"Sure, Fred," said the wearer of spurs. "What about a loan of five bob?"

Fred then said, "I caught it fair and square and had to 'lend' him that five bob. He did not pay it back and I have often wondered just how barmy he was."

The next story, which came from one of the local settlers, went thus:

This is a story about good old Sunny Southland and if you don't believe it I'll tell you where it happened and you can go and have a look yourself. The evidence will still be there – unless of course it has been washed away by a flood. This happened many years ago when my old man was working on a river protection job round about Lumsden.

They were building a stopbank, and one day a new man arrived on the job. One look at his hands showed that he wasn't used to labouring work, and the other fellows in the gang felt a bit sorry for him. Instead of putting him on to pick-and-shovel work they decided to give him a go at planting willow cuttings on a completed stopbank. He turned out to be a really keen number, and after a few hours he was planting these cuttings in good style. What's more, he was very quickwitted and a real humorist, and looked like becoming a firm favourite with the gang.

At the end of the day the ganger in charge of this section of the job came along to make an inspection of the work and was quite astounded at the progress the new man had made. This ganger was a nasty type and not too bright up top, but he had a cunning habit of being critical and complaining in an endeavour to keep himself in an advantageous position.

He had a good look over the job and instead of passing a favourable comment, as he might well have done, he complained that a number of willow cuttings here and there had been planted upside down.

This new man, however, was extremely quick, and in a flash he claimed that he had done this on purpose as he thought it would look much better, and break the monotony, to have a few weeping willows interspersed with the others. Caught on the hop, and not being sure of his ground, the ganger said, "OK then – leave them as they are, I just wanted to be sure that you had your wits about you." As an afterthought and in line with his usual practice of complaining about everything, he said, "In future, if you have any ideas, however bright they may be, I think you had better get my OK first."

Someone said at the end of the story – "That's a tall one, Jack," but Jack had a quick answer: "Not as tall as those weeping willows on the Lumsden stopbank – "that's if they haven't been washed away by floods."

By the time this story had been told it was getting late and mine host shouted for the crowd and closed the bar. We wanted to get away early so we asked him if we could settle our account. "I'd like you to be my guests," he said. "You boys are always willing to help me and I enjoy the little sessions we have in the evenings." We thanked him and were soon in bed and asleep.

Next morning we set off at seven for the Hollyford – about a day later than we had planned, but these things happened and it was just part of the job.

When I arrived at the Hollyford, Dan was waiting as usual with his titbits of information and was soon telling me about a character known on the job as Johnny.

It seems that a trip out to the races had been mooted for quite a time and arrangements had been made for seven men to chip in for the cost of the trip. One of them owned a big car and he was prepared to drive them out provided he got his expenses out of it. Came the day and off they set for Gore. As usual, all pubs en route were visited, but notwithstanding this they arrived on time and in reasonably good fettle. They had a pleasant if not profitable day, and after the races were over the programme was to be the same – a stop for refreshments wherever possible – numerous comfort stops, etc. On reaching Te Anau, which was the last hotel, they stocked up heavily with bottles of refreshment in case they should die of thirst on the final blistering fifty-mile dash over that scorching snow.

All went nicely till they were fairly well up the valley and overtook another vehicle also returning from the races. Somehow or other one of those mysterious skids occurred and one car, after passing the other, landed up with a nasty bump in a ditch. It was not damaged much and was soon pushed out of the ditch. Nobody seemed to be hurt, so another comfort stop was taken, but here it was discovered that old Johnny must have been suffering from shock. He just couldn't manage one, and everybody – except Johnny – was hilarious.

The seriousness of the situation soon became apparent however, and it was decided that a dash would have to be made to the nearest doctor, who was at Lumsden. The second car was to follow up in case it was needed.

Speed was of the essence and off they went, but it was a day of accidents. Trying to take another corner too fast the car again ran off the road, and this time hit a tree. Johnny was shot forward and hit his head on a crosspiece of timber on the roof. He was unconscious when they lifted him out but this was found to be a blessing in disguise, as apparently the shock he had previously suffered seemed to be relieved by the second accident and Johnny, unconscious, took his comfort stop.

By this time the second car had arrived. Johnny was coming to and was given a bottle of beer, this being all the first aid within the power of those present. After a few swigs from the bottle he seemed much better. He had a nasty lump on his head but refused to get medical attention and finally they got him back to his hut. He put a couple of days in bed but was soon back on the job apparently not much worse for the experience. The men in that Hollyford Valley were certainly tough.

After relating this story Dan suggested that we set off up the road and we were soon hard at it paying the men.

We finished late in the afternoon and I decided we would set off for Invercargill and make up some of the time we had lost. We arrived home in the early hours next morning.

11

ABOUT DAVE GUNN, KURT SUTER
AND OTHERS

IN ANOTHER CHAPTER I refer to the memorial plaque at the old
Marian Camp site commemorating the twenty-one hour dash made
by Dave Gunn from Big Bay on the West Coast to the Marian
camp. He did this epic journey to telephone for assistance to
passengers injured in a plane crash at Big Bay on the West Coast
on 30 December 1936.

On this day a small charter plane on a flight from Invercargill
crashed on landing on the beach at Big Bay. A young Invercargill
man named Walter Sutton Jones was killed and others were injured.
Help was needed urgently, and the nearest phone was at the
Marian camp.

Dave Gunn, a wellknown settler in this remote area, happened
to be at Big Bay at the time of the crash and he elected to go to
Marian for help. Experienced trampers reckoned on this being a
three-day trip, but Dave Gunn did it in twenty-one hours, which
involved rowing for twelve miles, walking for sixteen miles, and
covering the latter part on horseback, making numerous crossings
of the swift-flowing Hollyford.

On the morning of the day that news of the Big Bay crash reached
Invercargill I went to Riverton for the day with a mate from the
office named Jack McBride. I remember we called at the hotel and
had a few, just to acknowledge the holiday period. Feeling much
better we headed down the beach for a stroll, and no sooner had we
got there than a tiny high-wing monoplane dropped out of the sky
and landed right beside us.

I thought it was the tiniest plane I had ever seen – it didn't appear
to be more than about 4'6" to 5' high. I was told afterwards that
it was probably an early model Taylorcraft, constructed out of
tubular steel framing and fabric-covered.

What intrigued me however, was the general appearance of the
plane. If anybody had asked me for a description, I would have
said that it resembled a bunch of bicycle frames with a rag covering,
and I was thinking to myself, "Well, Harold, there's one joker here
that won't be going up in that crate – and that's you."

My thoughts were interrupted by the pilot and another man

Dave Gunn grazes his horse, near the Hidden Falls hut, Lower Hollyford Valley.
Weekly News, Bill Beattie photo

getting out of the plane right beside me. By this time several people had congregated around the plane and I was still gazing at it very critically when the man accompanying the pilot called out, "Who wants a ride – ten bob for a quarter of an hour?"

"We do," cried a voice at the back of me, and I looked round. It was my mate Jack and the "we" he referred to included "me". As I have already said, I didn't like the look of that plane one little bit – but there was worse to come. The man selling the flights then produced a pad of forms asking us to sign one each. I looked at one and found that it was a form indemnifying the owners of the aircraft from any claims should passengers be killed or injured in the crash. But that's not all – the name shown as the owner of the aircraft was the same as the owner of the plane which that very morning had been reported by the press as having crashed at Big Bay a day or so earlier.

I think I must always have been something of a coward, as I was more afraid of backing out than of making the flight, so up we went. Small and all as the plane looked it was a cabin type and took the three of us. It went very well except when we went over some high ridges, when it dropped alarmingly for what seemed about fifty feet. The pilot and Jack soon became good friends and were chatting very amicably, but what worried me was that the pilot, who sat in front, turned completely round and chatted with Jack and steered the plane without even looking where he was going. As a careful rider of a pushbike I thought this was a bit "on the nose". Jack was sitting in front of me and I poked him in the back once or twice to stop him from distracting the pilot, but all to no avail; and so friendly did they get that the pilot extended our trip from fifteen minutes to twenty-five minutes without extra charge. He said it was good for business on a first flight and it would give his mate time to sign up a few more victims. Actually he didn't use the word "victims" – that was my thought; he referred to "clients".

I remember thinking at the time that if the pilot had wanted to do me a good turn he would have cut the flight to ten minutes instead of increasing it to twenty-five minutes. It wasn't long however, before the pilot headed the plane back to a very nice landing on the beach and off the pair of us went to finish out the day in Riverton.

The next time I saw Dave Gunn at the Marian camp I told him about the flight. He smiled when I said it came a bit too close on the Big Bay crash for my liking. His comment was brief: "I'd rather go on horseback."

It is ironic that the Hollyford rivers, which played such a part in Dave Gunn's life, should, in the end, have claimed that life. He was drowned while crossing a ford on 25 December 1955. His body was never found. He had gone to join those Men of the Road who died in the Hollyford Valley in the years gone by.

Another wellknown name in the Hollyford Valley was Kurt Suter, and the following exploit illustrates the type of man he was.

The Homer camp and the nearby Forks camp were often visited by tourists who generally came in by the Railways bus. From time to time the area was also used as a base for climbing trips.

Experienced guides were available at the Homer camp, one very wellknown guide being Tom Cameron. On one occasion Tom arranged to take two young trampers named John Hunter McLean and George Chance to Milford Sound via the Grave-Talbot Pass. This involved an ascent to the Homer Saddle directly above the tunnel mouth. On reaching this point climbers veered to the right and ascended what is known as Talbot's Ladder, and then followed the well known Grave-Talbot Pass to Milford Sound.

This trip, led by Tom Cameron, proved very pleasant and the party, after a stay in the Milford Sound area, decided to return to the Homer camp by the same route.

84

It was the 9th day of February 1938, when tunnel overseer Jack Dawson, who was at the tunnel portal, happened to glance up towards the Homer Saddle and noticed a climber moving down the slope. When first seen he appeared to be no bigger than an ant and his progress down the mountain seemed very slow. On most days a climber would not have been visible, but the weather on this occasion was bright and the air was very clear. From time to time Jack managed to pick up the tiny figure and watch his gradual descent.

In due course the climber made his way down towards the tunnel mouth and over the last short distance Jack Dawson watched him continuously. When he reached the tunnel portal Jack discovered that he was George Chance, who had left for Milford Sound with Tom Cameron a few days before. Despite the considerable time he had been in view, Chance had made a hurried descent and he had a tragic story to tell.

On the return trip all had gone well until the party reached Talbot's Ladder. At this spot a boulder suddenly came crashing down the slope. It miraculously missed the other two climbers but struck and killed John McLean. Guide Tom Cameron elected to stay with the body and instructed George Chance to complete the trip to the Homer camp and fetch assistance. From the point where the accident occurred all that remained of the party's return journey was the final descent of 1500 or 1600 feet to the tunnel mouth.

On learning of the tragedy Jack Dawson immediately thought of Kurt Suter, who was the proprietor of the workmen's cookhouse at the Homer camp. Kurt was a Swiss alpine guide with years of experience at Mt Cook and Franz Josef, and in a short time he had organised a party. While he was doing this Jack Dawson contacted the police in Lumsden and it was agreed that the body should be recovered immediately.

Kurt Suter went ahead of the main party, which was waiting with a stretcher at the head of the valley. When he reached the scene of the accident it was confirmed that McLean was dead and Kurt tied a climbing rope to the body and hoisted it on to his shoulders. While on Talbot's Ladder Tom Cameron held the rope to stop the body falling down the precipitous slope into the Cleddau Valley on the western side of the Saddle should Kurt have stumbled at any spot.

On reaching the Homer Saddle Kurt began the final descent of 1400 feet on the eastern side of the saddle into the Hollyford Valley, and for two and a half hours he carried that body slung over his shoulders. He made the precipitous descent, picking his way, step by step, down the rocky slope till he finally reached the waiting stretcher party. Only then did he relinquish his burden.

This long-drawn-out and dramatic feat was enacted in the natural

Kurt Suter, who performed what was in veteran roadman Jack Dawson's opinion, "the greatest feat of strength and endurance he had encountered in a lifetime of heavy construction work". In this photograph Kurt is leading a party to the ascent of Mt Christina; the party bivouacked for the night on this ledge, over 5000 feet above Marian camp.

J.H. Christie

rocky amphitheatre at the head of the Hollyford Valley and Kurt's tortuous progress was watched by practically all the inhabitants of the Homer camp. At first only those with the keenest eyesight, or with fieldglasses, were able to keep track of Kurt, but as he got lower down the slopes he could be seen by all, picking his way down the face. On occasions he would be lost from sight as he rounded a bluff or disappeared behind a large boulder, but the weather was so clear that he would soon be picked up again a bit further down the slope.

The Homer was an isolated spot in those days and news travelled slowly and I doubt whether an account of Kurt's feat ever appeared in the press. Nevertheless this event will ever be remembered by those who witnessed it, and only recently, when I was talking to Jack Dawson, he said this was the greatest feat of strength and endurance he had encountered in a lifetime on heavy construction work. It was a feat that had to be seen to be believed – a feat that could be performed only by a superman. Jack's final laconic comment was, "There was only one Kurt Suter."

No story of the Hollyford Valley would be complete without some reference to the pioneer McKenzie family of Martins Bay. Daniel McKenzie and his wife Margaret lived in Hokitika in the early 1870s, Mr McKenzie being on the staff of the *West Coast Times*. At this time

Malcolm McKenzie, one of the "Pioneers of Martin's Bay", is talking to Bill Beattie (*seated*) who took many of the photographs in this book. The scene is on the track from the Routeburn to the Dore Pass.

Weekly News, Bill Beattie photo

he had a young family of three children and this is of extreme interest to the writer as my own maternal grandparents at this time also resided in Hokitika with a young family. My grandfather, Alexander Somerville, was an accountant in Hokitika and my mother was born in that town.

In 1875 the McKenzie family shifted to Jacksons Bay further down the West Coast and a year later they moved to Jamestown in the Lower Hollyford Valley, on the shore of Lake McKerrow. Within a couple of years they shifted a short distance to a site nearer the beach at Martins Bay. They had two further sons after leaving Hokitika.

The story of the McKenzie family has been graphically set out by Alice McKenzie, a daughter of Daniel and Margaret, in her book *Pioneers of Martins Bay*. Alice had one sister Helen and three brothers, Dan, Malcolm, and Hugh. The latter two, in due course, took over the cattle run from their father and later sold it to David Gunn.

Dan McKenzie junior, and a mate, Bill McPherson, were responsible for forming many of the tracks in the area and built the Homer Hut (earlier known as the McKenzie Hut) and the McPherson Hut in the Esperance Valley. Both of these huts were constructed of pitsawn timber to serve parties crossing to and from Milford Sound by way of the Grave-Talbot Pass.

Another job carried out was the fixing of wire ropes on the slippery rock face on what is known as Talbot's Ladder on the Grave-Talbot Pass. This was formerly a key route to Milford Sound, but it has lost its importance since the tunnel was pierced.

The McKenzie brothers also acted as guides for tramping parties and their names are closely linked with the area, right up to and including the tunnel construction period. *Auckland Weekly News* photographer Bill Beattie has told me of a trip he made with Dan and Malcolm McKenzie from the Routeburn to the Milford Track via the Dore Pass.

Mention must also be made of William Henry Homer, a landholder at Martins Bay, who discovered the saddle at the head of the Hollyford Valley which now bears his name. This occurred in January 1889.

Homer and his companion, G. Barber, attempted to cross the saddle and make a descent into the Cleddau Valley which leads to Milford Sound. They were unsuccessful and Homer also found that a crossing of the Gertrude Saddle, also at the head of the Hollyford Valley, on the other side of Mt Talbot, was equally impracticable. He was highly enthusiastic about the prospects of driving a tunnel under the Homer Saddle, but his pleas failed to convince the authorities. He died in 1894 and was buried in the Queenstown Cemetery.

In January 1891 a PWD survey party member, by the name of William Quill, was given the task of placing a flag on the Homer Saddle in a position where it could be seen from the Cleddau Valley. This flag was necessary to enable bearings to be taken in connection with investigations of the tunnel project first advocated by Homer.

Quill was an enthusiastic and capable man and had already achieved fame by climbing the 1904 feet cliff beside the Sutherland Falls and discovering the lake which now bears his name.

He chose to do the trip from his headquarters at the Greenstone without a companion, and placed the flag on the Homer Saddle as required. On his own initiative he then decided to climb the Gertrude Saddle and attempt to make a crossing to Milford Sound. On 15 January 1891 he left a note in his tent stating what he intended to do. On 19 January, when Quill failed to return to his headquarters, a search was made and from signs on the cliff face it was obvious that he had fallen to his death on the precipitous western slope of the Gertrude Saddle.

Many years later his relatives arranged for a commemorative plaque to be fixed on a large glacial boulder below Gertrude Saddle at the head of the Gulliver Valley where Quill had fallen.

Over the years the Homer and Gertrude Saddles defied the attempts of climbers to make a crossing, but in 1909–1910 two explorers, Messrs Grave and Talbot, after many excursions, found an alternative high-level route from the Homer Saddle to Milford Sound. Direct crossings however, continued to elude climbers.

Early in 1935, when John Christie and his PWD survey party were at the head of the Hollyford Valley it became essential to arrange for an accurate triangulation to fix the line and levels of the tunnel so that preliminary work on its construction could be begun. This triangulation made it necessary to set up two observation stations in the Homer camp, another two on the Homer Saddle, and another three in the Cleddau Valley. It was at this point that a serious difficulty was encountered.

To get from the Upper Hollyford, which would be the site of the inland portal, to the Upper Cleddau Valley, the site of the Milford Sound portal, was a full day's journey via the Grave-Talbot Pass, provided the members of the party had a good knowledge of the pass and were blessed with continuous fine weather. Neither of these conditions applied, and as John Christie was running short of time, he sought an alternative. A descent from the Homer Saddle direct to the Cleddau had still not been made by climbers, but John Christie, an experienced climber, was aware that permanent ropes had been established (by Dan McKenzie and Bill McPherson) on the trickiest part of the Grave-Talbot route and he decided to have a look at the possibility of fixing similar ropes from the Homer Saddle straight down the face into the Cleddau Valley. If this were possible the trip would be reduced to a 1500 feet climb directly above the proposed inland tunnel portal in the Hollyford Valley to the Homer Saddle, and a similar drop of 1900 feet to the vicinity of the proposed western portal in the Cleddau Valley.

To test out his theory, John ordered considerable lengths of manila rope and arranged for the blacksmith to sharpen large numbers of varying lengths of scrap steel from old rock drills. These were to be used as pegs to which rope would be tied. A direct descent was first tried but abandoned. This indicated a possible access to a basin in the north and after a while the party managed to place ropes and descend the precipitous face to a point about 100 feet above the scree slope which would provide reasonable walking access to the floor of the Cleddau.

Ropes on this last section were ultimately fixed by John Christie, John Grindley and Bill McCallum, and on 16 February 1935 these men succeeded in making the first crossing to Milford Sound by way of the western face below the razorback Homer Saddle.

This 'Homer Rope' route provided an answer to the survey difficulties, and was later used for a mail service to the Milford survey party, and for a telephone line. About 1937 the ropes deteriorated and this route fell into disuse.

John Christie's survey camp near the foot of Mt Talbot. *Left to right*: Bill Hall, John Grindley, George Jones, Gordon Miller (*kneeling*), Bill McCallum (*at back*), John Christie, Sid Mann.

Weekly News, Bill Beattie photo

John Christie and Sid Mann (*seated*) on the Homer Saddle making the triangulation survey for the tunnel.

J.H. Christie

In a later chapter is the story of a pay being taken over to Milford Sound by way of the Homer Rope route.

I have heard many tales of the survey party days and the primitive conditions under which they worked, but these are not mine to tell. John Christie loved and has continued to love the mountains of Fiordland, and the honour of trail blazing belongs to him and his intrepid survey party.

In a recent discussion with John Christie, he mentioned that with the completion of the Homer Tunnel few people would now visit the head of the Gulliver, where the plaque is erected to the memory of William Quill. John considers that it would be more appropriate if the memorial plaque were now removed to the Gertrude Saddle. I too am of this opinion as the Gertrude trip is a very popular one for climbers, and the Saddle is actually the area from which Quill fell to his death.

12

"COMPO"

Compo is the universal term for payments made to workers injured on the job, and denotes a payment under the Workers' Compensation Act. Many and varied are the stories told about compensation, and all I will do is to talk about a few of the cases I have encountered.

First of all was the case of one man who reported an accident and was supported in all his claims by evidence produced in the correct manner. It was a case of strain, and he had a doctor's report as well as reports from his mates detailing the time of the accident, the symptoms etc. It was an open and shut case, fully documented and checked, and was finally paid out. Not long after the compensation was paid out, this man came along to the foreman and said that something had come into his life and that he had now "seen the light". He confessed that he had deceived the Department and his workmates: actually the accident had occurred in the weekend when he was chopping wood.

In due course the money was refunded. "More power to him," said the foreman, "but he might have picked a more convenient time to 'see the light'."

In another incident a man swallowed a nail and my friend Dan was left with the initial job of making a case for payment of compensation. Bookwise there seemed to be a bit of a snag, as the instructions stated that the accident had to happen "during and in the course of the ordinary employment of the worker".

It turned out that the man was holding a nail in his mouth and suddenly he found that he had swallowed it. Dan took his job seriously and he was a little puzzled how to decide whether this accident actually happened "in the course of the ordinary employment of the worker". He wondered whether holding nails in the mouth was essential and in the ordinary course of the duties of a carpenter, and was not at all sure in his mind that this was the case. But he did come up with one bright idea when it would have been OK.

"Just imagine a situation," he said, "when the carpenter was in such an enclosed space that the only way he could drive a nail would be to hold it in his mouth and hit himself on the back of the head with a hammer. He would be OK then."

This caused a laugh but didn't really help Dan in making up his

Hard work – particularly if you were in a co-op gang like this and paid by results. Men who were not fully fit could all too easily sustain injury and become "compo" candidates.

Weekly News, Bill Beattie photo

report. In the finish he must have got round things all right as the man ultimately got his compensation – and the nail.

On the Hollyford job the road went through beech forest, but this was locally called birch. Woe betide us if we referred to birch trees in our correspondence with Head Office: we were reminded that it was *beech* and given all sorts of advice telling us that the botanical name was something like *Fagus fagusti,* and so on.

Some people are allergic to beech trees and the local name for this allergic condition was birch itch. On one occasion a compensation claim was sent to Wellington advising that the condition suffered was birch itch. Back came a reprimand about this use of the term birch – it should be *beech,* Head Office pointed out. Nothing was done about this until it one day came to the notice of our chief.

He was quick to reply and acknowledge that the trees were beech not birch, but the itch suffered by the men was birch itch not beech itch. It was locally named by them, and as far as his staff were concerned they used the term birch itch to describe the allergy caused by beech trees. There was no further comment from the Moguls in Head Office.

Accidents involving explosives were rare, as most men on this job had considerable experience in using them and there were a number of trained men holding PWD shot-firer's tickets.

The danger with explosives sometimes came from co-op gangs who were cutting down on time by using short fuses and a very quick sprint. One gang of young lads led by a headman from the Oamaru district had a reputation along these lines.

On two occasions I arrived in the pay car just as accidents occurred with explosives. One was said to be the result of ramming explosives into a hole in a rock with a steel rod instead of the copper rods usually supplied. Two men received fairly severe face and head injuries, but fortunately they recovered.

On the other occasion Dan and I were travelling round in a truck and the headman of the gang stopped us and said they were just due to light the fuses. Dan suggested we get under the back of the truck and I crawled under with him. The headman stood by the truck and after the shots were fired we crawled out, and there he was sitting on the ground with his head and face absolutely covered in blood. A small piece of rock had gone further than expected and ripped across his bald head, inflicting a long scalp wound. There was more blood than serious wound, but it was a good warning to all.

On another occasion we drove into a shingle pit and I was just paying one of the men and the others were shovelling gravel into a truck. All of a sudden there was a yell from one man and we looked over. There had been a sudden slide of shingle off quite a low face and it had covered his legs to just above the knees. His mates rushed in and pulled him free, but he had a nasty broken leg. From that day to this I have had the greatest respect for gravel faces, and can recommend my readers to do the same. It was the quickest thing I have ever seen.

Another accident which amused me at the time but which could have had very serious consequences, occurred in the Homer Tunnel itself. One of the tunnellers was standing on a crossbeam and swinging a 7 pound sledge hammer to knock away a prop. He made a mighty swipe at it, missed completely and the momentum of the hammer overbalanced him and he shot off as if he had been fired through a rifle, landing on the rocks below. His workmates were highly amused until it became apparent that he had received a fairly nasty bruising.

On every PWD camp there was a camp attendant and, as the name suggests, he was responsible for the general welfare and tidiness of the camp and its buildings. It was not uncommon to find that the camp attendant was a one-armed man and everybody knew the story how he lost his arm. He was working on a job and was attracted by the very fine trout in the river. He got a stick of gelignite and a fuse and detonator and away he went. Unfortunately things did not go just according to plan and there was a premature explosion and the arm was blown off. I accepted this story as being correct in one case, but some time later I was talking to an engineer who had known this attendant quite well and he said he lost the arm in the first world war. He was greatly amused by my story about the gelignite and he said he had worked in three PWD camps where there was a one-armed camp attendant and in each case the fish-and-gelignite story was whispered around on the grapevine but none was true.

One of our older and greatly respected foremen on a Southland job was stung by a bee while on the job and died soon after.

In the PWD there was a sprinkling of what were known as "compo kings". These were men who always seemed to be on compo and they fell into well-defined categories. There was the genuine unlucky type who always seemed to be at the wrong spot at the right moment or vice versa. Then there was the type who copped it whatever happened; today these men would be referred to as "accident-prone", but in the good old days of the 1930s this was called " b . . . . carelessness".

Then of course there was the professional compo king – the malingerer – the man whose injury generally consisted of a ricked back or something similar, well known among those types as being almost impossible for a physician to detect. These latter men were in the minority and soon became known to the Department, which in those days required such malingerers to sign an indemnity against this type of injury.

13

MILFORD PAY VIA THE HOMER ROPE

EASTER WAS APPROACHING and my room-mate Stan Scott broke the news that he had fixed on this traditional time to get married to his charming red-headed fiancée.

I was looking forward to this, but a week or two before Easter the Milford Sound timebooks arrived unexpectedly. There was also a request that the pay be made up and taken to the Homer Tunnel camp at the Easter weekend. If the weather was fine a message would be sent out over the Milford Sound PWD radio, advising that a guide would be sent up the Homer Rope at a specified time. The paymaster then had to climb the 1500 feet from the Homer portal to the Homer Saddle and meet up with the guide from Milford Sound. This guide would then take the pay down the precipitous 1900 feet Homer Rope route and deliver it to the engineer-in-charge at Milford Sound.

My boss, on receiving the message from Milford, called me in and broke the news that I would be required to do this rather unusual pay trip. I would also have to get somebody who was fit to go with me as it was a rule that two men must always go together on these long-distance pays.

So much for the wedding festivities – they were off as far as I was concerned.

I told the other lads in the office what was going on and was fortunate that Buster Uttley, a Southland rep. footballer and cricketer, volunteered to accompany me. There was no doubt about his fitness to do the climb and carry his share of the pay paraphernalia, but I wasn't so sure of my own capabilities.

Just as a point of interest I would mention here that on another occasion Buster also volunteered to do a trip and on that occasion it was right to Milford Sound. We had received a radio message from Milford, saying that they were short of certain vital commodities, one of which was yeast, and they asked that a plane be sent over and supplies dropped to them.

No time was wasted and a plane was hired. The pilot said he would like someone to accompany him to dump the parcels overboard as he expected a pretty bumpy trip and he would be occupied in flying the plane and dodging mountain tops if the weather was bad. Quick to volunteer was Buster, who had done quite a bit of flying and held a private pilot's licence.

This trip turned out to be something of a nightmare, and Buster later told us how the pilot flew round above the clouds over what he reckoned was Milford Sound. There were bumps galore and Buster was violently airsick. All of a sudden there was a break in the clouds and down swooped the pilot, overboard went the parcels, and up again went the plane and back to the Invercargill airport. A very chastened Buster came back to the office and related his story.

Having settled on who was to do the Easter pay trip, we got down to the question of timing and found that the pay in question covered almost two months' earnings. The only thing then was to get all available staff to work flat out and make sure that we could have everything completed and the money drawn and packaged on the Thursday before Easter. This we managed with a very small margin in hand and at about 9 am on Good Friday we left for the Homer camp in a Ford V8 10-cwt "tray". We had a leisurely trip and before we got to Mossburn we were hailed by two hitch-hikers who were also on their way to the Homer camp.

They were offered a ride in the back of the tray which they gladly accepted. One of the two turned out to be Mr. W.F. Sturman, Town Clerk of Invercargill.

On arriving at The Forks camp, which was just a short distance from the Homer Tunnel camp, we were advised by the engineer-in-charge that a radio message had been received from the PWD radio station at Milford Sound, reading as follows: *Weather prospects good, Guide Glasson will meet paymaster on Homer Saddle 2 pm Saturday. Must be on time. Will advise further if weather changes.*

The engineer-in-charge of the Hollyford job at this time was Donald Frederic Hulse, who resided at The Forks camp with his wife and two young children. Don had elected to remain in the Hollyford Valley over Easter and he invited Buster and me to remain at The Forks and do a couple of days' climbing with him – provided, of course, that the weather permitted our proposed rendezvous with Steve Glasson on the Saturday.

Fortunately the weather on Saturday was fine, and after sending a telegram to Stan and his bride-to-be, Buster and I set off in what we reckoned was plenty of time. We each had quite a sizeable pack and although it was a fairly easy fine-weather climb for experienced men, I think we rushed it a bit. I remember at one stage saying to Buster, "Can you hear my heart thumping?"

"No," was his reply, "but I bet you can hear mine." I couldn't, of course, but this was a reminder to us that perhaps, through inexperience, we were rushing the job.

We slowed down somewhat and ultimately picked our way up and

Aerial view of Homer Saddle (mid left centre). To the right of the Saddle is the rocky slope (Talbot's Ladder) leading to Grave-Talbot Pass. Below Saddle on valley floor to left of access road is the tunnel mouth (arrowed). Homer Camp is at bottom centre.

V.C. Browne

around a myriad of boulders and rock outcrops to reach the Homer Saddle. This is 1500 feet above the eastern portal of the Homer Tunnel, which was where we started the climb. This eastern portal is itself 3023 feet above sea level.

When we reached the Homer Saddle there didn't seem to be anyone there, but visibility was not really good for a short period as a light mist had floated over. We dumped our packs beside a rock and Buster moved a bit to the north while I went in the opposite direction to see if we could find anybody. The whole area was a razorback and very limited, and when we returned a few minutes later the mist had lifted and we were very surprised to find Steve Glasson sitting down beside the bags containing the pay.

He jokingly remarked that he should have grabbed them and headed back the way we had come. Although it had not been mentioned in the radio messages from Milford Sound, I had assumed that Steve would have a mate with him as he had to do quite a tricky climb up the Homer Rope.

What also concerned me was how he would be able to carry the two packs that we had brought. He soon solved this by stowing them in an enormous pack that he had, remarking, "This will be no trouble at all as it's downhill."

As we sat there, he told us, among other things, of a big bird which he had seen on some of his trips in the Lake Te Anau area, and said that one day he was determined to catch one or get a photo and find out what it was. I asked him if it was a species of kiwi and he said, "No – it's more like a big bo-kakka" the local slang for pukeko. I thought nothing of this at the time but, as events turned out, it seems clear that he had made early sightings of the Notornis – later rediscovered by Dr Orbell.

Up to this time the weather had been fine, but without warning a mist blew over from the Milford side and Steve said he had better

The Homer Rope. A heavily-packed George Jones (of the survey party) descending.
J.H. Christie

be going. We shook hands and off we went. It remained reasonably fine on the Homer side and Buster and I had a leisurely trip back to our camp.

We assumed that Steve did the same, but when I met him some months later he told me that he got into real strife on his return trip. "I nearly got drowned," was how he put it.

The Homer Rope at that time consisted of a series of ropes and pegs driven into the rock, and some of these were in channels down the rock face which had been gouged out by water over the centuries. The rainfall at Milford has to be seen to be believed, and an inch an hour is commonplace at times; Jack MacKay, a Milford Sound survey party man, told me that on one occasion his party recorded twenty-seven inches of rain in twenty-four hours. Official figures show a fall of 20.47 inches on 12 May 1958.

What happened to Steve on his trip back was that quite unexpectedly it started to rain very heavily on the Milford side as soon as he left us. This caused the rain to run down the channel in the rock face, virtually converting it into a raging stream and sometimes waterfalls. The fact that parts of the Rope were situated in this channel meant that Steve had to descend through the torrent. In doing so he took the full force of the descending water, and its effect was aggravated by the fact that he was carrying such a large pack. Steve told me that this was the most harrowing trip he had ever done, and he had been lucky to come out of it alive. I asked him what his mates thought about it and he said, "I didn't say much about it." That was typical of Steve. He was a fine example of those Men of the Road referred to by Dan Campbell. He later volunteered for overseas service and was killed in the Middle East on 14 July 1942.

When Buster and I arrived back we were just in time for dinner. That evening there was a social and dance at the Homer camp and I remember this quite clearly because of two incidents. I was with a party of wellknown Central Otago people, and one very attractive elderly matron asked me if I would take care of her handbag while she was away for a few minutes. Naturally I said I would do so and, tucking it under my arm, kept on talking to the group. A few minutes later I was approached by a hefty-looking specimen who said I had made off with his fiancée's handbag. I was of course taken aback and gave my version of what had happened, and just at that moment the dear matronly soul who had given me the bag, returned and volunteered the information that she had seen it sitting on the seat and planted it on me. I asked her why she did it and she said "My idea of a joke!" It wasn't mine at that particular moment, but it takes all sorts to make a world, and what a dull place the world would be without the odd joker and storyteller.

100

"No job was too tough for them". *Left to right*: Steve Glasson, Sid Mann, and John Grindley, with Dave Gunn's packman at rear.

J.H. Christie

The other incident I recall occurred later in the evening when I happened to get myself into a discussion with a group who were sitting in close proximity to the bar. Finally the discussion got on to the definition of a "king hit". Apparently during the evening someone or other was alleged to have administered a king hit, because he laid his opponent out cold. Then there came the man who said that one could administer a king hit without laying out the opponent. At this maudlin stage one of the gang, a veritable giant, grabbed me around the neck in quite a friendly fashion to demonstrate a few of the points about a king hit and every now and then I found myself more or less hoisted off the ground by my neck. Fearing that a king hit might be administered accidentally, I moved off fairly smartly.

A bit later that evening I learned more about the king hit incident. One of the gang had got fighting-drunk and asked, "Does anybody here come from the North of Ireland?" One chap said that he did, and it was at this stage that the king hit was administered. When the victim awoke his mates asked him why he said he came from the North of Ireland. His answer was quite simple and explained everything. He said, "I thought he said the North Island."

The next two days were fine and Don Hulse, Buster, a visitor to the camp named Leslie and I, tramped to the Key Summit and Howden Hut and climbed to the Gertrude Saddle (4870 feet).

The weather was perfect and we had a memorable holiday. The next day Buster, Mr Leslie and I left for Invercargill in the V8 runabout. We had just got as far as Cascade Creek when a vehicle swung round the corner on its wrong side and Buster, who was driving, had to swing to the left to avoid a head-on collision. This put us into a ditch and we stopped very suddenly. Young Leslie suffered a badly lacerated scalp, but we called into the first-aid depot at Cascade Creek and it was marvellous the improvement the attendant effected with a roll of sticking plaster. We dropped Mr Leslie (whose christian name I have forgotten) at Lumsden so that he could catch a bus for Dunedin. Some years later Buster wrote me from the Middle East and said that almost the first person he met in Alexandria when he arrived was our erstwhile tramping friend, Mr Leslie.

The most outstanding feature of this trip was the fine weather and the absence of snow even on the tops. This was at the end of March 1937. On 4 May there was a heavy fall of snow and an avalanche suddenly swept down at the Homer Tunnel mouth, killing engineer-in-charge Don Hulse and tunnel overseer Tom Smith, and injuring plant overseer Joe Lloyd, loco driver Jack Milne & others.

The author (*left*) with Don Hulse and Mr Leslie on the Gertrude Saddle, March 1937.

Author

102

14

THE MAJOR FISHES THE CLEDDAU

AFTER A HECTIC TEN DAYS or so we finished making up a pay for the men on the Milford Sound end of the road and posted it, registered and insured, to the engineer-in-charge at Milford Sound. This mail was then taken in by the MV *Tamatea*, (Captain R.J. Hamilton) together with new men for the job and the many stores and the food needed to stock up at the Milford Sound camp. The engineer at Milford Sound paid out the money and sent back the receipted paysheets, and the timebooks for the next pay. Sometimes these boat trips were delayed for up to two months, and on the return trip a number of workmen and staff came back to Invercargill, either because they wanted to finish up on the job or take some leave.

On this occasion, one of the staff timekeepers came out on leave, and when this had expired he was employed in the Invercargill office until he could return to Milford Sound by boat. Knowing that I was interested in trout fishing, he gave me a box of flies which he used to tie in his evenings at Milford Sound. He was an expert fly fisherman, and wouldn't use artificial minnows or live bait as we did in local rivers.

He fished the Cleddau, and at that time it was well stocked with trout up to 15 lb weight or more. There were a few fishing tourists who walked to Milford Sound over the Milford Track in the summer, but by and large the Cleddau was virtually unfished and was therefore well stocked. This timekeeper used to be a bit reticent about telling us of the big ones he caught, but his mates assured us that he kept the camp in fish and that many of them were "monsters".

One lunch hour, while working in the Invercargill office, this timekeeper told us about a fishing trip he made with an English tourist who walked the Milford Track just to get some real good fishing in the Cleddau River. This tourist was a retired English army "major" and "very much the type", according to the timekeeper. Despite this, however, he was said to be really a very likeable chap.

This major had heard about the enormous fish in the Cleddau, but having no local knowledge of weather conditions, feeding habits of fish, and suitable flies, he had spent about a week thrashing every available inch of water without any luck.

He told one of the staff at the Milford hostel about this and

103

was advised to call on the local expert for a bit of advice. The first the timekeeper knew of this was when he heard a knock on the door of his hut one evening and the major introduced himself and enquired if he could be taken out for a day's fishing. He wanted to pay for this, but the timekeeper explained that fishing was his hobby and it gave him the greatest pleasure to have a partner, particularly if he was able to assist him to catch some nice-sized trout.

The old major, however, was not to be denied, and a bit later that evening he returned with a bottle of whisky, and over this the plans for a day's fishing were discussed. During the evening the major was presented with a number of flies which had proved very deadly on the Cleddau – they were the timekeeper's own favourites.

Next morning saw the two fishermen up early. The major had a conventional English creel bag and a landing net which looked a bit undersized for the type of fish that could be taken in the Cleddau, but the timekeeper said nothing, however, as he had a hefty gaff slung on his back and a sugarbag in which to put the fish.

In telling us about the trip, he said he was very surprised at how it had turned out. According to his calculations, it was an ideal day, and in the ordinary course of events he should have taken a number of fish, including some fair-sized ones. But this was not to be. Try as he might, he managed to get only a few decent rises, and failed to hook a fish.

The major fared even worse. He did hook a fish and played it for about half a minute, but his trace broke. Instead of keeping on fishing himself, the timekeeper walked along beside the major and told him what to do. He said that the major could cast a long and accurate fly and there seemed to be no reason why they weren't getting fish. He even nominated the spots where the major should land his fly and the major managed to reach them.

It was no good, however, and as time was getting on, the time-keeper started to fish again in the hope that he would hook a fish, and if he did so it was his intention to hand his rod over to the major so that he could land it.

At last, just as the light was beginning to fade a bit, the timekeeper hooked a fish and off it went. The major was standing beside him, and when he was sure that the fish was well hooked the timekeeper told him to take his rod and land the fish. The poor old chap was flabbergasted. Here was someone offering to allow him to land a monster trout, probably well over 10 lb weight. To the major, the landing of such a fish would have been the greatest moment in his life and he must have looked upon this offer as a sacrifice that no man could ever be expected to make.

Much as he would have liked it, the major could not be persuaded to take the rod and the timekeeper played the fish out himself. It

Milford Sound staff, 1937. *Back, left to right*: H.M. Popplewell, J.R. de Lambert W.G. Pearce (resident engineer, Invercargill), R. Wells, T. O'Connell J. Paisley, R. Thomas, *Front*: G.H. Stables, J.F. Henderson, I.W. McKinnon, W. O'Keefe, W.L. Smith.

H.M. Popplewell

was a good fighter and it forced the timekeeper to move downstream for quite a distance. When he had tired the fish out, he found himself on quite a high bank and it would have been difficult for him to climb down and land it. It was easier for the major to do it, so he asked him to climb down the bank and help.

The old major was quite happy to do this and grabbed hold of his landing net, which looked to the timekeeper to be a bit small for the job, so he suggested it would be easier if the major took the gaff. The major looked a bit uncertain, hesitated for just a second or so, and then took the gaff and scrambled down the bank. The fish by this time was well and truly tired out, and when the major was down to the water's edge the timekeeper gradually reeled it in till it was in a deep spot just below where the major was crouching. "Gaff him now," yelled the timekeeper.

The major, never having used a gaff before, gave one mighty swipe, and instead of impaling the fish on the gaff, he missed it completely but neatly severed the very fine gut trace. The timekeeper said he did not know who was the most astonished – the major or the fish.

To the timekeeper it was all in the day's fun. It was the thing that made fishing worth while. He had caught them before and he would catch them again. To the fish it was a lucky reprieve, and it had hardly enough energy to swim out of the backwater into the fast-flowing stream where it disappeared from sight. But to the poor old major it was a catastrophe. He had come halfway round the world for such an experience; and having spoiled things, he was as ashamed as he would have been had he been caught shooting a fox.

The timekeeper said he might have been wrong, but he doubted whether the major had ever caught a trout much larger than 1 or 1½ lb on the fifty yards or a quarter mile of water which he probably fished in England. Words could not describe the major's chagrin, and whilst the timekeeper continued to assure him that it meant nothing to him, he said he was certain the major could just not believe him.

I gathered from the way the story was told, that the timekeeper was sorry it did not have a happier conclusion, particularly when he finished up by saying, "I should really have let him have a go with that landing net."

The timekeeper didn't mention whether the major managed to catch a fish later, so I enquired on this point and the timekeeper said: "Unfortunately not – he had to leave Milford Sound early the next day to continue his trip."

At this point he smiled and said, "I got a letter of apology from the major a bit later, and in it was £10 in English notes. I believe he felt he had to do something to atone for the loss of the fish. I sent the £10 back and with it I sent some photos of big fish I had caught. I told him I valued the thought behind the gift and would keep his letter as a memento of a particularly enjoyable day's fishing. I also added a paragraph to assure him that the loss of the fish meant nothing to me – but I doubt whether this did much to relieve his sense of guilt."

15

THE HOMER TUNNEL – AND AVALANCHES

As I MENTIONED EARLIER, the Hollyford Valley at its upper reaches splits into two small valleys. The one on the left leads to the Homer Saddle, while that on the right leads to the Gertrude Saddle. Each of these valleys ends in a cirque, and I cannot better describe what a cirque is than to give the definition from *Nuttall's Dictionary*, which describes a cirque as "a natural arena like an amphitheatre at the head of a valley".

To reach Milford Sound it was necessary for a tunnel to be driven under either the Gertrude or the Homer Saddle. After investigation, the decision was made to tunnel under the Homer, as a tunnel under the Gertrude would have resulted in its emerging high up the valley. This in turn would have made for a very steep road down to Milford Sound. The decision therefore was in favour of the Homer Tunnel, and this was approved by Parliament in 1934.

The 24 feet wide by 17 feet high tunnel was begun on 4 July 1935, with picks and shovels, when "Digger" Scully and a party of seven trundled their heavy wooden wheelbarrows up the valley and camped in the old Homer Hut. By early in 1936 the tunnel gang was working underground.

About October 1937 work was stopped on the full-sized tunnel and a contract for a bottom heading 14 feet wide by 9 feet high was let to Downer & Co., the idea being that this smaller tunnel would be driven at a greater rate than the full tunnel, thus lessening problems of drainage and ventilation.

The contractor provided the tunnel party only, and this consisted of a supervisor and three shifts of eight men each. The PWD provided all plant, plant attendants, drill sharpeners, fitting shop etc., and their staff outnumbered the contractor's men. The Department also maintained the road leading up to the tunnel and continued the construction of the Lower Hollyford Road which, at the time, was called the Hollyford-Okuru Road. This is the road that runs down the Lower Hollyford from the Marian Corner.

Downer & Co. recruited men for the tunnel from the Waihi mines, as they were experienced with rock work and explosives, but in time many of them were replaced by men recruited from our road works. Mr Arnold Downer spent considerable time on the job and his wife was there with him.

Birth of a tunnel. Picks, shovels and barrows – tools used by the ancient Egyptians—were later supplanted by 20th century machines.

Jim Sutherland

This smaller tunnel was broken through in February 1940 and ring-boring to take the charges necessary to blast out the full-sized tunnel was completed in 1942. Because of World War II the job was closed down and was not restarted till 1951. It was finished in 1953.

The tunnel is 62 chains long and runs on a downward grade of approximately 1 foot in 10 feet from the inland (eastern) portal, which is at an elevation of 3023 feet while that at the western (Milford Sound) portal is approximately 2600 feet.

The Homer Saddle is 1460 feet above the inland tunnel portal, and was named after William Henry Homer, who discovered it in 1889. In close proximity to the inland portal, are Mt Talbot, Mt Belle, and Mt Crosscut and further down the valley is Mt Christina. On the Milford Sound side there are a number of towering peaks, all of which are dominated by that mightiest of all the giants of Fiordland, Mt Tutoko, which towers to 9042 feet. In comparison Mitre Peak is 5560 feet.

Many difficulties were encountered on this tunnel job. First of all

Whistle in hand, tunneller Ernie Howell on the watch for avalanches. If the whistle blew, all hands scuttled into the tunnel for shelter.

Author

the tunnel mouth was right in an avalanche area and much time was taken in digging away masses of snow which cascaded down and buried everything in sight. Another unexpected factor was the amount of water which entered the tunnel. It had been expected that as soon as the tunnellers got into solid rock the flow of water would virtually cease. This did not prove correct, as there were extensive fractures in the rock which allowed water to enter from the vast permanent snowfields thousands of feet above on Mt Belle. It was estimated that this water entered the tunnel at between 6000 and 10,000 gallons per hour. As the tunnelling was being done downhill there was no outlet at the bottom of the tunnel and every drop of water that ran into the tunnel had to be pumped back to the mouth.

This meant that if the pumps failed, the tunnel would start to fill up with water. All this placed an enormous burden on the powerhouse, which had been built downriver, and it was necessary to hook up a battery of large portable Broomwade compressors to cope with the pumping, lighting, ventilating and drilling operations. Add to all this a rainfall of about 300 inches per annum, with heavy falls of snow and extreme frost in the winter, and you have a picture of some of the difficulties faced by the engineers and men at the Homer Tunnel.

Having given this brief survey of the tunnel, we return to those days of the 1930s when it was under construction.

As I have mentioned, the tunnel portal was in an avalanche area, and in 1936 considerable damage was done by repeated avalanches of lumpy wet snow. These avalanches could be seen and heard coming down the mountainsides, and it was the practice of the Department to post an observer – generally Ernie Howell – outside the tunnel, with a whistle in his hand. If he spotted or heard an avalanche coming, he would blow the whistle and the idea was for all and sundry to scuttle into the tunnel like rabbits into a burrow.

Despite this and other precautions taken, an avalanche came down on 6 July 1936 and killed a man named Percy Leigh Overton. Others were injured. As previously mentioned, a further tragic avalanche occurred on 4 May 1937 when Donald Frederic Hulse and Thomas William Smith were killed, and Joseph T. Lloyd was injured. All three were married men living with their families in married quarters.

Although the facts were not fully understood at the time, and there is still much to learn even now about avalanches, it appears that there are two main types. The first are known as wet-snow avalanches and they come down the mountain relatively slowly, with a loud noise, and consist of masses of the permanent snowfields sitting high up on mountain slopes. These generally slide down the slopes like an ordinary slip on a road and may contain hundreds of thousands of tons of snow.

The other type, dry-snow avalanches, consist of recent snow precariously perched on top of the deep permanent snowfields. When changes of wind or temperature occur, this massive blanket of "dry" snow is thought to cascade right out into space in blanket form, like a skier taking off on a long jump. This massive body of snow then plummets down and as it does so, it compresses the air under it and a vacuum is created above as the mass of snow falls away. This creates a wind of unbelievable force and in the fatal avalanche of May 1937 it lifted men distances of up to 300 feet. The force is such that the snow-laden air will skin the bark off trees hundreds of yards away. Hardwood poles were splintered into matchsticks where they fractured, and a $5\frac{1}{2}$ ton diesel locomotive was blown right off the tiphead and over a bank. A motorcar went the same way.

These avalanches are noiseless, and the first intimation is the catastrophic blast of wind, whereas in the main, the damage from wet-snow avalanches comes from the mass of compacted snow.

I remember one pay trip to the tunnel when I was accompanied

Two tunnel overseers, Jack Dawson and Tom Smith, near a building wrecked by an avalanche.

Kurt Suter

by one of the younger boys from the office, as well as Mac as driver. The lad was taken on the trip so that he could get an idea of what was doing on the job.

My idea when paying was always to get to the tunnel mouth at the change of shift, as this served a double purpose: I could pay both the shift going on and the shift knocking off all at one spot without having to carry that heavy paybag down the long slope to the tunnel face. On this day, however, my luck was out and I was an hour late, so I had to set off down the steep slope right to the face where the men were drilling. The lad decided he would come down with me, so off we set. The lighting was not too good and the rail sleepers were slippery, and we had to watch that we did not fall. We slowly picked our way down and finally came to a point where there was a screen of massive iron chains hanging right across the tunnel like a curtain. These were used to stop rocks from shooting up the tunnel after a round of shots was fired. Apparently, in the earlier stages, some eager beavers fired some shots which cleaned out ventilators, pipes etc. for a considerable distance back.

We parted the chains and came on the men drilling holes for

111

Massive wet-snow avalanche caught in the act, 1936. A unique photograph by Kurt Suter.

After the avalanche. Taken by Kurt Suter immediately after the preceding photograph. Tunnel mouth, right centre.

shots at the tunnel face. Their pneumatic drills were supported on a steel frame and as the drilling progressed the drills were wound forward to keep the bits in contact with the rock face. There were a number of drills being operated in a cramped space and the noise was terrific. There was water pouring in from the roof and water was also being played on to the bits to stop the dust rising. There was also the noise of the pumps. I had seen this often and had got quite used to it, so I turned to tell my companion a bit about what was going on. To my surprise he had vanished, so I went back and parted the chains and shone a beam from my big torch up the tunnel. I picked him up in the distance and he was hotfooting it for the tunnel mouth – he had seen quite enough.

I paid the men and then had to hump that paybag all the way back up the slope to the tunnel mouth. I had been saving that little job for the lad, but he was too quick for me.

We had dinner at the cookhouse and by the time we had finished our meal it was about 8 pm. With the pay finished we had a free evening on our hands, so off we went to the social hall. When we arrived they were playing a pool game which they called Chinaman. Both Mac and I were invited to join in but I was not up to their class and Mac said he was a bit rusty and would rather watch. I found out some time later that Mac was a first-class billiard and snooker player but he then told me that he made it a rule not to play for money. "I've learned my lesson in the past," he said with a smile. "In any case a former chief justice, Sir Robert Stout, is said to have made the statement that 'Proficiency at billiards is a sign of a misspent youth' and I wouldn't like you young chaps to think that this applied to me."

Soon afterwards we left the hall and went over to the staff mess, where about a dozen or so of the staff were reading, playing cards or just having a chat.

Dan, the timekeeper, raised the question of how long it would be before the tunnel was finished and one pessimist said, "About twenty bloody years at the rate we're going," and how nearly true this later proved to be. The tunnel theme continued to be discussed and gradually the talk came round to what form the opening ceremony would take. Someone suggested that the Minister of Public Works would cut a ribbon in the time-honoured style.

"Would you like to hear the story about the opening of a bridge when I was up on that East Coast job?" asked one of the foremen named Joe.

"Yes," was the general answer and Joe started off.

I was working on the final section of the road at the time and we had just completed a decent-sized bridge. The local MP, who was a cabinet minister, was invited to cut the ribbon. Afterwards there would of course be a few speeches and the usual refreshments.

At the last moment it was discovered that although the ribbon had been purchased, there were no scissors available, so there was a real scurry and I was given the job of tearing back to the office in the truck to get a pair. The storemen at the time was one of those dyed-in-the-wool old public servants, and when I told him I wanted some scissors "pronto" he produced a pair but made it quite clear that they belonged to the Department and were on loan only and had to be returned.

The opening ceremony went beautifully. The local MP made his speech, the ribbon was stretched across and duly cut with the scissors. Refreshments followed as per schedule – gallons of it – and good stuff too!

About a week later the storeman came along to ask about the scissors as they had not been returned.

"Don't worry about that, Dick," I said. "I saw the old man (meaning the local MP) shove them in his pocket. You'd better issue him with a LUF docket."

This docket was a form used by the PWD for charging workmen and staff who failed to return tools or other items loaned to them. The form got its name from the initial letters of its title – Loans Unaccounted For – and the money owing was either paid in cash or deducted from the men's wages.

"OK, I'll charge him," said Dick the storeman, and off he went. Little did I realise that he had taken me seriously.

This car was blown off the tiphead by an avalanche-wind on 4 May 1937. Its owner, Don Hulse, and Tom Smith lost their lives in that avalanche.

George Jones

About a week later we were having our lunch in the office and along came Dick again. When he saw me he said, "You know, Joe, that old buzzard (meaning the MP.) hasn't paid for those scissors yet."

"What!" I yelled. "You don't mean to tell me you actually charged him for them?"

"Of course I did," he said. "You told me to, and in any case I'm responsible for everything on stock."

I was horrified and immediately got in touch with the chief clerk and told him what Dick had done. "The dopey old bastard," was all he could say, as he was in a complete dither.

Having told Dick to make the charge I wasn't feeling too happy myself, so I thought I had better try and help. "I tell you what I'll do," I said, "I'll go down to the MP's place myself and explain the position and see if I can straighten it out before he starts squawking to Head Office."

This was a fairly desperate move on my part but I had met the local MP and I thought maybe I could talk my way out of the trouble. The chief clerk, clutching at a straw, agreed and off I went.

The local member's house was only a few hundred yards from the office. Gingerly I opened the front gate and walked very slowly up the path. I can remember this as if it were yesterday. The house was a very big old one with a heavy front door with coloured glass side-panels.

I lifted the big cast-iron knocker gingerly and dropped it, but got no answer. My next knock was a bit harder, and after a minute or two I was really thumping. This produced an unexpected result, as the woman next door popped her head over the fence and said there was no one at home. "He's been away about a week and won't be back for a day or two," she said. "Can I give him a message?"

I assured her that this was not necessary and I returned slowly to the office. Suddenly I had a bright thought: if the MP had been away for quite a time it could be that his mail would still be in his letterbox and I might be able to recognise the PWD envelope and get it back without his knowing.

I must admit that the legal penalties for robbing His Majesty's mail did enter my mind, but things were desperate and desperate remedies were necessary. Back I went to the front gate, but there was no letterbox. On the front door however there was one of those cast-iron flaps held shut by a steel spring, and it was the postman's job to come to the front door and push the mail through this opening. Surely this was my unlucky day – but on looking down at the bottom of the door I noticed that there was a fair gap underneath.

There was nothing I could do at the time, and I was dead scared the woman next door would poke her head over the fence again

Tunnel mouth all but buried by an avalanche. Overseer Tom Smith stands at the top of the arch, engineer Duncan White peeps out from inside the tunnel.

George Jones

and want to know what I was doing, so I turned and left as fast as I could.

I had one or two jobs to keep me occupied for the rest of the afternoon but after tea I pocketed a small torch and got a piece of thin wire and bent it over so that I could push it under the door and hook out the letter I was after. It was some time before darkness fell, but finally I was back at the MP's house and quietly crept up the path. I poked the wire under the door and managed to extract a dozen or so letters but none in the familiar OHMS window envelope. One more go, I thought, and then I'll have to leave it. I hooked again with the wire and to my delight a window envelope clearly showing inside it the LUF docket came into view. This was enough for me. I pushed the rest of the letters back through the hole in the door and fairly ran down the path and didn't stop till I was almost home.

Next morning I went to the chief clerk and handed him the docket. All he said however, was, "Give this to the storeman and tell him to cancel it and not be such a damned fool in future." He didn't ask for any details and I didn't volunteer any.

Joe's story was well received and to show their appreciation the members of the staff mess voted that he should be allowed to make the tea and serve supper. Joe reckoned this was a bit "on the nose".

Lost one tunnel! The two figures show where the portal is.
George Jones

Tunnel regained. Clearing avalanche snow from tunnel mouth.
George Jones

A "barrel extension" was built at the portal to give protection from avalanches. An avalanche crushed it and it was never rebuilt.

N.J. Dawson

While he was making supper we were told that a suggestion had been made to the engineer-in-charge that steam or hot-air pipes should be run up the mountainside above the tunnel and under the snowfield. The idea was that this would melt the snow and if there was no snow there would be no avalanches.

This amused the crowd and someone suggested that the pipes should be connected to the union meetings, as this would be the only place where sufficient hot air could be generated. Apparently this remark filtered back to the union and an official protest was lodged at the resident office at Invercargill. The matter was trivial and was dealt with accordingly, but unfortunately the letter in reply, through a typing error, was addressed to "The Secretary, New Zealand Wormers' Union" instead of "New Zealand Workers' Union", and of course there was a further blowup. As usual however, these things fizzled out in favour of some later event.

Supper was then served by Joe, and with this over I quote a favourite phrase of diarist Samuel Pepys: "And so to bed."

16

THE AUDITOR DOES A
HOLLYFORD PAY

MY BOSS CAME ALONG one morning and said he'd had a phone message from the Audit Department. They would send one of their staff up on the pay trip and wanted him to do the actual paying. This was within their rights, although it was not very often done. In fact this was the only occasion it was done on the large number of pay trips I made to the Hollyford Valley.

I was told to dot my I's and cross my T's and generally let the Audit Department know that the accounting and pay procedures at the Public Works Department, Invercargill, were second to none. I was also given a broad outline of what situations could arise, and a few helpful suggestions. I was told that the auditor would "take the mickey out of me", but the boss said to try and slip an odd ace or two up my own sleeve.

Jack the chainman was our driver and I decided on a 4 am start. This wasn't too well received by the audit man but starting times etc. were my prerogative and if the pressure was on in the office and the weather was good it wasn't unusual for us to do the trip right to the Homer Tunnel and then immediately head back for home. Our usual time of arriving home was about 2 am next day, and this meant that we travelled up to 380 miles, paid several hundred men, ate what snacks we could get, and got back home in twenty-two hours. This on paper may not sound a great achievement, but I had good drivers, knew every man on the road, where they were likely to be and had everything prepared, and that was the best I could do.

On this occasion I decided on a there-and-back trip if the weather was right. (This weather proviso held for every Hollyford trip because if the elements were against us we could not move. On one occasion the trip took four full days.)

On this occasion I must admit that my decision to do the "up and back in one day" trip was to let the Audit Department man know that he was not on a picnic. Had we been too kind to him he might have enjoyed himself and wanted to come again.

Anyway, we got away right on 4 am in the V8 sedan. As soon as it was daylight I checked over the pay with the auditor and got him to sign a receipt for the full amount, which I then handed to him. If anything was lost from then on, I was in the clear. This was our usual procedure if we handed over the pay to anybody, because mistakes could happen. Strictly speaking, the paymaster was not supposed to leave envelopes out on the job if the men were not there on pay day. This caused no strife on town pays, but at the Hollyford it sometimes happened that odd gangs might be miles out in the bush on survey, or a workman due to return next day from leave. On these occasions I used to leave the pay envelopes and a receipt on the job. I would of course have to know that the men were genuinely on the job and would always get a receipt from the person to whom the envelopes were handed.

If this were not done the pay envelopes would have to be taken back to Invercargill, paid into a trust account and cheques then sent to the men back on the job. This could take a week or ten days and in the meantime the man would be without his money. In any case a cheque was something of a nuisance in the Valley.

On this particular pay we had fine weather all the way, although it had snowed at Hollyford on the day before we got there. We did not start too well as a tyre blew out and we had to change it at an awkward spot on the road. Later we had to wait for it to be repaired at Te Anau.

While we were doing this we wandered along to the hotel and went into the bar. "What will you have?" I said to the auditor.

"A whisky please," was his answer.

"One whisky, two sarsaparillas, please," was my order. I haven't heard much of sarsaparilla for years but this used to be the non-alcoholic drink that teetotallers would order when they lined up at the bar.

This wasn't a bad start as we felt we were one up on the auditor. I remembered that old saying "If you're not one up you're one down." I am sure, however, that the auditor sensed that this was a bit of a "ready".

He then wanted to shout for us but we thanked him and declined saying that we would like to have one but "couldn't spare the time". He had to grin at this but didn't say anything.

The men at Te Anau were duly paid and off we set, paying the maintenance men as we went along the completed stretches of the road. Near The Bluffs, in the Eglinton Valley, we stopped and stretched our legs.

While we were there Jack pointed out a vertical rocky formation right at the side of the road and showed us that this cliff face was covered in glacial scratches. This fascinated me, and on quite a number of later trips I pointed this out to people who accompanied me. It is a shame that features of this nature are often missed by casual

A tricky wicket, at the Homer camp, and the odds are all in the bowler's favour.
Jim Sutherland

visitors. How long ago was it that those glaciers moved down that valley? Unfortunately questions like these often remain unanswered.

All went well till we got a bit further up the valley, and one man complained that his canteen account was excessive. Before we had got to the Marian camp three more men had the same complaint, and the auditor had this noted in his book. So had I for that matter and, what is more, I knew that on this pay I had a new arrangement for all the canteen accounts to be checked on the job instead of being sent to Invercargill as had been done in the past. This was to save us time in checking at Invercargill.

When I got to the Marian camp the first thing I did was to get hold of the canteen accounts for the four men who had complained, and in each case there was an error and they had just cause for complaint. I got hold of the chap in charge of the canteen and he assured me that all the additions had been checked by a man who had been working in the store. He promised to let me know what had happened and he came back with a quick answer. The man who had done the checking was quite indignant about the whole matter. He produced a pad showing hundreds of little sums scribbled on it and said that he was sure that all the totals had been checked.

121

On looking further it turned out that if the total of a man's dockets was not correct on the checker's first add-up he had another go. If he didn't get it the second time he had a further go, and so on. His arithmetic was so bad however that as soon as he managed to get an answer that was near enough to the total on the sheet, he left it at that. This explanation satisfied the auditor but not me. As we proceeded I had to agree to another half dozen or so claims that the canteen account was wrong and had to adjust the whole lot on the next pay.

Our next trouble occurred when we came to a couple of chaps who had a co-op contract for the first time. The headman said we had put an extra man's name in the contract and had paid this man 32s. I knew this was not right but I thought I had better sort it out, especially as a refund of the 32s. was being demanded.

"What's this extra man's name?" I asked.

"G.Z. Holiday," was the reply, "and he's never worked for us." There was a simple answer to this: the two items "G.Z. Holiday" appearing on the sheet meant "gazetted holiday", and the 32s. was the eight hours day wages at 2s. per hour the Department had paid to each of the two men on the co-op. contract. I explained the position and everybody was happy. This sort of complaint was not a usual thing with co-op contracts, as I found that in most cases there would be one or more in the gang who could go through the contract sheet and follow it to the last penny.

By this time Dan Campbell had joined us and the auditor asked him how many men were on the job. Dan then came across with the standard answer, "About 900 – say 300 here, 300 coming and 300 going." When pressed however, he was able to supply the exact number, which the auditor noted in his book and I presume he did some check with the paysheets later.

Our next call was at the canteen, which was quite a sizeable building set up like a grocer's shop. There were no customers when we got there and after a word or two we made a move to go. The chap at the counter said, "When you go out, give the door a really hard slam as the lock is sticking a bit."

When Jack and I heard this we moved fairly quickly to the door and got out before the auditor. When he left he obeyed instructions explicitly and gave the door a mighty slam. This had the effect of dislodging a great lump of compacted snow from the sloping corrugated iron roof just above the door and down it came all over him. This was a wellknown trick at the canteen and Jack and I were awake to it.

Our next port of call was The Forks camp and the auditor by this time was getting pretty tired of lugging the heavy bag around and rushing from place to place to keep up with the clock. We were cracking on the pace, "to keep him out of mischief" as Dan put it.

Dan and I got into the car beside Jack while the auditor was standing at the front with his paysheets open on the radiator, doing a check to see that he hadn't missed any signatures. When he was finished he hopped in the back seat and we set off up the hill on the final short stretch to the tunnel portal.

As we were getting out I told the auditor the name of the headman of the co-op gang we would be meeting and suddenly he said, "Where's the paybag?"

"You've got it," I said and looked over the back. It wasn't there and the auditor said, "I must have left it at the last stop."

What a ker-fuffle! You can guarantee that no time was lost in getting back to The Forks, but when we got to our previous point of departure there was no sign of the paybag. I don't know how that auditor felt, but I was in a complete panic. "Bang goes a good job," was my thought and I shot out of the car and started for the office at a run. I had only gone a few steps when I saw Bill the camp attendant, and I said, "Have you seen the paybag lying around?"

"Yes," he said, "I put it in my hut," and with that he opened the door and passed over the big leather bag. The auditor said he wanted to check over the envelopes again so I gave him a hand with this. Fortunately there were not many left by this time and the check didn't take long. There was a very relieved auditor and paymaster after that small incident and we all set out for the tunnel again.

The V8 gave a warmer ride than the old Model A. Big Bill Pearce's car outside the office at The Forks camp, where on this occasion the paymaster was "snowed-in" for two days.

George Jones

The steep faces above and to the left of the tunnel entrance. The permanent snowfield at the summit is a breeder of avalanches. Homer Camp at bottom centre.

Weekly News, Bill Beattie photo

We finished paying the main groups just as the men knocked off, which was very satisfactory under the circumstances. We had already gone thirteen hours with only a few breaks for cups of tea where they were available.

We had a final check of the envelopes and paid a few stray men we had missed on the way up. This invariably occurred and we used to look these men up on our way back.

The auditor then asked whether it was our practice to leave any pays if men were temporarily absent. He was quite awake to what went on as he had been firing the odd question here and there to staff as he met them on the way in. I admitted that we did this on occasions, gave him the very good reasons for doing so, and promised not to do it again.

I added that there was one thing we never did – we didn't leave the whole pay sitting on the side of the road. He grinned a bit and made a note in his book.

The only criticism we had from the Audit Department as a result of this pay check was that the practice of leaving pay envelopes and receipts on the job for absentees should be discontinued.

We stayed for dinner at the staff mess and then headed off for home. The auditor had spent quite a full day and slept quietly in the back seat while Jack and I shared the driving, getting to Invercargill round about 2 am.

"We've done it in even time again," said Jack as we pulled in to the Invercargill office.

Next day we took the auditor out to Invercargill's famous White House and insisted that he should buy us a few drinks. I explained to him that "We just don't drink intoxicating liquor in working hours."

That slow grin appeared on his face once again and he said, "I do – especially if I can find someone mug enough to pay for it."

That auditor man had been on the road for a year or two and it was hard to ruffle him.

17

FUN AT THE OFFICE

MOST OF MY STORY has related to events out in the field but, depression days or not, we had lots of fun at the office too.

When I first started on the pay job I found that one chap in the office had a most unusual hobby. He saved the torn-off ends of £1 notes. He was unable to get very large pieces as this would mean the number of the note was interfered with, but as time went on his stock grew steadily. He had a contact at the bank who supplied a few ends, and in the finish he must have had about thirty or more. One day he got them out and started to paste them on to a backing sheet. As he pasted each piece down he left a bit of the previous note showing. The ultimate result looked as though he had a big wad of notes thumbed a bit so that the ends overlapped. He then slid this into a pay envelope and stapled it into position.

His next move was to get the office boy to sidle across the road and plant this packet on the footpath just outside the Railway Hotel. We worked in the old Government Buildings opposite the railway station, on the first floor, and this gave us a very good view.

For quite a time the package lay there and not a person passed it. Then along came a couple of middleaged housewives and they must have had two or three days' gossip to get off their chests as they stood right above the packet and talked for about twenty minutes. Finally they parted without noticing anything.

The next move was quite dramatic. Along came a very fat boy, walking quite fast for one of his bulk, and as he passed he swiftly bent down and whipped up the packet. He then kept on going and shot round the corner from the south end of Esk Street into Leven Street. From our vantage point we were still able to see him. He quickly extracted the packet from his pocket and feasted his eyes on it, but only for a second. He was disgusted and fired it on to the ground and went on his way. The office boy was immediately sent to retrieve it for use on another occasion.

This same office boy featured in another bit of fun a few days later. There had been quite an epidemic of measles and a certain family man was very frightened that he might take them home to his children, so he was avoiding all known contacts like the plague. Not only did he avoid people, but his obsession was such that he was always talking about measles.

One day this young office boy said, "There's one thing anyway, I haven't got them," and to prove his point he whipped up his shirt and there, all over his little fat tummy, was a myriad of spots. The measles-avoider went about five shades whiter and suggested that the office boy should go immediately to the doctor.

These were depression days, and the office boy swore he didn't have the 7s. 6d. necessary to pay the doctor. The measles-avoider then said he would contribute 5s. towards the cost if the rest of the crowd would chip in the other half-crown. There were no takers so the avoider's offer was increased to the full 7s. 6d.

The young measles suspect agreed to go to the doctor, and headed off for the rest of the day with the 7s. 6d. in his hot little hand. Here he showed a bit of that shrewdness that has since stood him in good stead over the years. That evening he went to the doctor who used to handle all the Workers' Compensation Act claims for the Department and who knew all the lads through his frequent visits to the office.

By this time the spots for some unaccountable reason had disappeared, and as he had no temperature, lumps or bumps, the doctor gave him a certificate to the effect that he was fit for work. Knowing the boy quite well, he charged him only 2s. 6d., so next morning the measles suspect landed back at work with a medical certificate of fitness and a clear profit of 5s. In those days that was real wealth.

One day we had a visit from a little wee lad about fifteen who wore a pair of those very large round hornrimmed spectacles. He wanted a job in the office and, as he measured up in all respects, the clerical boss took him on. He then brought him into the office to instal him in his new job.

"What christian name do you use?" asked the boss.

"John," answered the lad.

"We'll call you Jack," said the boss.

"My name's John," persisted the little fellow – and John it has been from that day to this. Not one of the other lads would have dared to lay down the law to the boss – especially on his first day at work.

Another incident in the office which amused me, was when one of the wives came in wanting her half-pay money a bit earlier than usual. We had no timebooks in from the job so we didn't know how much she could get. When the lad told her this, she cut up pretty rough and was going to do all sorts of things.

She finished up her tirade by saying, "That's not good enough – I've got six or . . . (a long pause) . . . seven children."

At this stage the office boy rather amazingly said, "Now make up your mind, lady – it's got to be one or the other. What is it – six or seven?"

This sudden sally completely took the wind out of the lady's sails because she answered, "W-e-l-l, if you want to know I've got six . . . " – there was another long pause, and then she added " . . . or seven."

The boy looked at her and said, "That's *much* better – now we know exactly what we are talking about."

One day one of the draughtsmen came in and told us about a young boy who had called at his home selling swede turnips – quoting a price of six for 6d. or nine for 1s. His wife was a bright young lass and she told the boy she would have two lots at six for 6d. The boy was obviously a bit puzzled at this one but finally handed over the twelve swedes and collected the shilling. A few days later there was a small paragraph in the local paper about a young boy who had run away from home and had been supporting himself by stealing swedes from a market garden and selling them.

At the maintenance workshop we had a couple of men who travelled around a bit doing repairs to lighthouse dwellings and outlying properties. At one of the lighthouses the keeper's wife was a very strict sort of woman who would not tolerate a lot of things – one of which was swearing, or anything even bordering on it. The carpenter who was in charge always warned any tradesman to mind his language when on this particular job. One day he came back to the office and told us this story.

He had taken Sam the paperhanger out to do some work on the lighthouse buildings. The keeper's wife was providing meals and bed, and for a day or so the paperhanger had not blotted his copybook. One dinner hour the keeper, his wife and his son aged about two, were sitting down at the table and in came our two tradesmen and joined them. Before long, Sam the paperhanger said to the little boy, "'Ere, – stop that!"

The boy's mother looked over at Sam and said, "What's he doing?"

The carpenter sitting beside Sam simply shuddered at the reply. Sam said "He's scratching it."

"He's scratching what?" asked the woman.

"His dingle doodle," says Sam, without batting an eyelid.

The woman's face assumed a look of horror. "His *w-h-a-t*?" she asked.

Sam said, "His dingle-doodle – *you* know – his doodle-dasher."

The carpenter by this time was ready to dive for the door and head for home, but to his surprise and relief the humour of the situation suddenly seemed to strike the keeper's wife and she burst out laughing.

In telling us the story the carpenter said Sam got away with it that time but he finished up by saying "That's the last time I'll take that b . . . out to the lighthouse". Sam, who was within hearing distance, grinned slightly. He had just told me a few minutes before how he hated jobs which took him away from home for several days.

As I have said, we often worked overtime in the evenings, and on occasions we treated ourselves to supper at one or other of the local restaurants. On the first occasion that this happened we went to Son Tall's restaurant in Dee Street and had a couple of dozen raw oysters. One of the boys then said he was going to have another half dozen and he wondered whether I would do the same. I said I would, and out came the proprietor. Obviously this operation had been pre-arranged, because each of those oysters I got was about the size of the palm of my hand and correspondingly thick and luscious. I had many adventures and unusual experiences in Southland, but this particular incident sticks out clearly in my memory and I think it is because I felt it as part of that wonderful welcome I had to this new life in "Sunny Southland". No doubt the taste of those luscious oysters also contributed something.

I remember another visit we had to a restaurant for a spot of supper. This place was run by a Hindu named Charlie, who used to work at the Hollyford. At the time I am talking of he had just started in business and things were obviously a bit slack. When we arrived he said, "Good evening Mist' And'son – what will you have – eggs and orsters (oysters) or orsters and eggs?" After a bit of discussion one ordered "eggs and orsters" while the rest of us settled for "orsters and eggs". It was obvious that the menu was fairly restricted and Charlie was set on doing a bit of promotional work.

As time went on the menu was extended and the next time when we went in we had the option of "eggs and orsters", "orsters and eggs" or "fried turkey". Now, here was something really new that none of us had tried, so there was a hundred per cent vote in favour of fried turkey. After a while out came Charlie with our order – four plates of nicely fried fish with a few chips and a piece of lemon on each for good measure. I couldn't understand this so I said to Charlie, "But what about the fried turkey?"

"That's it, Mist' And'son," he said in his piping voice, and in support of this he pulled out a menu card and there it was clearly set out in black and white – "Fried Tarakihi". The only trouble was that Charlie's pronunciation was a bit astray – but not to worry, the fried "turkey" was very nice.

I remember one incident which happened soon after I was married. Lola, my wife, had said that we must have a vegetable garden, so I had to spend a few of those lovely long Southland evenings in tilling the soil. After I had dug a fair patch she inspected it and said the soil was very poor and it needed some form of manure or compost. I was no gardener so I couldn't argue my way out of it. I happened to

Fun at the office – an informal celebration in the draughting room, Invercargill. The author (*in doorway, wearing hat*) had just returned from a pay trip and homed in on the party, "lured", he thinks, "by the scent of hops".

Robert Robb

mention this at work and one of the chaps said he knew of a sheep farm run by a titled namesake of mine, somewhere out in the country, and he would arrange for a couple of sugarbags of dry sheep manure to be loaded up for me. I arranged to pick it up in the dinner hour and took my trusty Austin 7 to work with me. At noon, off we set and met the donor of the manure out at the farm. He loaded it on the small carrier at the back of the Austin and tied it on with a piece of rope. I remembered that the manure was described as "dry", and while it may not have been exactly wet it did look a bit moist on parts of the sack. But no worries – it was loaded and tied on and I wouldn't have to touch it till I had got home and changed into old clothes.

That afternoon Sunny Southland belied its name somewhat, and we had a good downpour of rain. After work I started the car and drove up Tay Street, and following the tramline I was slowly turning into Conon Street when there was a bit of a bump behind me and a chap at the side of the road called out for me to stop. I got out and found that one of the bags of manure had fallen off on the tramline and the other had slumped a bit and was likely to fall at any moment. I went back to pick up the first bag and then discovered the trouble. The rain had soaked into the manure and softened it so that it had oozed through the sugarbag. It was just a slimy mass, but I could see a way out: I would lay one sack flat on the carrier and the other on top of it, and then tie them in this position instead of their standing vertically as before.

There was only one difficulty; the sack on the ground was so slippery that it was hard to lift. Not to be outdone I started to roll it, and had got it about halfway when round the corner came a tram. The driver stopped and watched the operation for a few seconds and then he started to ding the bell. This of course rattled me, and I tried to hurry things and finally rolled the sack up behind the car. I was in my office clothes and was trying to avoid getting them dirty. *Ding-ding*, went the trammie, and I was getting hot and flustered. *Ding-ding* once again as I tried to untie the ropes on the carrier and re-secure the load. *Ding-ding* – by this time I'd had it. I could see that it would be a long and slippery operation to get the bags securely tied on the carrier so I opened the car door, wrapped my arms around sack no. 1 and poked it inside on to the back seat. *Ding-ding* once again, and I picked up sack no. 2 and into the car it went. By this time my coat and trousers were a stinking slimy mess so I hopped into the car and drove off.

Little did that trammie realise that I had just reached the point where one more *Ding-ding* would have precipitated a tribal war in Conon Street, Invercargill.

By the time I got home to Tweed Street I had cooled down a bit and I drove the car in and unloaded the two sacks. Lola had come outside and, sizing up the situation, she got out the hose, screwed on the high-pressure nozzle and, after relieving me of my wallet, watch and hat, she hozed me down for about ten minutes. Then we pulled the mats and detachable seats out of the car and also gave them a thorough hosing. Happy days!

In due course I put that manure on the garden and a bit later I bought a bag of seed potatoes. Somehow or other I didn't get round to putting them in, but one fine Saturday, Tony Officer, brother-in-law of Stan Scott with whom I used to board, came round and wanted me to go fishing.

"Not till you've planted those potatoes," said Lola. I grabbed the bag, picked out a potato, dropped it on the ground, trod on it, dropped another one, trod on it and so on till the bag was empty. Believe it or not, as Mr Ripley used to say, that effort produced the best crop of potatoes I have ever grown.

Another event of note was the office farewell party given to Russell Rawle, who was going into camp prior to overseas service. At this party the opportunity was also taken to farewell Ray Hesselyn, who had volunteered for service in the Air Force. Ray was the son of George Hesselyn, who was in the architectural section of the PWD in Invercargill.

What struck me at the time was Ray's extremely youthful appearance and his fresh, almost girlish complexion. This did not seem to fit into the role of a fighter pilot. That appearances are deceptive was proved by Ray's war record: he became the leading RNZAF fighter ace of the second world war, and the only RNZAF pilot to win the DFC, DFM and bar. He had $21\frac{1}{2}$ confirmed aerial victories and was also awarded the MBE in 1946. He later served as a squadron leader at RAF Fighter Command Headquarters.

He was one of Southland's greatest sons, and the exploits of this Malta Spitfire ace are recorded in *The Fighter Aces of the RAF 1939–45* by E.C.R. Baker (publisher William Kimber, 1962). He was also well known for his own book *Spitfires Over Malta*.

After Russell Rawle's farewell was over, he and I walked home to his lodgings pushing our bikes beside us. I remember him telling me of his Cornish ancestry and I told him my father was Norwegian and he later said, "We Nordics must stick together, Harold." Apparently he had by this time renounced his Cornish ancestry and become a Viking.

As we neared his boardinghouse he said "Hey, Harold – do you want this bike? I won't have much use for it on the Western Desert." As it was I would have found it a bit hard to ride the one bike I had with me so I saw no chance of negotiating two of them. I told him this and just at this moment we were going past a six feet galvanised iron fence. Russell stopped and grasped his bike by the handlebars and the seat and swung it round about three times like a discus thrower. He released the bike and it shot over the fence like a rocket. It may still be there.

Some years later I was walking along Lambton Quay in Wellington when a voice cried "Hullo, Harold." I looked around and saw a man in uniform. It was Major Russell E. Rawle, MC, recently back from the Middle East.

Turning now to gardening again, it is well known that Invercargill has that warm current running along Oreti Beach which helps its climate, but somehow or other it is still difficult to grow tomatoes unless one has a warm north wall or a glass house.

Most people however, like to have a go at growing a few tomatoes, and when one of the fellows in the office said he had a lot of fine plants in boxes there were plenty of takers. It then became a bit of a competition for who would get the best results. I was never really in the race. I didn't realise that latitude played a part in these things and I planted mine outside in a cold spot and that was it. A few of the locals however, reported very good results and competition was keen. Nobody had troubled to ask what breed of tomatoes they were and I suppose that this was because the price was right.

In due course each budding horticulturist got his answer. Some tomatoes were the yellow variety – some were shaped like a teardrop, while others resembled a pear, or as one fellow put it – like an electric-light globe. The pick of the bunch were the ones that were about the size of a grape and they grew in the shape of a bunch of grapes except that instead of the bunch being round like grapes it was flat in the shape of a triangle of snooker balls.

Some of the successful growers were irate while others were quite pleased with the results. All however questioned the donor about their origin. "I saw an advertisement in a nursery catalogue so I thought I'd try them out," he said. Then, with a bit of a grin, he said, "Try them out on you jokers."

Another incident was when one of the engineers came into the office and asked me to come out into the street and talk to a man. This engineer was a big tough sort of chap, and without any other explanation he said to me, "I don't know whether to laugh or to cry about this lot."

It was a very hot day, and when I got outside I found I knew this workman and he started to tell me his story. Someone had run off with his wife and as he told me about it the tears absolutely welled out of his eyes, rolled down his cheeks and splashed on the hot bitumen pavement below. The remarkable thing was that this man, although charged with emotion, was not crying in the ordinary sense. The tears simply welled from his eyes and poured down his cheeks. I was completely flabbergasted – and I too just didn't know whether to laugh or cry.

One day one of the local boys suggested we get an office crowd together and do a bit of fishing out at Oreti Beach. It was all arranged for one Saturday and the programme was to dig for toheroas and then net some flatfish. The equipment was gathered and the organiser told us to bring as much old woollen clothing as we could manage.

In due course we arrived at the beach and as the tide was right we started to dig for the toheroas. It was soon apparent that on this operation the gear we had wasn't altogether appropriate. I had a new Skelton spade, and I dug it in the wet sand and gave a mighty backward heave as though I were digging my garden patch in Tweed Street. To my surprise and horror the steel spade just bent as though it were rubber, so I didn't try my luck further and changed my digging tactics. We soon had a pile of toheroas, and as I look back I wonder whether there just weren't any fishing regulations for toheroas those days. Perhaps we were just blissfully ignorant of them.

The next phase of the activity appealed to me, as I was very fond of flatfish and was assured that they were plentiful. We had a long net about three feet deep with a round pole on each end, and the

133

idea was for one end to be carried out as far as possible and then walked along parallel with the shoreline. After a reasonable distance had been covered the seaward end of the net would be walked back to the shore – thus forming a big loop. The whole net was then hauled in and with it the flounders or soles.

At this stage I found that the "netsmen" all donned about three woollen jerseys and a couple of old overcoats etc. I was helping with the net and on the first haul I was given the landward pole to hold. All I had to do was to hold the pole firm and upright while the seaward man moved out and along and back to form the loop.

I don't know exactly what month this was, but if it was the 22nd June I wouldn't be surprised. I found out one curious fact: while the portion of me from the waist down in the water was freezing, the top half of my body was simply petrified with the cold. It was at this stage I discovered one of the great secrets of life – why little boys wet their nappies – it keeps them warm. I made this discovery known to one of the other fishers and he said he had just made the same discovery.

On the next haul of the net I swam out with the seaward end and found that when I was totally immersed I was not quite as miserable as I had been when I was in the half-in-half-out position. Perhaps it was that when I was totally immersed I was not affected by the cold biting wind – or perhaps it was that warm current! – that runs along the Oreti Beach.

Cold day or not we got a very good catch of piper (garfish) and flatfish, and finished off a good day with a roaring fire on the beach.

Now about Rugby. Bill was organising a trip to Dunedin, and word flashed from house to house right throughout Invercargill. It soon reached the PWD.

This bit of news may not convey much to people "up North", which often meant the rest of the world, but to Invercargill residents it was a message loud and clear. Bill, of course, was Bill Graham the famous Invercargill pie-cart proprietor. His cart was always parked opposite the railway station and right outside the PWD office, and was very handy for us boys particularly when we were working overtime. The "trip to Dunedin" was the invasion of Southland Rugby supporters annually organised by our worthy pie-cart man.

Bill was an enormous man and the invasion matched his physique. A train was hired and the people marched to Carisbrook Park led by the indomitable Bill plus a brass band or two playing the *Invercargill March*.

As soon as we heard about the trip at the office, we started off to organise a party. Our first idea was to go on the train, but one of the boys named Mick said he could borrow his father's car and would take five or six of us if we would chip in for the petrol – in advance. He made no secret of the fact that on his last trip he'd had to do a lot of reminding before he finally collected all the "subs".

Mick was bringing his brother and this brother was an ex-medical student. According to Mick, the reason that his brother was an "ex" medical student was that he had a bad habit of developing every symptom that the lecturer would be discussing. Mick said this wasn't so bad on temporary complaints such as pregnancy or earache, but his brother wasn't so keen on those permanent jobs such as kidney disease or cancer – the symptoms persisted for weeks afterwards. In the end Mick's brother got fed up and turned in any thought of being a doctor. To date, however, he hadn't thought of being anything else.

But why I mention Mick's brother is this – he used to stay at a boardinghouse in Dunedin, along with a lot of other medical students and he was reputed to be the firm favourite of both the landlady and her lovely daughter. The landlady had told him that any time he came to Dunedin for a night there would be a bed available for him and a couple of his mates "free, gratis and for nothing".

Mick's brother had never availed himself of this offer and he said he would do so now. The chosen three to get this free accommodation were Mick, Mick's brother and I. The other three in the party had to book their own accommodation.

We set off from Invercargill after work on the Friday and were soon lapping up big lungfuls of that Southland dust. Mick was driving fast but safely and while the light lasted we played a few hands of draw and show poker. Finally we all lost interest in the game at the one moment – and speaking for myself, I had a very good reason – I felt carsick and, as it turned out later, so did all the rest. Roads in those days had short up and down steep patches and taken at speed these could produce carsickness in a flash. Fortunately nobody succumbed to the complaint and in due course we were chatting quite happily once again.

When we got to Dunedin we went to the pie-cart and had a meal and then set off for the boardinghouse. When we got there it must have been nearly midnight, but Mick's brother opened the front door and conducted us upstairs to an enormous room set out like a dormitory. There must have been about a dozen beds, of which six or seven were occupied. When Mick's brother came in there were shouts of joy followed by shouts from a few bottles of beer. There was a terrific din and a bit of a tune on the bagpipes.

Before long there was a sharp knocking on the wall from the landlady. Apparently all the boys were medical students and one grabbed a very large medical tome and thumbed through it for a few seconds. He then gave a diagnosis: "*Symptoms*, knocking on wall

135

at night; *Complaint*, dung on the pluck." With this he put the book away, but I must say that from that point the noise level dropped a bit. Perhaps one of our eminent medical men may still remember this early diagnosis.

For the next half hour or so Mick's brother and the students filled themselves in on all the current doings on either side.

One story told was of a student who hadn't done too well in an exam on heart troubles and had been brought back for another try. The panel of examiners had a man in the room who had some form of heart trouble, and they asked the student to listen in with the stethescope and let them know what he heard. He hadn't done that essential half-hour's homework to become a heart specialist but he wasn't going to give in easily. He said, "I hear *gluggety-glug*." The panel was not satisfied and told him to have another listen and tell them what he heard. "More *gluggety-glugs*," was his answer. Apparently he didn't pass.

Sometime later we got to sleep and I remember being wakened by a young lass who turned out to be the landlady's daughter. "Who are you?" she asked.

I said I was Mick's brother's friend and said I thought that they were expecting us. By this time Mick's brother and Mick had popped their heads from the under the blankets and Mick's brother broke the news that he had just popped in as a big surprise to her and her mother. The daughter seemed pleased but the landlady certainly wasn't, and after breakfast we found that we were without board for the next night and that we had been charged 6s. each for bed and breakfast. "Extortionate," was Mick's brother's comment.

This was a bit of a financial blow as Mick's brother did not (or said he didn't) have 6s. to spare so I paid it for him. This made quite a hole in my exchequer. As we had no place to stay we were going to have to return to Invercargill that evening after the match, and this would have spoiled our plans for an evening out in Dunedin.

Mick's brother wasn't perturbed, however. He had another girlfriend whose father owned an hotel where he was sure that the three of us would be very welcome. When I questioned him how much it would cost he assured me that it would be free. If it was like the previous evening it might be free for Mick's brother but I would be called upon to again help out, and I just didn't have too much spare cash.

However we went to this hotel, which was out in the suburbs, and this time Mick's brother was made very welcome by Mum, Dad, and particularly the daughter. All the rooms were booked up by Southland supporters but we were told we could sleep in the staff quarters. So far so good. We set off for the football match and hadn't gone more than a few hundred yards and we had a blowout in the back tyre. We changed the tyre but the spare wasn't at all good and we had no option but to buy a new tube and have the original tyre fitted on again at the garage. Mick's brother said he had no spare money so Mick and I shared the cost of the tube. This cut my funds to bedrock and I was by now genuinely worried whether I would have enough to last out.

After the match we moved around the town as young chaps do, and filled in the evening very nicely.

We got back to the hotel before midnight. Mick's brother managed to find some cold lamb in the kitchen and we made a few sandwiches; somehow or other during the evening I found myself paying for cigarettes etc., and by the time we got back I had only 1s. 6d. left. I told Mick and his brother and they said they were in the same box. I was still not sure whether we would have to pay for accommodation but Mick's brother again assured us both that it would be OK. This was poor consolation to me as I remembered what had happened that morning at the boardinghouse.

I slept very little that night and when I did I was plagued with all sorts of disturbing dreams which apparently sprang from my worries. I wasn't much better at breakfast, and could only manage a small piece of toast. We were to leave early, and the nearer the time of departure came the more apprehensive I became. This state of mind wasn't relieved when Mick whispered to me that he hoped that what his brother had said about the accommodation being free was correct. I was sure then that we were going to be asked to pay.

Finally the time for departure came and all the family assembled to see us off. This ceremony seemed to stretch on and on, and momentarily I expected the account for the night's accommodation to be produced. But no, with a final wave we were off – there had been no charge.

From that moment on I wished I'd had a good breakfast like the other two. By the time I got to Invercargill I could have eaten an ox.

18

NIGHT FISHING ON THE MAKAREWA RIVER

IN BETWEEN PAY TRIPS and my efforts to establish a vegetable garden to my wife's satisfaction, I found that there was still time to get in a bit of trout fishing around the Southland rivers. I was aided and abetted in this by a friend named George Stupples, who was always coming to light with some new idea or new place to fish.

From time to time he would meet some old stager who would tell him of a pet method for catching trout, or of some spot where they were so plentiful that "limit bags were commonplace". Unfortunately, I would also fall under the spell of these stories, and it took little time for George to convince me that any scheme he put forward was a good one. From time to time we had our disappointments and I remember one particular evening when we did 120 miles in the Austin 7 after our evening meal, sat about 4 hours in teeming rain, caught one trout about five inches long by foul-hooking it in the eye, and lost ourselves on the way home. The dam we had been fishing was, according to George, "full of trout up to about sixteen pounds weight, and so hungry they will snap at the lure as it hits the water".

One Friday evening Lola and I were doing some shopping when we met George and his wife, and the first thing he did was to bring out an envelope and show me some fish hooks he had just bought. They were like ordinary hooks except that they had a type of safety pin fitted on to the back of the hook.

"I suppose you know what these are for," said George in a slightly superior manner. I did not, and was forced to admit my ignorance.

Having established his superior knowledge, he informed me they were specially made for fixing shrimps to the hook, and he went on to say "Shrimps are deadly bait on the Makarewa River after nightfall." This bit of information sounded very like an extract from the local sports dealer's catalogue, but I didn't mention this to George for the simple reason that I didn't want to find any loopholes in his story. He was already preaching to the converted and any tale, however thin, which gave promise of new horizons in fishing was good enough for me. I wouldn't have dared to express any doubts in case an opportunity was lost.

Our wives, by this time, were catching up on the events of the week and had decided we should go to George's place for supper. This was right up our alley, as by this time George and I had decided to go out fishing the following evening and this obviously necessitated a planning session.

Before we left town, George purchased a yard or two of mosquito netting, as we would have to make a net to catch bait.

After supper our wives got their heads together again, and George and I were free to plan the expedition.

The first thing we did was to ask the wives to run up a net on the sewing machine.

For newly-married men, we were no doubt the two most privileged fishermen in the country. Both our wives came from families where fishing was considered a way of life for husbands, and never on any occasion did they have any objections to our excursions. Always on our return we were treated with kindness and consideration even if the bag was empty, and accorded full honours on the less numerous occasions when we came home with a good catch.

George's request to have the net made met with a ready response from the women and he and I settled down to finalise our plans.

The idea was to get to the Makarewa next evening about an hour before dark and scoop out some shrimps for bait. George, who was still silent as to the source of his profound knowledge of this new type of fishing, assured me that, "One scoop with the net will yield a pint or two of shrimps, bullies and sprats – all of which are very good bait for trout."

Here again I seemed to sense a rather unusual turn of phrase for George, and once again it reminded me of the words used in those catalogues issued by sports dealers. However, I was not there to disbelieve anything that was said. I was happy to believe it all and would be even happier to find out later that it worked out in practice.

When the net was completed, we fixed it on to a wire loop at the end of a long pole, finishing up well after midnight.

Next evening I took Lola round to George's place as company for George's wife and we soon had his Austin 7 loaded with our gear. This consisted of the usual paraphernalia of bags, rods, torches and landing nets, and on this particular occasion we took two pint jars for the shrimps. Strung on the side of the Austin was the long pole net and our two long bamboo rods which in those days were so popular in Southland for fishing with live bait.

Finally we set off for the Makarewa, and by this time my enthusiasm had reached such a high pitch that I was almost starting to worry about whether we would be able to carry home all the fish as well as our gear. Apparently George's mind was also on other things as both of us were rudely jerked back from our mental wanderings in a fisherman's paradise when the old Austin went into a hectic skid in the heavy gravel, then shot on to the grass beside the road and bumped along for about twenty yards till George took control again and edged it back on to the road. A skid of this nature was a most unusual event for George, although he invariably seemed to drive with the accelerator flat down and was an expert in making the most of the gravel for cornering.

He completely ignored the whole event however, and just kept the accelerator flat to the boards as usual. I didn't say anything either – mainly I think, because I was speechless with fright and also because I felt that if he could take it, so could I. As a matter of fact George often tried me out to see just how I would react to various situations and, being aware of this, I often had to put on a much bolder front than my inner feelings warranted. George was a thin, tough, hardy type, who would spend a week or two in the bush on his own, on a shooting trip, often in wet weather, sleeping in his sleeping-bag under hollow logs and more or less living off the land.

We soon arrived at the Makarewa, parked the car, and unloaded our gear.

We found what looked like a suitable backwater to get our bait, and on the first scoop we had quite a few bullies and shrimps. Certainly not a pint at a scoop as George had predicted, but quite a fair haul. I had the job of picking out the shrimps and putting them in the bottles. Before long we had enough shrimps to keep us going for days, so we gave up the shrimping and sat down and waited for darkness.

At this stage George, like a general before a battle, went carefully over the night's operations. The first and main essential was that we must locate a trout which was feeding; this didn't seem to present much difficulty to me as in most decent-sized pools in the Makarewa after dark, the odd large fish could be heard or seen rising with a resounding splash as it broke the water from time to time. One of the difficulties, however, was that more often than not, these splashes were just out of range, or, if they were near, an overhanging tree or a steep bank would make it difficult to get a line near.

George explained that few difficulties would be experienced with his new method as it did not involve casting a minnow, bully, or big fly in the usual manner. All we had to do was to fix a shrimp on to the special safety pin type of hook and then creep up to within a few feet of the edge of the river, preferably behind a bit of high ground, in a spot where we could hear a fish feeding, and then slowly shove our long rods forward and dangle the shrimp as near to the fish as possible. George was careful to explain, that, according to his informant – who by the way still remained anonymous – it was preferable that the fisherman must not be observed by the trout.

These requirements did not appear insuperable, and as it was then dark we set off on a course parallel to the river. I had not gone fifty yards before I stepped on a rotten log, the outside shell suddenly gave way, and I fell over. After picking myself up I took stock and found that one jar of shrimps had tipped over in the long grass. I wanted to switch on the torch and recover a few of them but we decided that we had plenty in the other jar. In any case George pointed out that his expert informant (still anonymous and still in my opinion closely related to a fishing tackle catalogue) had told him that in this type of fishing, a light, once lit, put an end to any chance of successful fishing for the night.

To give full weight to his remarks, George also informed me that on a clear night, the light from a match could be seen up to some figure like $2\frac{1}{4}$ miles away, although I am not at this stage prepared to swear that this was the exact distance. I could have argued that the river had a few bends in it, or that it would be a good fish that could see up a steep bank and then out on to a paddock, but I was in no mood to argue. My main thoughts were on the fish we would soon be catching.

Before long we heard the heavy splash of a big fish feeding, so we dumped our bags and gear several yards back from the steep bank on the river's edge, dipped into the jar, selected a shrimp each and fastened it on to the safety pin on the hook. George then dropped flat on his stomach and started to worm his way towards the edge of the river like a commando in action, and I followed suit. I had not gone far in this fashion, however, before I found out to my sorrow that there had been some cattle in the area recently, but having made this discovery there was little I could do about it. From muffled remarks, it seemed that George had also struck similar trouble.

By this time we were getting near the edge of the river and soon forgot these minor upsets. We were fortunate in that at this point there was a small fold in the ground about five feet high between us and the point where the bank dropped away to the water.

"This will do," said George, and we both edged our rods up in the air and slowly slid them forward in the general direction of where we thought we had heard the fish. By this time we couldn't hear the fish breaking the water, but were hopeful that it would start feeding again very soon.

For about ten minutes we lay there with the shrimps dangling in the water till George leaned over my way and said, "There's something at mine."

"Let him get a good hold of it," was my advice, and no sooner had I said this than there was a scream from George's reel and the line was torn from it at a great pace.

Alas, our luck was not to hold, as no sooner had George raised his rod to a perpendicular position than the fish got off. What

141

The author with two brown trout from the Makarewa – one of 11 lbs, the other 9 lbs.

Author

George said is better left unrecorded, but when he reeled his line in he found that his hook was still there and he baited up with another shrimp and edged his rod forward once again.

Things were quiet for about five minutes and then I felt a number of gentle tugs at my line and suddenly away it went with the reel screaming in the style that brings joy to the heart of any fisherman. I was rather more fortunate than George, as my fish was well and truly hooked. It made off upstream for what, in the murky light, looked like a patch of weed. I was determined that if at all possible I would keep it away from the weed. For the next ten minutes or so there was a real tug-of-war, but my rod and line withstood the heavy strain and finally the fish tired and I was able to steer it downstream to a small beach where I managed to net it.

"Eight pounds if it's an ounce," I found myself saying aloud as I stowed it in the bag. I then started to grope my way back to where I thought George should be. I had not gone more than a couple of yards when I felt a few drops of rain and within half a minute or so there was a real deluge. I had on my oilskin coat and immediately buttoned it up to the neck, pulled my sou'wester out of my pocket, and jammed it on my head. Then I faced into the wind and let the rain beat on the front of my coat, which was still carrying a very pungent reminder that the paddock we were in had very recently been occupied by cattle. After a while I found that the coat was very much more tolerable and I decided to rejoin George and get on with the fishing.

By this time it was impossible to see any distance at all but I knew, or thought I knew, roughly the direction to take, and I headed off, picking my way over rough cow tracks and clumps of blackberry. After I had groped around for about ten minutes and fallen over in the mud a couple of times I decided that I didn't have a clue where George was, nor did I even know in what direction the river lay as I had moved away from it. Luck was with me however, as just at that moment a car came down the nearby road and swung round the corner and shone its lights on the Austin 7. This gave me a rough bearing and I was able to get back to the river's edge and work upstream.

I was still groping along when I heard the scream of a reel ahead of me and I yelled out, "Is that you George?"

"Yes, come here quick," was his reply. By this time I had tripped over once more and did not feel inclined to move at anything much above a slow shuffle. I did however, speed up a bit and soon came up to where he was hanging on to his rod and having a battle royal with what was certainly a very lively fish.

"See if you can pick him up with your light," was George's next request and I fished out my big torch and shone it out on the water. The fish was really going to town in the middle of the pool but every now and then it would head towards the patch of weed, which was shown up by the spotlight. George meantime, was doing his level best to keep it away. Finally however, the fish did get into the weed and was either sulky or the line was entangled, and George was unable to make any headway.

There was only one thing for it and that was for one of us to wade out and endeavour to untangle the line or net the fish if it was still there. Being placed as we were, I was the obvious choice to do the wading out into the stream. I slid down the bank and let myself into the water and found it quite a bit deeper than I thought. I edged my way out gingerly and finally managed to get a hold of George's line where it entered the water. I traced it into the weed and found it was twisted around a dead willow branch in the weed. I freed the line and drew it in slowly and there was the fish, still firmly hooked. Most of the fight had left it however, and I managed to net it without much trouble.

"Got him!" I yelled, and started to edge my way back. This was no easy task as I had the net in one hand and the torch in the other, but I finally made it and handed the net and torch to George and clambered up the bank.

While all this had been going on, the rain had been pelting down and I was feeling pretty uncomfortable. I had been unable to stop some water running down my neck and had also taken in a few cupfuls over the tops of my thigh boots while wading in the river.

We shone the torch on the fish and George said "I bet that goes eight pound." I told him mine was about the same size and I asked him whether we should continue fishing or head for home.

"Home for mine," said George. "No good keeping on now we have shown a light."

So we packed up our gear and headed off in the direction of the car, aided this time by two very powerful torches. We soon had our gear stowed away and reached home without further incident. There we were rewarded by the praises of our wives on the successful catch.

The official weigh-in was a disappointment to me, as George's fish was 7¼ lbs and mine was 6½.

After a good clean-up we sat down to a nice supper, and before I left for home we had tentative plans made for a trip the following night, and had even discussed the possibilities of bottling some of our future catches in view of the assured supply of such well-conditioned pink-fleshed trout.

Unfortunately it rained all next day and we didn't get out again till the following Saturday night.

Having already landed two good fish on our previous trip, we had no trouble in convincing ourselves that, with a bit more planning and average luck, we could do much better than this.

Although I was loath to admit it, I really had begun to believe that George did have a secret informant well versed in the wiles of the Makarewa trout – and that he had not culled his ideas from some fishing catalogue.

On our second trip we took my Austin 7. The night we selected was a pitch black one and this, according to George, was just what was required. As far as I could remember, George had not previously mentioned this point and I was even unkind enough to think that he must have had another browse through his fishing catalogue and suddenly come upon this extra titbit of fishing "know-how".

In due course we arrived at the Makarewa a bit before dark and had soon scooped up enough live shrimps to provide bait for the evening.

We then sat down to wait till it was properly dark, which in Southland's mid-summer, can be after 10 pm. When darkness fell we headed off to the spot where we had successfully fished on our last trip. This again necessitated our crawling along on all fours till we arrived at the rear of the small mound on the edge of the river. The technique was the same as before – to keep out of sight of the water and not to show any lights. All that we then had to do was to fix a shrimp on the hook and gently slide the rod up over the bank, letting the shrimp dangle in the water.

From the very nature and size of the hook and the bait, we were fairly sure that any fish we would catch would be quite sizeable, and this fact alone was enough to get our imaginations really going. How big would the fish be? Six pounds? Eight? Or ten? We even got to the stage where we hoped for some of each weight.

Our hooks were soon baited and we both slid our rods up in the air and over the top of the bank in the approved style. Then we waited expectantly. We could hear the odd fish "plopping" in the distance from time to time, and prospects seemed bright.

For a while we did not get any bites and I decided to reel in my line and see whether the shrimp was still on the hook. Just as I lifted the rod into the perpendicular position I felt the line tighten appreciably and there was quite a reasonable tug. I struck with the rod but there was no weight on it and, of course, no fish. I wound in my line and there was a very damaged shrimp hanging half on and half off the safety pin.

"It must have been a small one," I said quietly, and George agreed with my diagnosis.

I baited up again and slid the rod up and over the mound in front of us. We left our lines dangling for some time but neither of us had any sign of a bite. Nevertheless we were not worried as we knew there were good fish in the river and we were sure we had the techniques necessary to catch them.

After a while George decided to check on his own bait but found that it was intact. He changed it however and we both again settled down expectantly. A bit later George decided that it might be a good idea if we shifted upstream a bit, but I was not in favour of this. I argued that this spot gave us the cover so essential for this type of fishing, and after a bit of discussion we decided to stay put. This was a wise move apparently as George, while moving his rod to a new position, suddenly struck with the rod and there was a short scream as the line ran off the reel. George wound in but failed to hook anything and when he finally hauled his line in and got the hook into view he found that his shrimp bait had gone.

"That must have been a better one," was his comment and, ever an optimist, I agreed with him. He then had a bright idea: "Perhaps they are more interested in a moving bait tonight."

I thought this was a possibility so we agreed that we would move our rods about a bit to see if that would help. As a matter of fact it did seem to result in our getting a number of small "touches", but we did not succeed in actually getting a fish really well hooked.

By this time it was getting near midnight and it felt as though it could rain anytime, so we decided to turn it in and head off home.

To assist us in packing up, we switched on our torches and, out of curiosity, we climbed up to the top of the mound and shone the lights into the river to see if we could locate any fish breaking the surface as they were feeding. Imagine our reactions when we looked down where we had been dangling our lines. Instead of seeing an expanse of slow flowing river, we looked down on a grassy ledge, about ten feet wide and completely devoid of water. It was on this ledge that George and I had been dropping our shrimp baits for a couple of hours. When we had hit upon the bright idea of moving the baits about a bit they must have caught on the grass and given us the illusion of a slight tug.

What we had not been aware of was that the Makarewa at this point near its mouth, was backed up by the tide in the adjoining estuary. On the other evening we had fished at this spot it had been a high tide, but on the present occasion the tide, like our luck, was definitely "out".

"Well – what do you know?" was George's reaction. I was speechless.

However, it's a poor fisherman who cannot see some ray of hope even in circumstances such as this and by the time we had groped our way back to the car, our spirits were high once again. I summed up the position thus, "It isn't as though we have been fishing and caught nothing – we just haven't been fishing at all."

Having got over our frustration by this very logical bit of deduction, we were then in that glorious mental state that we had been in prior to this latest trip – we knew how to catch the big ones, and we knew where to catch them. In fact we had even progressed a little – we knew when to catch them, and this was certainly *not* at low tide.

With all this in mind, plans for a further evening excursion on the Makarewa were laid before we reached home that night.

As time went on we had many an evening out on the Makarewa and a variety of experiences. On occasions we would no sooner get the shrimp into the water than an eel would take it. If this happened it would set the pattern for the evening and we would pack up quickly and leave for home.

On odd occasions we did catch good fish on our later evening excursions on the Makarewa, but they were never easy – and that, I think, was where the attraction lay.

19

CARPENTRY WORKSHOPS

PAYDAY WAS AROUND again and it was one of those days when we couldn't go wrong. Everybody seemed to be at the right place at the right time. Nobody even complained that their hours were wrong or that the co-op contract rates were too low. (This was the day when one of the men on the job presented me with the beautiful fly rod he had been making for some time.) The sun was shining all day.

I got to the Hollyford in good time and there again was Dan waiting to join me on the trip around the job.

When I met up with him the first thing he would do was to fill me in on the local pieces of scandal and funny incidents and this particular day was no exception. He had a tale about one of the men who had a reputation for being something of a "dodger". Dan said he was doing his round of the job, taking tallies of the hours worked, and happened to be walking round in the dinner hour when he saw a man stretched out on top of a low stack of timber. For a moment Dan thought he might have been injured, but on getting up to him he found he was asleep, so he shook him and said, "What are you doing here, Charlie?"

Instead of answering this question Charlie countered with "What's the time, Dan?"

Dan looked at his watch and said it was half past twelve.

"Well I'll be damned, Dan," came the exclamation, "I must be getting old – here's me been sleeping half an hour in me own time."

Dan then mentioned one of the young chaps in the staff mess who was rumoured to be a bit of a lad with the girls, and in fact he had a rather rude nickname which could indicate that this rumour may have had some substance. One evening when the scarcity of females was being discussed, someone asked this chap how it was that a man of his reputation was quite happy to stay on this isolated job.

His answer, if not strictly mathematically correct, certainly conveyed the message: "I'll admit that only a few sheilas come up this way, but there's one important thing you've got to remember – their regard for the male increases not in direct relation to the increase in altitude, but according to the square of the increase in altitude."

Next morning it was rumoured that the engineer-in-charge had received three applications for a transfer to the Homer Tunnel area, which was much higher up the valley. Dan then remarked that it was always said on the Hollyford job that when the bus came in the cry of the married men was "Any mail arrived?" while the single men asked "Any female arrived?"

After Dan had got this off his chest we set out up the road. As we went along he was telling me of various odd incidents that had happened in his experience. One in particular was that a man in single hut accommodation had complained bitterly that his hut was too small, and so cramped that if he wanted any furniture he would have to paint it on the wall. What amazed Dan was that at the time the chap complained he was living in a hut with canvas sides and an earth floor. This didn't seem to worry him.

Another point which Dan commented on was that many single men on these jobs were not single by choice. They wanted to marry but just didn't get the opportunity to meet any women. I had noticed this, and years later, as Chief Clerk in the Rehabilitation Department, Wellington, I found the same thing amongst returned servicemen. I then took the matter up with the Hon. Hilda Ross, Minister of Social Security, who was very sympathetic and asked me to write a report for her. I did this but although she had ideas on the subject, she told me that she could not get Cabinet support for them.

When we called at the canteen, the chap in charge complained that he was having trouble with two "alkies", who were wanting to buy ingredients for a cocktail and he wouldn't supply them. He said they had threatened to go to the union. We asked him what sort of things they wanted and he said, "Flit, Brasso, worcester sauce, painkiller and meths." How much of this was true and how much imagination I couldn't guess.

He also complained that one man was buying so much chocolate and other lollies as well as his ordinary groceries that he was not earning enough to pay his canteen account. Dan knew this chap and explained that he was a bit of a hypochondriac and would lie in bed on the slightest pretext. As Dan put it, "He enjoys bad health."

After dinner that night we were watching a game of poker and all of a sudden one of the players dropped his hand on the table and said "Look at *that!*" He had a flush with a pair in it and he was horrified. The matter was soon explained however, as there were two similar packs and one or two cards from one had got mixed with the other. As the holder of the unique hand said, "It's just as well is wasn't 'guns on the table'."

This evening at the mess was productive of quite a number of stories and as sometimes happened, one story often triggered off another by bringing to mind some long past incident and that is what occurred this evening.

Paying out at the tunnel. *Left to right*: Ian McLachlan, Joe Lloyd, Roy Hunter, Bill Ryan, author.

Author

"That reminds me," cried one of the gang and off he went with his story—which I tell in his words!

As you all know, there are tricks and secrets in every occupation and walk of life. Take for instance that age-old secret that the Scotsman has never divulged – what he wears under his kilt! And so it is with the PWD in the joinery and carpentry workshops. The secret referred to is not one that is spoken about outside the confines of these workshops and I have no certain knowledge that it is even spoken of inside the workshops. I gained my knowledge not by the spoken word but by what I saw with my own eyes.

I haven't told this story before and I am only doing so now because I trust all you chaps and know you won't repeat it.

The secret that has never been divulged or set out on any plans and specifications is this – What is the measurement of the hole in those hundreds of seats made annually by the PWD for its outside privies, and how is that measurement determined?

I'd enquired for years but could never get an answer, and had almost given up hope when I shifted on to the Waitaki Hydro job. One day I was passing the joinery shop and noticed fifty-seven of these toilet seats, all completed except for one vital feature – the hole had not been cut out. At last I had the chance to get an answer, and I wasn't going to be beaten. I haunted the joinery shop and just

149

by accident I learned a piece of news which could provide a vital clue. The Government Architect was making a flying visit from Head Office to Waitaki that night but would only be staying an hour or two. I won't say I'm psychic, but I was definitely guided by intuition and I decided that I would keep a close watch on him as he was the High Priest of Building Construction in the Public Works Department.

He arrived by car and had his evening meal at the staff mess, which cut his available time down considerably.

I was watching him closely and saw that as soon as dinner was over, the buildings overseer furtively handed him a key, and he left the room. Again by intuition I knew his destination, and I was ready. He was going to the joinery workshop, and I slipped round the back of it and climbed up on an old 44-gallon drum so that I could see through the window. The light was switched on and I had a perfect view. The Government Architect turned around and carefully locked the door. He then picked up a carpenter's pencil in one hand and with the other he took off his beautiful black homburg hat and placed it on one of the unfinished lavatory seats. He quickly ran round the brim of the hat with the pencil and the hole for the seat was clearly marked out. He swiftly did this with the other fifty-six seats and then left the building smartly and locked the door. At last I had learned the Great Carpentry Workshops Secret.

At this point, the teller of the story finished up by saying – "I've trusted all you chaps with this great Departmental secret, and I hope you will never divulge it."

Somebody then asked if there was anybody else who could tell a new story – they didn't want any old chestnuts they had heard before. There was quite a long pause and all of a sudden a voice piped up, "Could you stand one which starts off 'When I was on the South Island Main Trunk Railway down Parnassus way'?" There was a roar of laughter as this member of the mess was one of those fellows who had a wealth of good stories and the ability to adapt them to suit the circumstances.

On this particular evening there had been quite a discussion on politics and electoral procedures, and this must have brought this story to his mind, and away he went with his time-honoured opening –

"When I was on the South Island Main Trunk Railway down Parnassus way – " This caused another laugh but finally he got under way.

The story he told concerned a parliamentary election and a timekeeper who used to earn a pound or two acting as returning officer or poll clerk on polling day.

At this election he was given a job at a remote PWD camp where there were twenty-two employees. He received all his gear from the local returning officer on polling day and duly stationed himself at the polling booth. He had as his helper one of the local Public Works gang. All the local men called early in the day and voted. As far as they knew, this was all the voters and this was how it turned out, but to comply with the regulations they had to wait until closing time when they themselves cast their vote. This made a very monotonous day but at last it was over and the count was made.

During the day the local helper had made it clear that he was a strong Labour supporter, and the timekeeper had not expressed any contrary view. In a predominantly Labour community the time-keeper felt it was wise to keep his own counsel and his political views to himself. On the count-up however he did get a bit of a shock as the result was 22 to 1 in favour of Labour.

The timekeeper telling the story said that his assistant at the time made no comment. When he next visited the job however, one of the men told him that when the result was known all the twenty-two at the camp had got together and sworn a solemn oath that they had all voted for Labour, and this meant that the timekeeper was a Tory. The timekeeper, not to be outdone, as he was the only one of the twenty-three who knew positively how the voting had gone, said, "I'm very surprised that you should all think so harshly of me and I have no way or intention of trying to prove you wrong – but just look at these receipts and then go back and see if any of the twenty-two men at the camp can match them."

The receipts were for subscriptions to the Labour Party for many years past and the last one was only a week or two old. This apparently created some doubt in the camp and the episode was never referred to again.

The timekeeper, with a smile on his face however, said that he would never take on a poll clerk's job on a small Public Works camp again in similar circumstances. He also said he could just as easily have produced a bunch of receipts for subscriptions to the National Party over the years.

20

MONOWAI - A SPORTSMAN'S PARADISE

GEORGE, MY HUNTIN', shootin' and fishin' cobber, had been talking for some weeks past about a couple of pig dogs which a friend of his "a wellknown breeder", to use George's words, had let him have for a nominal sum. At the price I had grave doubts as to whether the dogs would be any good but George was confident. He said he had been out on a trip with these dogs and they were "just the berries". He was all for making an early trip and he suggested I should go with him for a two-day outing.

I had a few reservations. George had a lot more experience than I had and was inclined to make some fairly extensive trips and expected me to be up with him all the way. He also had better and lighter gear than I had and was remarkably fit. In fact he was just too much of the expert pighunter and tramper for me to qualify as an ideal mate for him, but he genuinely wanted me to go with him so I agreed.

The spot we chose was the Lake Monowai area which was renowned for the number of pigs, deer and fish it provided.

No sooner had I agreed than George suggested a get-together to discuss plans and this was arranged for the next evening. First of all there was the transport to be considered. I had my Austin 7 but no spare petrol as the war had broken out and rationing was in force. George also had an Austin 7, of somewhat earlier vintage than mine and, being mechanically inclined, had installed a gas-producer unit with a burner at the back. He admitted that the car "hadn't quite got the herbs she used to have" but finished up by assuring me that "She'll do us, boy – we'll get there."

A possible reduction in speed seemed at that time to be quite a good thing as George had a frightening habit of driving over Southland's shingly roads with the accelerator very close, if not flat to the floorboards for most of the time.

Next evening we finalised our plans and decided to set out the following weekend. I had some reservations about the car as I felt it might be overloaded, but George assured me that all would be well. After all there was only our personal gear, rifles, packs, sleeping bags, two medium-sized shooters in George and myself, two dogs, the gas producer and a bag of fuel for stoking it, plus our food.

152

George was quite happy however, and pointed out that we were not carrying a lot of petrol, which according to his calculations weighed about ten pounds per gallon.

The arrangement was that George was to pick me up at 2 am, so I got to bed early and put the alarm on for 1.15. I awoke just in time to switch it off before it rang. By two o'clock I was ready and George arrived right on time. I was certainly not too far wrong about the car being overloaded. The two dogs were sitting on the back seat with gear packed all round them. The back carrier was loaded with gear, including the bag of charcoal for the gas producer. I managed to stow my gear in somehow and off we set.

I noticed that it took George quite a time to get into top gear and before changing up he got the maximum revs and then whipped it into the next gear as though he were on a racing circuit. These manoeuvres ultimately produced a maximum speed of about 37 miles per hour, and having achieved this I felt that my fears may have been groundless.

There was more to come however. The going at the start was flat and the speedo stayed steady at that magical 37 miles per hour. We soon found however, that as we reached even the smallest hill the speedo reading dropped back considerably. I mentioned this to George but his only comment was, "We'll be right – you watch me get up to fifty when we get on a good downgrade." He certainly did just about that, irrespective of the state of the road. As we came to the straight flat stretches, the speedo reading would gradually drop and became static at the same old 37 mph.

So far so good, but in time we came on to some steeper patches and the speedo reading of the old bus dropped further and further until George suggested that I hop out to reduce the weight on some of the tougher spots. I even had half-hearted ideas of giving the old bus a push if necessary, but somehow or other we always just managed to make the last final efforts and reach the top.

When we came to a very winding part of the road I found out that the larger of the dogs, called Blacky, would persist in leaning his head on my shoulder and licking my neck and as far around my face as he could manage. George thought this was a good joke and said that the dog must like the taste of my face cream. Today this remark would probably go unnoticed but in those times the thought of a man using a face cream was unheard of. I countered by informing George that the dog knew a good man when he met one.

However there was worse to come, as the dog seemed to develop some internal rumbles and every now and then he would belch in my ear. I mentioned this to George and his reaction was to turn half round and give the dog a thump on the nose to try and make him stay further back on the seat. This took George's eye off the road and made things decidedly dangerous so I came to the conclusion that it was better to put up with the dog and leave George to attend to the driving.

It was not long however before more trouble developed. The dog started to get spasms somewhat akin to a very bad dose of hiccoughs.

The road was getting worse and worse and at this stage consisted of what looked like two clay sheep tracks with a grassy hump in the middle about a foot high. Unfortunately these tracks had been made by the tyres of vehicles with a track considerably wider than an Austin 7 and George was doing a spectacular if terrifying job in keeping the car on its four wheels.

Every now and then it would leap out of the tracks and the only thing that kept it upright was the heavy manuka scrub on either side. George had to keep up the revs to keep the car going and I have never experienced a finer or more terrifying piece of driving. The dog behind George was quite happy but the brute behind me was still shuddering like an erupting volcano, and by this time had a paw on each of my shoulders and his head alongside mine. There was nothing I could do as it was panic stations all around. The worst happened. The poor old dog behind me had reached the limit of canine endurance and became violently carsick. George's eyes were glued on the road but even so he realised what had happened. "Hang on, Harold – we'll soon be there," was all he could say. "Hang on" was right. I had been hanging on like grim death for the last half hour or so and this was the final straw. From that point on for the next ten minutes, the dog and I were sick in turns, and at times simultaneously.

Finally George brought the car to a stop in a clearing beside a tramper's hut on the bank of the Monowai. I struggled out of the car and peeled off my light oilskin coat and dumped it in the river. I then stripped off the rest of my gear and had a cold dip – and cold it certainly was. However this revived me and that was all to the good.

Meantime George had grabbed hold of the dog and heaved it into the river, which at this point was running fairly fast. The dog disappeared downstream but after about ten minutes it ambled back looking very dejected. George rather rudely remarked that the dog smelt a lot fresher and as an afterthought said, "And that goes for you too."

After my dip I grabbed some clean clothes from my pack but owing to the extreme cold I did not take sufficient time to rub myself dry with the towel and my clothes refused to slip on easily. George could see that I wasn't doing so well so he grabbed a towel and just about rubbed the hide off me. "Take it easy," I said but he kept on and in a few minutes I started to feel better and was soon fully dressed again. My oilskin was in such a mess that we decided to leave it in the water and anchored it down with a few large stones and left it to soak. Fortunately I had a lightweight parka with me.

On our arrival George had tied up the fit dog Ginger and suddenly he grabbed Blackie and tied him alongside.

"I don't want them setting off after a pig before we're ready," was George's explanation. "Wishful thinking" was my unspoken reaction, but I was sufficiently enthusiastic as to the prospects to be greatly encouraged by his comment.

Despite our troubles it did not take us long to get ready and we were soon on our way. George had a beautiful high-power .22 rifle, while I had my old heavy army-type short Lee Enfield .303 purchased from army stores at some ridiculous figure of £1 or thereabouts – and reputed to be fitted with a new barrel.

George again assured me that the dogs really knew their job and the way they trailed along a few feet behind us and obeyed him certainly backed up his remarks. Blackie seemed to have profited from George's cold water therapy. He was reputed to be half collie and half something else but certainly did not look like a collie. On the other hand Ginger, who was also half collie, had both the colouring and look of a collie. Ginger had one particular feature – his tail was only half there and George said that in his youth his tail had been caught between a bike chain and sprocket and was so mangled that an amputation was necessary. George, ever an optimist, could see virtue even in this, and his comment was "less weight to carry".

The first stage of our trip was up a bit of a slope and then over some flat scrubby swamp country. The dogs were dead quiet and trotted behind us for about half an hour, then off they went like a shot out of a gun. We heard no sound for a while and kept on going and after a short time found that both dogs had come in from the rear and were again at our heels. This was the pattern of the next half hour or so. A few more minutes and off they went again and in no time we could hear them barking flat out. We headed off in their direction. We must have travelled something over a quarter of a mile before we came up with the dogs and no sooner did we get near them than they were off again.

"I'll bet this is a bottler," said George. "These dogs don't usually let a pig get away on them."

After another couple of hundred yards of fast scrambling, we came up with the dogs again and there was no doubt this time that they had got a good hold of the pig because all we could hear was an agonised squealing.

"Hang on to my rifle," said George. "I'll go in and knife him."

He handed the weapon to me and although we had already agreed that we would not shoot unless we were in sight of each other, he

155

apparently wanted to be reassured and yelled "Don't start shooting!" With this, he pulled out his knife and walked warily through some beech trees at the edge of the bush where the pig was baled up. At this stage we had seen neither the pig nor the dogs. About three minutes later George came back moving fast and said, "Give me the gun – this is the biggest boar I've seen for years and I'm going to shoot him."

I handed him the rifle and he beckoned me to follow quietly. The spot where the pig was baled was in fairly open bush with plenty of small trees, and I decided that if the pig made a break in my direction I would shin up one of these like the old rat up a drainpipe. As I moved in I checked that my safety catch was on so that we wouldn't have a bullet flying if I happened to drop the gun in the rush. I walked a few paces behind George and ultimately got a glimpse of the pig. It was certainly a monster boar but by this time the dogs had chopped it down to size. Blackie had got it by the ear and Ginger had a very strong hold of its nether appendages and the pig was really squealing. I felt almost a wave of compassion as I could not imagine a more agonising or ignominious situation.

George was intent on business and crept fairly close in and took very careful aim, as it was quite possible that the pig would make a break at any time and he was taking every precaution to ensure that he did not account for one of his dogs instead of the pig. He pulled the trigger and the pig slumped over. For good measure he put another shot into it.

I was no expert on pig sizes but this one was a monster in anybody's language and George decided to keep the tusks as a trophy. He has them to this day. He cut out the jawbone and hacked off a hind leg, remarking that it would make a lovely piece of bacon. I had my doubts on this but said nothing. We hung the leg up in a tree and off we went with the dogs trotting at our heels.

We hadn't been going for more than about a quarter of an hour and the dogs were off again.

"Hang on," said George, "and see what happens. We might as well have a spell while we can."

We heard nothing of the dogs for quite a time and finally they came trotting in from the rear, along the track we had just traversed. We waited a while as they had obviously covered a fair distance and were puffing hard.

A bit later George said, "I suppose we'd better be on our way," so off we set with the dogs bringing up the rear.

Within twenty minutes or so they were off again, but apparently it was an old scent as they soon trotted in again at our heels. George had certainly acquired a great pair of pig dogs and he was very proud of them. A bit later they were off again and in a short time we could hear them barking so we again headed off in their direction at full gallop. They were quite a distance away and had baled up a medium sized sow in a bit of a clearing in a swampy area. Neither of the dogs had a hold of the sow but they were obviously enjoying themselves by heading her off every time she attempted to make a break.

George shed his pack and rifle and before I realised what he was going to do he had run in and made a flying tackle at the pig and grabbed her by the back legs. He tucked one leg under each arm and stood up and the pig just tottered on its front feet and seemed completely helpless. This was one of the funniest sights I had ever seen and George, who was always ready to put on some sort of an act, started to trundle the pig around like a wheelbarrow.

All this happened in about as short a time as it takes to tell the story. The next thing we knew was that the dogs had left us and we could hear barking and crashing noises all around us.

George immediately stopped clowning and yelled out to me to help him secure the pig while he knifed it. He did this in short time and we then tried to take stock of what was going on. Both dogs were barking and we could hear noises from all directions. Finally things sorted themselves out somewhat and we could definitely locate a pig squealing quite near us. I ran over and there was Blackie with a young pig. I grabbed it by the hind legs and George came up and stuck it in quick style and off went the dog again. By this time Ginger had baled another pig of similar size just nearby and we soon reached the spot. George again knifed this one and off went the dog again.

No more barking for a while so we sat down and started rolling a smoke, expecting the dogs to come in as usual.

We heard nothing for a few minutes more and were just about to light up our cigarettes when another small pig, the same size as the others, shot across in front of us, going like a cannonball. About ten or fifteen seconds later along shot Ginger – hard after the little pig.

"Hang on," said George, "He'll soon get him."

George, despite his experience and fitness, was feeling the pace and was quite happy to take an opportunity to get a break. Needless to say this also went for me.

Before long we could hear both dogs barking and George said, "Hop over and see what's doing." "Hopping" hardly described my weary trudge over the two hundred yards to where the dogs were, but when I got there I found out that George's predictions were correct and that the dogs had baled the small pig that had previously run past in front of us. I grabbed the little fellow and carried him back to where George was still sitting and I went to hand him over to George for sticking.

"Not me," said George. "You've got to learn to do this yourself – comes in handy when you're on your own."

He had been patiently waiting for an opportunity to initiate me in to this art of pigsticking so I had no option but to ask him to instruct me in the gory act. He pulled out his knife and indicated the spot where the blade should be inserted and also the direction of the thrust. I can still hear that poor little pig squeal as I stuck him. I shuddered but George seemed to be quite proud of his pupil.

"The first is the worst," was his laconic comment, and then he said, "I've seen this pig hunting pretty good but never any livelier than it is now."

Then he made a remark that sounded like sweet music to me: "I'm stonkered," he said. "Pigs or no pigs I'm going to have a cup of tea".

"You'll do me, boy," was my comment as I suddenly realised that I hadn't had a drink since about 1.30 am and it was now after midday. By this time the sun was quite hot and with the heavy going in swampy ground most of the time, and the fast following up of the dogs, we'd had enough.

We tied up the dogs and got out the thermos, and after eating our sandwiches we had a short snooze. After we woke up we gutted the three small pigs and George and I hung them up in a tree. "As long as they're fourteen feet up in the air the blowflies won't get at them," said George.

We then headed off again but although the dogs followed a number of scents they did not get on to any pigs for the next hour or so and finally we agreed to head back to the hut where we had left the car.

George checked with his compass and set a track for home. This compass of his was always a bit of a mystery to me, but he was never in any doubt as to what direction to take, so who was I to question his navigation? After a while we struck the spot where we left the three young pigs and we cut them down. George carried two and I carried the other and he set a direct course for our camp.

On arrival we stowed our gear away, got out our sleeping bags and generally tidied up.

The previous occupants of the huts, in true tramper's style, had left us a large pile of manuka saplings, cut to correct lengths and neatly stacked by the fireplace. George started to cut some replacement firewood while I strung the three pigs in a tree – fourteen feet up according to George's instructions, and generally got things ready for our next meal. This was a large pan of fried onions and a big piece of steak which we divided equally. By this time there was a very cold wind blowing and as soon as we had our tea and cleaned up we got into our sleeping bags and were soon asleep.

We were up at daybreak next morning and fortunately the wind, which had howled all night, showed signs of abating.

I stoked up the fire while George boiled the billy and heated up what was left of the onions. This looked a bit miserable when compared with our appetites, so I landed the additional job of grilling a few sausages on a stick and making toast in the same fashion.

We then cleaned up our cooking gear and stowed as much as we could in the car as we reckoned on leaving for home soon after midday. It was about an eighty-mile trip back to Invercargill, but bearing in mind the fun and games we had on the trip in, we wanted to be able to take things easy and provide for any contingencies en route.

By the time we had finished our chores the dogs were all excitement, and Blackie started to bark. A cuff on the ear from George soon silenced him however, and before long we were away again on the uphill trek. George's theory was that as we had been in the scrubby swamp area most of the previous day the pigs would probably have moved away from there He suggested that we should move into the more rugged forest area.

As we went on it seemed that his theory had some substance, as the dogs headed off on quite a number of occasions but did not bale a pig at any stage.

In the open area the sun had been shining quite brightly from low over the hills but as we entered the bush it was as though we had suddenly gone into a tunnel. The tree tops met overhead and cut out most of the light while underfoot there was a deep carpet of soft spongy moss.

We had not gone for more than a mile or so when George stopped quite suddenly and raised his hand, indicating that he wanted me to stop also. He very slowly slipped his rifle off his shoulder and turned left and half pointed with the barrel of his gun. He then raised it very slowly to his shoulder and I automatically followed suit and simultaneously slipped off the safety catch.

So far I had not seen anything and the dogs were quietly standing behind us and obviously had not scented anything. My guess was that George had either caught sight of an opossum, which would be an unusual thing in the daytime, or that perhaps – and I am ashamed to admit even thinking this – that he was going to take a pot shot at a wood pigeon. (I could well have dismissed this latter thought as George was a true sportsman but I am merely recording my thoughts as they occurred to me.)

Suddenly I too saw what had attracted George's attention. Not thirty feet away was a beautiful hind standing perfectly still with her head raised high in the air.

159

She was side on to us and, apart from the camouflaging of the trees and the light, it was a perfect target. George was still slowly raising his rifle for what must have been one of the easiest shots of a lifetime, when suddenly there was action. The deer leapt and George's rifle cracked and both actions appeared to be simultaneous. I expected to see the deer drop in its tracks. Instead it was off like lightning. George had registered a complete miss. Almost in the wink of an eye the deer was heading off in the direction from which we had come. At this spot the bush was not particularly heavy but at the speed the deer was moving it would have merged into the maze of trunks in almost fractions of a second.

Acting automatically I swung round and brought my rifle up and as I did so the deer leapt high to clear a small stream and on landing would have been out of sight. I was able to press the trigger however while the animal was in mid air and to my surprise I registered a hit, and the deer crashed to earth on the far side of the creek. George and I and the dogs covered the intervening distance in quick time but it was clear that the deer would not move again as I had hit it low down in the back of the neck.

George was an expert shot but had made one of his rare mistakes, while I had been particularly lucky, especially as I had hit it at full speed. The deer was originally up wind and apparently had not scented us and must have been curious, and this was her downfall.

George said later that as soon as he had unslung his rifle he should have had a quick snap shot rather than ride his luck to the extent of hoping that the deer would remain still until he had her perfectly lined up in his sights.

He gave me full marks for my shot however and proceeded to carve off the choicest cuts of meat and stow them in his pack.

We then sat down for a smoke and before long we were away again.

From this point we tramped up ridges and along valleys for some long time but not a pig did we get. We were getting very tired so we decided to head for the flatter scrub country again.

No sooner had we headed off in this direction than off went the dogs down a steep creekbed and we had to go after them. This was really steep country and it took the dogs some time to bale the pig. It also took us some time to get up with them and it was only then that we got a sight of the pig. It was baled up in a stream and we first caught sight of it from a bluff about fifty feet above. It was almost a sheer cliff and it would have taken us some time and considerable effort to get down to despatch the pig. It was a sow and she was standing in the water, which was about a foot deep. The spot where she was standing was shingly and at this point the stream bed was level. The poor old sow could not retreat as the stream behind her deepened quite considerably. The two dogs were standing on the bank facing the pig and every now and then they would rush her and she would retreat back into the water. On finding that she was getting her hind quarters into the deep water she would reverse the procedure and rush at the dogs and then they would retreat. George and I at this stage were pretty blown and sat down for a while to watch proceedings and have a bit of a breather.

After a while however we came to the conclusion that there was no joy in just sitting there, and George suggested that I should climb down the bank and stick the pig. "What then?" was my query and George's idea was that I should return the way I had got down. I thought that this was such an excellent idea that I offered him the opportunity to go down himself. George, as ever, was trying to take the mickey out of me but on this occasion I wasn't having any. He therefore decided to call the dogs off and leave the pig to its own resources.

Calling the dogs off was another matter however. As I have already indicated we were above them on a high bluff. There was by this time a bit of a wind blowing and the noise of the water cascading down the rock face all went to diminish George's whistling to the dogs. In any case the dogs were thoroughly enjoying the fun and I doubt whether they would have obeyed had they heard us.

George's next move was to start throwing stones down to try and break up the party. I joined in but we could not get any result so George said, "The only thing is for us to shoot the pig." I agreed, thinking that he would be the marksman but he insisted that I should do the dirty work. I say "dirty work," as this is the only way I can described this operation. The sow, as I said before, would make a lunge forward at the dogs and they would retreat and then they would attack her head on and she would go into reverse and back quickly into the stream bed. George was for ever putting me on my mettle on these trips, and I think it was his rough and ready method of converting me from a new chum into some degree of competence.

On this particular occasion he didn't spare me one bit, and kept on reminding me that I would have to be careful not to shoot his precious dogs. I was only too aware of the possibilities and tried hard to get him to do the shooting himself, but he was adamant, and I still wonder to this day whether he was not himself scared of shooting the dogs.

At last the message came through to me that George did want me to shoot the pig, so I took careful aim when it was well back in the water and not likely to retreat further. It was a good shot and the pig floated downstream about fifteen feet into deeper water and lodged in a dead tree. I put two more shots into it to make sure it was properly despatched. At this point the dogs were well clear so George and I had no further fears for their safety.

We then headed off in the direction of our camp. It took us some time to get to the scrub country again and no sooner had we done so than the dogs were off again. They baled a pig and this was where the fun really began. When I say "baled" we never really knew what happened, because the pig was in an absolute tangle of bush lawyer overlaying some very thick scrub. George and I had to skirt this sort of growth but for the dogs and the pig it was ideal going. It was full of tunnels and in went the pig and after him went the dogs. Then out came the pig from another tunnel and hot on his heels were the dogs. Finally they stopped the pig in a small clearing about eight feet across, but this clearing was completely surrounded by the thick scrub.

From the noise that went on we could have believed that there were a number of pigs baled up. Every now and then the dogs would come hurtling out and just as quickly they would be in again for more. From the way they were yelping and being tossed around it was clear that they were not getting their own way and George was afraid they might get ripped.

Both he and I had to stick together if we were to use our guns, but finally he got me to move well back and he said he would go in and see what he could so.

I did shift well back and George told me later that he skirted round the patch of scrub till he found a spot where it was matted so thickly that he was able to worm his way on to the top of it and get a sight of the pig. It was a young boar and George was able to drop it with his first shot without any harm to the dogs.

I remarked that this was a pretty agile type of pig and George said, "Look at the lice on it – you'd be agile too if your were as lousy as that pig!" And lousy it was: the lice were sliding all over it like skaters on ice and we shifted off smartly in case they took a liking to us.

Before long we came to a spot which seemed familiar and on rounding a bend in the track saw the remains of the big boar George had shot on the previous day. The hindquarter was still strung up in the tree and George cut it down and gave it to me to carry. I was still very doubtful whether it would be any good, but he was quite certain that it would make "a lovely piece of bacon". I pointed out that we had the three small pigs and all the best of the venison steaks and that should be sufficient. George I still felt, was having me on over this leg of pork but I did not openly say this.

When he pointed out that he had been carrying the venison all day I had to give in.

The only thing I had with me in which I could put the leg was a flour-bag, so in it went and off we set. I don't know how much that hindquarter weighed, but I do know that there are better ways

162

of carrying heavy weights than in a thin flourbag. Going up a slope was not so bad except that the bag would roll around a bit from side to side. Going down a steep slope however, I had to lean back to keep my balance, and this meant that I had to take the full weight of the load on my fingers as the bag hung freely behind me.

Nevertheless I was not going to be beaten so I said not a word and struggled every inch of the way. I was just at the point of exhaustion as we reached the top of the rise above our camp site, when George spoke. "You know, Harold, I have been thinking about that leg – I reckon it will be too strong and tough for bacon – I think we should dump it."

"OK," I said and dropped the bag and tipped out the leg. I never batted an eyelid or mentioned the matter again. To this day I'll bet George doesn't realise how thankful I was to drop that load.

He may have been putting me through a "trial by fire" but I had one consolation in that very trying time – I had shot that deer after the expert had missed, and for me this was a wonderful thrill. As a matter of fact this one shot alone had made the whole trip for me – all the rest of the fun came as a bonus.

When we reached camp there was plenty to do but first of all we boiled the billy and had a meal.

I then retrieved my oilskin coat from the river and stowed it in the car and George, who was attending to the gas-producer, suggested that I should cut down the three small pigs from the tree and wrap them up.

I climbed the tree and there were the three small carcases in good order, without any sign of flyblow. George had stipulated that fourteen feet above ground level would ensure that they would not be flyblown, and this proved correct. What still puzzles me is, first, how these blowflies know how to measure fourteen feet and, second, why they have picked on an odd figure like fourteen feet – why not say twelve feet or fifteen feet, which are good round numbers? Finally comes the sixty-four dollar question – why *don't* flies blow meat when it is fourteen feet or more in the air?

While I was getting the meat ready George had fixed the gas-producer and we stowed the final bits of gear and set off for home.

Having in mind the car-sick dog, George took things a bit easier and we had a relatively quiet trip home. One small incident, however, did lighten the monotony of the trip. In those days the majority of Southland roads carried about six inches of loose shingle on top. There were however odd places where the road was tarsealed for a couple of hundred yards or so. This would perhaps be in a small settlement; outside a country store or dairy factory or – if one was to listen to local ratepayers – outside the farms or homes of local county councillors.

It was on one of these stretches of tarred road that George decided to rake out the gas producer fire, as experience had taught him that this was a very dusty job if carried out on the shingly stretches.

Doubtless what he did was without due thought. It wasn't without drastic results however. Some of the hot coals fell on the soft tarry road surface. I don't know whether any particularly inflammable road oil or similar substance had recently been spilled where we stopped, but what I do know is that in a few seconds the road surface was burning merrily and George and I had to shove the car smartly off the sealed surface to save it from catching fire.

By this time he was really moving fast attending to the gas producer while I was doing my best to beat out the flames. He had more success than I had and he soon finished his job and came to help me put out the blaze. After quite a battle we did beat out the flames and were just going to roll a smoke when we saw two men come running out of a nearby farmhouse and head in our direction.

No doubt we were prompted by a sense of guilt, but we stood not on the order of our going – into the car – into gear and off.

About a mile or so down the road George broke the silence. "I wonder what those chaps really wanted?" And then he smiled and said "Perhaps they wanted to shout for us."

"Like hell," was my reply, "my bet is that they wanted to shout at us."

By this time we were pretty tired and lapsed into a long silence which lasted almost till we reached home in Invercargill.

We did however, promise ourselves another shooting trip and I was all for a return to the Lake Monowai area but George said that he wanted to take me on a trip to Lake Hauroko and we left this suggestion for later discussion.

A BAD BEND

JACK MACKAY was my driver on this trip and we had decided to do a bit of exploring – if we could make the time. This idea arose from remarks made by Jack every time we passed what he called "the worst corner on the road". It was a tricky bend on the Eglinton section of the road, and was quite out of character with the others. Jack told me how it happened. He was on the road survey with "Smithy" (Harold Welton Smith) when they came upon a deep hole in a ridge and found great difficulty in deciding how to avoid it. They could have gone right through it, but this would have involved expensive cuts and fills, and was just not on in those days when money was so tight. The alternative was to finish up with a rather nasty curve in the road, and that is what happened.

Smithy's theory was that this hole had been caused by a meteor, and this intrigued me so much that I determined to have a look at it when time permitted.

I checked with Smithy and this was his story: "When we were doing the survey of the Eglinton Road we found this hole in the ridge and were able to sidle round the batter of the hole instead of climbing over the ridge. The hole is about three or four chains across the top and about sixty or eighty feet deep, with water at the bottom, with no outlet. It is overgrown with large red beech trees so it's pretty ancient. It is about the 46-mile peg at map reference 203384 in the Eglinton Volcanics of the Wakatipu Sheet of the recent Geological Maps. It isn't a limestone soak hole though it slightly resembles one." (The map reference was given to me by Smithy at a later date, but the balance of the information was as he detailed it originally.)

Smithy favoured the idea that this was a meteor crater and Jack and I thought we would have a look. Jack was able to pinpoint the hole and we scrambled off the road and had a look at it and satisfied my curiosity. I didn't know what caused the hole but if Smithy thought it was a crater caused by a meteor I was prepared to go along with that. I knew him for years and never found him to be far wrong.

It was a very nice little diversion, and who knows that one day a track may be made from the road just to allow travellers to look and speculate as Jack and I did on that pay trip?

"Smithy" (*standing erect*) on survey. Mr. H.W. Smith succeeded Mr W.G. Pearce as resident engineer, Invercargill.

Mrs H.W. Smith

We got back to the car and before long we had reached the Hollyford and met up with Dan Campbell who was waiting for us. We started paying the men and before long Dan was handing out tips right and left on the race meeting to be held at Invercargill. I knew nothing of racing but he would insist I should be able to "talk the language" and, just to satisfy him, I used to do a bit of a study of the racing column. It never profited me much when I went to a meeting. I am one of those all-up-on-the-last-race punters, but to date the last race has never treated me kindly.

The sandflies were very bad on this day, and most of the men had their arms plastered with lysol. I was a victim of hayfever and found the smell of the lysol more annoying than the sandflies. I had always associated sandflies with hot sea beaches in the summer but I reckon they are really at their worst in snow conditions in the bush. I now associate them with Lake Manapouri, The Bluffs and Cascade Creek, but Jack MacKay said these were only "little boys" to what they had at Milford Sound. Having said this Jack was then impelled to tell me about the mosquitoes at Milford Sound. He told me the story was that they were so big they could stand on their hind legs and drink out of a four-gallon kerosene tin, but Jack denied this stoutly and said it was a gross exaggeration. He said that to

166

drink out of a kerosene tin the average Milford Sound mosquito would have to stand on its mate's shoulders. He was a stickler for the truth in matters such as this and I had no hesitation in accepting his revised version of the story.

When we reached the next gang, one of the men extracted five shillings from his pay packet and handed it to Dan, and I later asked him about this, as it was a regular occurance every pay. He said this chap borrowed small amounts from all his mates and was most meticulous about repaying them. Dan told him he was only about one pay behind, and suggested he make an all-out effort to catch up; but he never managed it despite the best of intentions.

We next called in at the canteen and found the canteen attendant to be in a really bad humour. His stock had just been checked by the storekeeper, and the canteen attendant was not happy about the result. First of all he knew he was short on prunes, as everybody – including himself – would nick a few as they went past, "just for their health's sake". He intended to arrange for a write-off one of these days but never quite got round to it. Contrary to his expectations, the storekeeper did not check the prunes, but took a couple of handfuls himself "just to keep his works in order".

On doing a preliminary check, the canteen attendant had found that his stock of 2 lb tins of jam was twenty-five tins in excess. He didn't know how this came about, but to keep his books in order he took these tins of jam out of the canteen and stashed them away in a hut next door. When the storekeeper checked up, almost the first thing he found in the stock cards was an error in addition, so he checked up on the number of tins of jam on the shelves. These were then found to be twenty-five tins short and the poor old canteen attendant had to admit that he had planted them in the hut to keep his tally right. He rather shamefacedly produced them and put them back on the shelves. "Shot in the pants," was his way of summing up the position.

Before I left the Invercargill office, the costing clerk told me that one of the machine plant items, (PWD No. 1011) seemed to be frightfully expensive to run and it also had a variety of unusual charges against it. He asked if I would enquire what it was all about. So as we were going along, I asked Dan if he knew what this plant item was and I gave him its number. Yes – he knew it and said he would show it to me later.

On arriving at the tunnel tiphead, he pointed out a piece of machinery lying at the bottom of a bank. It was smashed almost beyond recognition and Dan explained that this was Broomwade Compressor PWD Plant item No. 1011 that I had been enquiring about. He said it had been bowled over by an avalanche, and that it was apparently smashed beyond repair. I enquired how it was that

Few "men of the road" or their families were indifferent to the wild beauty of the country in which they lived. Here Val Walker studies placid Lake Gunn in the Eglinton Valley.

Weekly News, Bill Beattie photo

so many items were being charged against this old wreck, and rather sheepishly he said that the foreman and overseers had lots of small items which they found hard to charge against any particular job, so the general idea was to spread them around a bit. It was a case of "think of a number", and what could be easier than the plant number on that old compressor? There it was, clear and shiny, PWD 1011, clearly visible from the road for the world to see. In further explanation, Dan said it was such a simple number that "even an engineer could learn it off by heart after a few months".

Some time before I arrived on this particular pay the job had been visited by the Minister of Works, the Honourable Robert Semple. "Bob" had apparently been in particularly good form when he addressed the men, but reactions to his performance varied. They ranged from virtual hero-worship to the laconic comment "Consummate acting!"

Whatever one's political views it could not be denied that Bob Semple was a colourful character with an unusual turn of phrase. He used such terms as "a snivelling snufflebuster", and had been

168

known to say of his opponents that everything they knew "could be written on the back of a postage stamp with a ballot pencil".

Bob had a habit of potting off rabbits, hares, hawks and other game from the fast-moving ministerial car on his trips around the country. He invariably had a tight timetable to work to, and this proved very handy when he met up with some of his associates of his earlier and more radical "Red Fed" days. This enabled him to say "Hello Bill – nice to meet you – But I must be on my way as we are due at . . . in an hour's time." One old mate in the Hollyford Valley had just experienced this, and what he said about the Hon. Bob was certainly unprintable.

Bob Semple certainly pushed ahead with the programme of Public Works and missed no opportunity of letting people know what he had done. One of his favourite claims was the number of bad bends in the road that had "been straightened". Somewhere along the line this came to the notice of the proprietors of *Punch* and they thought that "straight bends" were a very good thing to have in roads and wanted to know if Bob had any for export.

Bob Semple never liked the Homer Tunnel job and he went to considerable trouble to point out that this job had been started by the previous Government. It was not a spectacular success story, and Bob was more inclined, when dealing with tunnelling, to refer back to his own co-operative efforts in the Orongorongo area, which he invariably referred to as the "Rong-a-rongs".

On this trip to the Homer the minister had been accompanied by photographers, and just before he left, these photographers had one of the jack-hammer men posed on the top of an enormous boulder in the act of drilling a hole to place explosives. This was just too much for the Hon. Bob; he hopped out of the car, climbed up on the rock, took hold of the drill, and click went the cameras.

After dinner we went for a bit of a walk round the camp and found a two-up school in progress. This form of entertainment was always popular on payday but diminished between pays as surplus funds became less. We were invited to join the party but declined. These schools were taken very seriously and had well established rules and procedures, but not being fully acquainted with these I always felt that my position should be on the sideline. Later we joined the usual get-together in the staff mess and I remember somebody "shouting" as it was his birthday.

On this particular evening Dan Campbell had a story to tell and he said he wasn't breaking any confidences in doing so as the man involved had been telling this story against himself to all and sundry.

This man, whom I will call Tom, was separated from his wife and she had a maintenance order out against him for a certain amount per week which was always paid on due date. What tickled Tom, however, was that he could live on the Hollyford job, pay the maintenance order, and still save a bit of money.

Over quite a period he had saved about £120, and as his savings increased so did his desire to go and see his wife and let her know how well he was doing without her. In the finish the urge to do so became so great that he applied for leave and off he went. He took his money with him and as "his skin was cracking a bit", to use the expression of the time, he called in at a few "boozers" on the way. By the time he got to his wife's house he was drunk or, to use his own words, "pretty rotten". He also had a bottle of gin with him as he said he wanted to impress his wife with his affluence.

His original intention was merely to call on his wife and let her know how rich he was by showing her his roll of notes and then to leave her lamenting.

He knocked on the door, and when she opened it he just stood there and said nothing. In explanation afterwards he said this was probably because he was getting to the state where his head was really starting to buzz round, or perhaps he was just "too full for words". As he said afterwards, "I'd been on the wagon for about a year and the grog got to me." His wife apparently sized up the position very quickly and asked him in and sat him down at the table. He said his last recollection was that she took the bottle of gin out of his hand and poured him what must have been a sizeable "snort".

Next morning he woke up and found himself fully clothed on a chesterfield suite and beside him was his wife. She was really irate and said that in terms of the separation order he was not allowed on her property. She threatened to call the police if he did not leave immediately.

Thinking discretion the better part of valour, he took off promptly. It wasn't till he went to book in at an hotel that he found that during the night his wife had extracted the roll of notes from his wallet. On telling the story later he said, rather ruefully, "Not to cry – there was nothing I could do about it."

Following Dan's tale, one of the overseers had a story about a man who opened the firebox door of the coal range in his home and shovelled in a very generous scoop of beautiful shiny Southland coal. Unfortunately in that shovelful was a stick of gelignite left there somewhere along the line, and the inevitable happened. The range blew up and this man was injured, but fortunately not fatally, and before long he was progressing quite well. When talking to his wife a bit later, in a lighthearted way, thinking to cheer her up, the overseer said "It was almost a case of *Riding the Range in the Sky*" – this being the words of a cowboy song which was very popular about that time.

The construction camp at Monkey Flat, Mt Crosscut towering above.

Weekly News, Bill Beattie Photo

A national pastime particularly popular in the camps. "Two-up" will always attract an interested crowd.

Kurt Suter

Apparently, however, the wife had not herself got over the shock and instead of recognising the attempt at a joke she thought the remarks had a religious connotation and, to keep up the image, she said that in times of real trouble the words of those good oldfashioned hymns certainly took on an added meaning.

After this story the party broke up and went to bed.

Next morning we had one or two men to pay on the way back and I mentioned to one that I was going to the Invercargill races next day. He handed me £3 and said, "Put this on Lucky Lee for a win." It wasn't till we got going that I thought how foolish I was in taking this money. If I didn't get the money on the race I could be in trouble, but as it happened I did get to the races and put on the £3. Lucky Lee paid about £33 and I delivered £99 back to this man next pay.

In those days this was real wealth, and I often wonder what would have happened if somehow or other I hadn't got that money on the tote. "Lucky Lee – Lucky me" has ever been my thought. Never again did I accept money to place on a horse.

22

THE PWD AT WAR

THE *Official War History of the Public Works Department* has been written and lies safely in the archives, and what I have to say about the PWD at war will be entirely on the lighter side.

After the outbreak of war the first impact on the Invercargill office was a request from Wellington to order a number of 10 ft × 8 ft army huts which were to be made to standard plans and specifications.

These plans were dished out to local builders and it was found out that we could get these huts built for some ridiculously low figure of £31 or thereabouts with almost immediate delivery. This pleased the powers in Wellington, and they told us to go ahead and order them thick and fast. This we did, with full instructions as to where and how they were to be delivered and how they were to be branded.

Speed was the essence, and patriotism was the goad to the builders. In no time piles of hut parts were arriving from all sources and they were dumped here, there and everywhere despite all our explicit directions. In many cases they were not marked as to the source of origin, and Bill & Co's roofs got mixed with Jack & Co's floors. How it was all sorted out I don't know, but I heard it said that someone counted every section, whether it was one side of a roof, a side, a back, a front, or a floor. This grand total was then said to have been divided by seven and the resulting answer was the number of huts we had received. Fortuitously, it is said, this exactly equalled the number we had ordered and everybody was happy and all bills were paid. How true this was I wouldn't know, but nobody sued the Department so it couldn't have been far out.

The PWD was of course involved in all sorts of defence work construction and before long it had organised a sort of Dad's Army of its own. This was called the Defence Engineering Services Corps (DESC for short), but it differed in one respect from the Home Guard in that it was an army unit and as such it was entitled to much more liberal supplies of equipment than the Home Guard.

At Invercargill there was already an Army territorial unit known as the No. 7 Works Company, New Zealand Engineers, so instead of setting up a DESC unit in Invercargill, the Army said that PWD employees could join this territorial unit, and in no time we were drilling one or two nights a week and at weekends.

A lot of hard work went into this unit's activities, but like Dad's Army it had many amusing interludes. To illustrate this I am quoting an article I wrote for the NZBC. This was featured in the Open Country session on all YA stations on Sunday 5 December 1971, and repeated later, and was entitled "Dad's Army Radio".

The story went like this:

The location was New Zealand's deep south. The day was a Sunday and a perishingly cold one at that, but despite half a southerly gale the winter sun was shining feebly.

The manoeuvre was a combined one. The No. 7 Works Company – a home service territorial unit – was ordered to erect a bridge over a small river, using local timber and ropes supplied by Army. The plan was for the timber to be felled by the Works Company and the local branch of "Dad's Army". The Works Company, which was an engineering unit, was then to build the bridge in a specified time and the "Dad's Army" men were to observe how the job was carried out. On the completion of the bridge "Dad's Army" had the task of mining it and ultimately blowing it up. Official plans were for the CRE, a high-ranking Army officer from "up north", to inspect the bridge and then to see it demolished by "Dad's Army".

I was a member of the Works Company Engineering Unit and we were busily employed for a considerable time in felling trees and building the bridge. This work was ably carried out in the time allotted, and our CO was very pleased with the job we had done. He then officially handed over the bridge to the CO of the Home Guard for the placing of the demolition charges. This Home Guard unit had specialised in demolition work and had its charges well and truly laid within the time allowed. The charges were to be fired electrically with an exploding machine, and all the wiring was ready to be plugged into the exploder long before the appointed hour of 2 pm, when the high-ranking Army officers were to arrive for their inspection and the subsequent demolition.

By the time the mining of the bridge was completed, the wind had increased to a full gale and it was bitterly cold. Over an hour remained however, before the Army top brass was due to arrive and all sorts of methods, from hip flasks to spells of physical training, were tried in an effort to combat the bitter cold. At long last our watches showed 2 pm and we gazed over the Otatara sandhills in the direction of the road, expecting each minute to see the Army chiefs coming into sight. But the time went on – five past two, ten past two, quarter past two and so on. By about 3 pm we were absolutely frozen and much of our enthusiasm for the big occasion had abated.

Hitler however had still to be conquered, and morale was fairly high, and nobody seemed to be reaching the point of mutiny. The fact that one of the Home Guardsmen casually walked over towards the exploder was hardly noticed and his action in plugging in the wires was probably thought by most of the spectators to be part of the overall plan. His next action however, really claimed everybody's attention. He bent down, grasped the handle of the exploder with two hands, pulled it up to the full extent and then – without even a "permission to act, sir" – he shoved it down again with a mighty heave. As he did so there was a terrific explosion and the whole bridge seemed to lift up into the air in one piece, but as it got higher into the air it started to disintegrate and by the time it had reached full height it was just a wild mass of flying logs. It was a wonderful sight and, I think, a welcome sight to most as it indicated that the day's manoeuvre was over and we could head for home and mother.

On second thoughts however the horror of the situation seemed to strike us. It was probably due to our Army discipline, and many eyes turned back to the gap in the sandhills. Horror of horrors – there, on the brow of a small hill, was a group of Army officers just coming into sight and the splashes of red on the uniforms clearly indicated that they were the high-ranking officers we had been expecting.

I will not dwell on the immediate reactions of the respective COs of the Works Company and the Home Guard Unit. Some things are best left untold.

I have no doubt that subsequently the matter was somehow or other ironed out, as the local group of "Dad's Army" continued to parade in full force and carried on with its good work.

The matter however, was often discussed at subsequent parades and whereas all of us could think of lots of forms of penalty which could have been imposed on a duly attested soldier for such unorthodox action, we came back to the conclusion that "Dad's Army" had not been in existence long enough for rules and regulations to be formulated to cover such unusual situations.

The official Army reaction to the events of the day will never be known but my guess is that reason prevailed and that Army records, even to this day, would not record this unscheduled event.

On another occasion the No. 7 Works Company joined in a manoeuvre with the Invercargill Home Guard Demolition Unit.

This time the exercise was carried out at Greenhills, which is between Invercargill and Bluff. Army Intelligence had notified us that an enemy raider would probably parachute a number of saboteurs between Bluff and Greenhills and that these saboteurs would probably move towards Invercargill where they would carry out strategic demolitions. This was a very serious state of affairs and we were ordered out to counter this invasion. Fortunately we got there before the invaders and were able to place a mass of booby traps in the area of bush through which we expected the approach would be made. Sure enough, after a few hours there were detona-

"Closed for the Duration." Never a garden suburb at the best of times, the Homer camp is forlorn in wartime.

Free Lance Collection, Alexander Turnbull Library.

tions and every now and then a large cloud of smoke from booby traps would be seen to arise from scattered spots which would pinpoint the invaders, and these were soon disposed of by strategically placed Mills grenades.

Towards the end of the day it seemed clear that we had accounted for all saboteurs and a careful "recce" through the bush area confirmed this. In the circumstances our respective COs called us together and we formed up and marched back to our "headquarters" in a clearing at the far end of the bush. As we entered this clearing there was a burst of machine gun fire and our whole force was wiped out. We had suffered a crushing defeat in "The Battle of Greenhills".

What had actually happened was this. The Bluff Home Guard, who were the "invaders", had sent most of their forces through the booby-trapped area and if these men tripped a wire they exploded a small charge of gelignite safely placed well up a tree and they were then "dead". If they trod on a flat tobacco tin this broke a phial of liquid and when it combined with impregnated pads there was a large cloud of smoke. This gave away their positions and they were quickly disposed of by a "Mills grenade" which was a small paper bag full of flour.

Having disposed of all invaders we thought we were OK but our troops on the road had let us down. They had stopped all and sundry and questioned them – and let them pass. When I say all and sundry what I really meant was *nearly* all and sundry. It so happened that a number of ladies riding pushbikes came along and as they were reluctant to dismount when called upon they were allowed to pass and this was where the battle was lost. These "ladies" were in fact invaders from the Bluff Home Guard and when they passed through the forward defences they were able to approach our headquarters from the rear and lob in a few "Mills grenades" and capture all those at headquarters who were not killed. It was then a simple matter for them to dispose of our small returning force by machine gun fire.

Thus ended another combined exercise by the No. 7 Works Company and the Invercargill Home Guard Demolition Unit.

Early in the war years a German raider sank the *Turakina* in the Tasman Sea and a bit later the *Holmwood* coming from the Chathams was accounted for. Soon after, the *Rangitane* was sunk off the New Zealand coast, and at this stage Cabinet decided to set up coastwatching stations. The first we knew of this in Invercargill was when we were asked to interview likely personnel to man these stations. We were not told where these were to be situated but the personnel required had to be hardy types used to cold climates and able to tackle anything. The code name for this scheme was the "Cape Expedition" and we did not know where it was and did not care. The members of the expedition were not to be told of their destination until after they had left port, but years later one of the members told me how he and his mates learned of their destination before putting out to sea.

The boat was waiting at the wharf when a butcher's boy arrived with a parcel of meat and asked "Is this the boat that is going to the Auckland and Campbell Islands?" They were unable to answer his question but took the meat on the off chance that it was meant for them. As it turned out the butcher's boy was right in his destination.

Another PWD war effort was the Civilian Construction Unit (CCU), which was recruited by the Department to construct an aerodrome in Fiji.

A large number of men were required, and as the medical standard was below that for other forms of overseas service there were plenty of applicants. The Invercargill office, along with other offices throughout the country, had the job of recruiting men for this unit.

Speed was the main yardstick and we worked night and day. Overtime for staff men had not been invented in the Government service in those days but if ever I was paid in full it was for the overtime I put in over that two or three weeks recruiting. My payment came from the variety of experiences we had over the period and the amusing incidents.

Chaos was the order of the day. We would get requests for all sorts of employees. One day it would be for say six cooks, and after scouring the whole district and bringing them in by bus, taxi etc., we would have a medical board set up perhaps at 2 am and then find out that the men on arrival, were in no state for a medical exam due to calling in for a few beers on the way in. Next day we would perhaps line them up again for medical examination and if they passed we would pay them an advance on wages and give them £20 to buy a "tropical kit". This was of course courting disaster when some of the men had been at Milford or Hollyford for six or twelve months without a break.

Assuming we got the six cooks all medically boarded and passed, and paid up, we would ring Wellington and often found that cooks were no longer required. All we did then was to change their designations to something else and hope for the best.

On many occasions we had men all ready to go and we would then have solicitors approaching us on account of wives who were owed money on maintenance orders – or for some other reason.

On one occasion we had a medical board in the early hours of the morning and the doctor had rather a unique way of testing eyesight. He had a chart with a large number of circles on it. Some circles were complete but others had gaps in various parts of the circumference and what the doctor wanted to know from each man was whether the circle was complete or whether it had a gap in it. All went well for a while till we came to one man and he was asked whether the circles were complete. He seemed to disregard this question and started off something like this: "Ort," "Ort," "Nought," "Oh," "G," "Q," "Ort," "Ort," "Nought", etc.

Try as he would these were the only answers the doctor could get, so he failed the man. I have an idea that the recruit involved may have had pressures from home to remain in New Zealand and that he had evolved a unique system to ensure he failed his medical examination.

This was the pattern for about a fortnight or more and by this time we were exhausted.

Needless to say the CCU soon sailed for Fiji and in time the aerodrome became a reality.

23

AN HISTORIC MOMENT

The construction of the Homer Tunnel, situated in a region where the climate is extremely severe, is the most difficult job ever undertaken by the Public Works in New Zealand.

Hon. Robert Semple, Minister of Public Works, 16 April 1940.

As TIME WENT ON I shifted on to other duties in the office and I had not done a pay trip for a long time. Early in February 1940 however, it became necessary for me to do the Homer trip and on this occasion I was accompanied by a driver and Mr Huia Perrin, manager of Hannah's Ltd., Invercargill, as a passenger.

We did not get away till 8 am which was much later than I liked, but by this time other factors had started to influence my operations. I have already mentioned that I had married, and events had now progressed a stage further and our first son, Lester, had just arrived on the scene.

The weather was dull but looked promising enough and we set off in the 10-cwt Ford V8 runabout. We had not been going for long when a rabbit ran across the road in front of us and I thought of an old trick I had often played on pay trips in the past. To be doubly sure of myself however, I waited till a few more rabbits had crossed the road. I then said, "Let's have a competition to see who can guess which way the rabbits will run – left to right or right to left." Then, without waiting for a reply, I said, "I'll take from left to right", and my companions said "OK", and the count was on. By a bit of luck the others scored the first point and then as the miles went by there was a succession of left to rights. When the score was about seven or eight to one in my favour, Huia, who knew me well, said, "I might have known. How did you work it out?"

Strange as it seems I had been on pay trips for about eighteen months before I noticed that there was a pattern to the way rabbits ran across the road in front of a fast moving vehicle. One had only to count the numbers and would find that on one day it was predominantly left to right and on another the opposite applied.

I have never had an answer as to why this should be and in fact I have never enquired, but on thinking it over later I came to the

The tool-sharpening shop at the mouth of the tunnel. From this shelter the gelignite charges further down the tunnel were exploded.

Alexander Turnbull Library

conclusion that it might have something to do with the wind direction. Perhaps it is that rabbits prefer to go down-wind from their burrows?

When we got to Te Anau it was lunchtime and the surfacemen were spread all over the area, so we had to travel round the loop to Lake Manapouri – an extra thirty miles or so. We called in at the Te Anau Hotel and I remember the barman telling us of all the attributes necessary to make a good publican. One I thought worth remembering was that the publican should himself "drink enough to pay the rent".

As we left Te Anau I was sorely tempted to get out my casting rod and hop down to the lakeside at the 4-mile peg and have a few casts in the hope of picking up a nice rainbow trout or Atlantic salmon. Time was short however, and I could not spare the twenty minutes it would take, so I determined I would have a cast at The Bluffs in the Eglinton Valley as there was an excellent spot only a few yards off the road.

We made good progress up the Eglinton Valley, but I had told Huia of its beauties, so I was a bit disappointed that it was overcast with low cloud. As we moved right into the beech forest however, he pointed out some blue sky ahead and from then on it became clearer.

We stopped at The Bluffs and I had a cast, but I got my minnow

180

snagged in a log and had to break the trace to get the line free. Time again plagued me so I shoved the rod in the back of the runabout and off we went. I had been warned that there would be no staff accommodation available at the Headquarters camp in the Hollyford so we called in and booked in for the night at Cascade Creek. This would mean that we would have to go right to the Homer Tunnel, paying as we went, and then return the sixteen miles or so to Cascade Creek for the night.

When we got to the Homer Tunnel, overseer Jack Dawson told me that they would be firing a round of shots and he invited us to watch proceedings. All in all there would be eight rounds fired and this would involve the use of 136 lbs of gelignite.

Before long everything was ready and all precautionary checks had been made. We moved into the tool-sharpening shop at the mouth of the tunnel where the switchboard was situated. As Jack Dawson prepared to plug the power into the circuit everything was strangely quiet and the whole atmosphere became tense. Quickly his hand moved and there was a mighty roar which shook the ground beneath us. A terrific blast roared from the depths up the tunnel and out the mouth, but being round a corner and not in the direct line of detonation we were protected from it.

This initial blast was followed by seven others and the tunnel overseer and the shift boss carefully counted the detonations to ensure that no misfires occurred.

On this day there were several overseas visitors present and they were very interested in the firing procedures. They questioned Jack Dawson on a number of points and he went to quite a bit of trouble to answer their queries. Huia and I found the discussion very interesting so we waited to hear what was said.

The first question was what would happen if say only seven of the eight charges detonated. Jack said they would lock the switchboard, and wait one hour for safety and pumping out water.

He and the tunnel shift boss would then check that all electric power was switched off and would enter the tunnel with carbide lamps. About a third way down the sloping tunnel they would earth a plug from the firing main as an extra safety precaution. About two-thirds of the way down they would earth another plug. When they got near the face they would reach the lead from the power main and they would then check that the leads to the charges had been properly coupled up. If they had not this would be one reason for a misfire.

The next procedure would be to go to the face itself and inspect the unfired charge and withdraw it with a copper screw and spoon. Jack explained that this was similar to the procedures in operation for many years at the Australian Mt Isa mines.

At this point it turned out that there were a couple of overseas journalists present and their enquiries round the job had apparently left them with a number of interesting leads on which they wanted further information.

They wanted to know more about the water problems in the tunnel, and Jack explained that at one stage in the tunnelling operations one of the drills tapped a spring of water and the pressure from the one-inch hole was such that there was one big squirt for about forty feet or more. It was estimated that this one spring yielded about 6,000 gallons per hour. To counter this problem a number of other holes were bored and this resulted in what Jack called "a lot of smaller squirts". Further holes were then bored in the sides of the tunnel to reduce the pressure of the "squirts" even further.

To contain all this water a deep sump was built across the tunnel to trap the water, which was then pumped from the sump to the tunnel mouth. The pumping was done with compressed air and electric pumps, and when the holes on the tunnel face were to be loaded with gelignite the electric pumps were shut off so that there would be no chance of a power leakage prematurely firing the electric detonators. The compressed air pumps would still be working but they were unable to cope with the full volume of water and the tunnel would start to flood.

The procedure for placing charges was to shut off the electric power in the tunnel, carry the explosives and electric detonators into the tunnel, using carbide lamps for lighting. The charges would then be placed in the prepared holes in the tunnel face and the detonators wired into the mains. By this time the water would be so deep at the tunnel face that on occasions Jack Dawson said it came over the top of his thigh gumboots, and he is a very tall man.

After all charges were placed and wired up, the men would make their way uphill to the tunnel mouth. By the time they got out of the tunnel the flow of water inside would be such that the whole tunnel face and the charges recently placed would be completely submerged. Nevertheless it was considered that this had at least one advantage as it provided a first class tamping for the charges and gave a much more effective breakout of rock.

Jack explained that during the winter of 1938 the tunnelling operations were suspended and the tunnel filled with water right up to the mouth. It was found that the effort needed to de-water it was so great that a decision was made to work right through the 1939 winter.

One of the journalists said he had been told that there had been a number of quite severe earthquakes during the tunnelling operations, and he enquired about the reactions of the men underground.

Drifter drills set for boring shot-
holes in the tunnel rock.
Murray Gunn

In reply Jack Dawson said that the only way he could answer this
was to say that they "saw" the earthquakes rather than felt them.
He went on to explain that with the inflow of water and the drilling
operations, there was always a misty haze at the tunnel face and in
an earthquake this haze could clearly be seen to move sideways and
then return, as though the air were drawn up the sloping tunnel and
then allowed to return.

A further question asked was about the effect of lightning, which
in the tunnel area seems on occasions to run along the surface of
the ground rather than to earth directly. This is quite an unusual
and frightening thing to watch, and one theory advanced was that
it had something to do with the clear air, lack of earth in the area,
and the fact that the rainwater was a bad conductor, being more or
less distilled.

Whatever the reason was for this, the Department took no chances
and Jack explained that elaborate precautions were taken to provide
for earthing the railway tracks and various ducts at the portal.

Finally there was the inevitable question about any humorous
incidents which had happened.

First Jack told the story of an occasion in the tunnel when there
was what he called "an explosion of pulverised rock". This was
caused by pressures released by the tunnelling operations. The
result was a sudden shooting out of this pulverised rock and it was

so extensive that it practically buried a man standing beside him. Fortunately there were several men present and the victim, named Harry De Latour, was quickly extricated and he managed to get to his feet.

"Is everything OK?" asked Jack anxiously.

"No," said Harry, and he kept patting himself all over as though feeling for a fracture.

"Well, tell us quick, what's the matter?" screamed Jack.

"I've lost me bloomin' pipe," said Harry – and he wondered why his mates laughed.

Jack had one more incident to relate and it was about a visit to the tunnel made by the then Governor-General, Lord Galway, who was invited to fire a round of shots.

There was quite a crowd present and the hum of conversation and the congestion were such that it was very difficult for Jack to trot out his usual line of instructions on firing procedures. In addition the Governor's aide was present and this more or less involved a three-way effort.

Added to this was the fact that the Governor-General himself wanted to be doubly sure that he understood the drill properly, and this took a fair amount of time.

The essentials were that the power plug should be inserted at the top of the board. If the circuit was OK a light would show. The next move was to withdraw the plug from the top socket and plug it into a socket at the bottom. All that then remained to be done was to throw over the large main switch and the charges would be fired.

Having got these basic essentials firmly established under the prevailing difficulties, Jack decided it would be unwise to complicate the position any further with additional explanations. He therefore nodded to the Governor-General to go ahead. His Excellency plugged in at the top of the switchboard and the light showed clearly. Jack nodded again and the plug was withdrawn and plugged into the bottom socket. The Governor's aide, ever helpful, then made a movement with his hand indicating that the final act was to throw over the large switch. His Excellency did this and nothing happened. He was just in the act of turning quickly to find out what it was all about when there was one almighty roar and a blast of wind up the tunnel.

This caught the Governor off balance and he had to make a sort of half hop to recover himself. No sooner had he done this than there was another mighty detonation and another hop, and so on.

Jack then explained to us what had actually happened. When the main switch was thrown, the first blast, although theoretically instantaneous, was not felt immediately as there was a fractional delay while the blast and roar travelled the long distance up the

184

tunnel. This apparently gave the Governor the impression that nothing had happened and caused him to quickly swing round to find out what was wrong. Jack said he gained the impression that His Excellency was also thrown off balance by the extra seven delayed detonations, which he probably had not expected. Jack said that after that episode he determined that he would give his deputy shot-firers a full rundown on procedures whatever difficulties presented themselves, or whatever delays were involved.

Jack was then thanked by those present and we told him we were heading back to Cascade Creek.

For the rest of the trip we had an uneventful time. I got back to work at about 3 pm and was just clearing up the odds and ends of the pay when the office was electrified by the news that the round of shots that had been fired in our presence the previous day had enabled a breakthrough to be made to Milford Sound. We had been present at an historic moment – the breakthrough of the famous Homer Tunnel – a mighty achievement for the "Men of the Road", and the realisation of the dream of William Henry Homer.

This was also a great moment for me, and I was proud to have stood there as Jack Dawson fired that dramatic round of shots. My mind went back to the day some years before when I went up to the Hollyford with the first payment on the Homer Tunnel co-operative contract. These tunnellers had a tough job, and the Department at that time was still on a tight budget. Despite a large "inexperience allowance" granted by the Department, the rate earned by the tunnel gang on this first contract payment was not good. I well remember big Jack Dawson having a look at the contract sheet and saying to me, "Nobody's going to be happy about this lot – I'll come round the job with you," – and this he did, taking the brunt of the criticisms and, believe me, there were plenty.

Even though a break had been made through the solid rock, the opening at the Milford Sound end was buried by fifty-seven feet of scree, and this had to be removed by the fifty men working on the Milford Sound side. On Monday 11 March 1940 Mr O.H. Pearce of Downer & Co led a four-man party to make the first trip through the hole.

Even though access to Milford Sound was now available, this was only a fourteen feet by nine feet heading and the next task was to ring-bore the whole length of the tunnel in readiness for shooting out the hole to the full size of approximately twenty-four feet by seventeen feet, and the contractors, Downer & Co carried on with this work.

The war situation resulted in the Homer job being closed down "for the duration" in 1942. As it turned out, work was not recom-

Breakthrough. The tunnel's first emergence at the Milford Sound end.

J.F. Henderson

menced till 1951, when a further contract was let to Downer & Co and the job was completed in 1953.

Rather appropriately, the trip on which the breakthrough was made was the last visit I made to the Homer Tunnel as paymaster. I have since driven through it as a tourist and I stopped once again at the tunnel mouth. I read the plaques commemorating the deaths of Messrs. Overton, Smith and Hulse and I thought of Dan, and Duncan White, Alec Duncan, and of Harry and Roy, Doug Stewart, and all the others. A lump rose in my throat and I walked to my car – and back to present days.

Sitting on the bonnet of my car was a fairly bedraggled kea, and he was doing his best to peck a large lump off the rubber moulding round the windscreen. This again took me back to the past when, years before, a kea at the Homer had pecked a hole in the bellows of my 1A pocket Kodak camera. Suddenly a thought came into my head – parrots can live as long as humans. Would it? – could it? – be possible that this was the same old bird who had done me wrong in the past? Was he also the bird that poked his beak through holes in the galvanised iron roof of the guest hut at 5 am one morning, and then skidded down the roof to take off for another roof and more skids?

I took another look at that bird and as I did so he slowly cocked his head sideways, nodded, and winked his eye. He recognised me – we were birds of a feather and a bit the worse for wear, but we were both "Men of the Road".

Instead of giving him a clout off the bonnet of my car, I threw down some licorice allsorts and he hopped to the ground and pecked at them. He was a wily old bird – he nibbled off the lolly parts and left the licorice.

He still enjoyed the peace and freedom of that Valley. Nobody was going to hurry him along.

24

WOMEN OF THE ROAD

When I told my wife that the title of this book would be *Men of the Milford Road* her immediate reaction was that I should also make reference to the "Women of the Road". She had shared a room in Nurse Young's maternity home in Gala Street, Invercargill, with Iris Jones (who lived in the Hollyford Valley) when each was having her first child, and had learned about the difficulties facing a young mother in this Valley.

While compiling the book I also received considerable help from Jim and Beryl Sutherland who spent some years in the Valley. Beryl too mentioned the part played by the women, and I invited her to supply me with some first-hand information. This she has done and it is so typical that I am including it just as she wrote it. Here is her story complete with the title she assigned to it –

NEW LIFE IN THE HOLLYFORD

In 1938 I was married and started my new life in the Hollyford Valley. We were to live in the Marian camp, situated where the Homer road and the Lower Hollyford road meet. As the house allotted to us was not quite ready I stayed in Invercargill for a short time and then travelled by bus to join my husband. Seated beside me was a young mother with a lively eighteen-month-old baby. Naturally I helped nurse the child as the day wore on, but it was not till we were ready to alight at Marian that the mother remarked, "I'm so glad she has been good all the way – she has measles, and I wondered how she'd stand up to the journey." The result for me was that, two weeks later, with my house scarcely in order, I was struggling to entertain my first guests and endure a dose of measles myself.

Setting up house when one is so far from civilisation is in itself a hazard. When our bed arrived, the bed ends proved to be a different measurement from the wire mattress, so that for quite some time we were supported by four appleboxes.

I found it necessary to learn a new form of housekeeping – with shops a hundred miles away plans had to be made well ahead and tins kept well filled in readiness for chance callers.

I experienced my first snowfall not long after I entered the Valley

187

and I can remember it still – huge flakes falling vertically, and swiftly turning everything to a picture-postcard beauty. That day I had accepted a ride to Cascade Creek with "Ambrose" (truck driver Les Palmer) on his delivery round, and coming back down the steep grade into Marian every tree was laden with snow and all the telephone wires sagging white. The snow of course, was not always so beautiful: when it cut us off from the world, and supplies ran low, when avalanches threatened or, worst of all, when it thawed slowly, some of the glamour wore off.

I remember once travelling in from Lumsden after a particularly heavy fall. The road across The Wilderness had been so ploughed up by heavy lorries that Jack Moore wasn't prepared to trust his "tray" to it. With an injunction to me to hold tight, he drove across The Wilderness itself, knowing quite well that if he once got stuck we would be there till the next traveller chanced along. We must have made an odd sight bouncing and lurching along, Jack with his window wound down and his right hand banging the door, after the manner of a jockey urging on his mount, and his cheerful voice calling, "Come on old girl, you can do it!" Luckily "she" did.

My two babies were born during our stay in the Hollyford. Luckily I kept good health, partly I think, because a nurse told me, early in my first pregnancy, "Remember, this is a natural thing. Just go home, lead an ordinary life, but don't do anything to excess." I obeyed her, but I doubt if she quite realised that to me an "ordinary" life included a certain amount of mountain-climbing.

Trips to the maternity clinic were made as and when possible. On one particularly eventful occasion I started off late in the afternoon with one of the PWD engineers. My son was just toddling and the next baby due in a few months time. As we came down the Eglinton Valley we were stopped by workmen who told us that the approaches to the next bridge had been washed away in a flash flood. There was nothing for it but to return. At the camp at Cascade Creek we discovered that in the intervening time, part of the roadway on the Marian Hill had been washed away, so we couldn't even return home. Luckily there was accommodation available at Cascade, so I was given a meal and settled into a tent for the night.

I went to sleep to the sound of steady mountain rain, and woke to brilliant mountain sunshine. At breakfast I discovered that during the night the Creek had overflowed its banks and rushed down the camp roadway, leaving our row of tents stranded. While I slept on, almost every man in that camp had at some time come out in the rain and waded across to the tent, just to make sure that I was not anxious or afraid. This was typical of the consideration and respect shown me the whole time I was in the Valley.

The sequel to this adventure was a long hot sunny day playing

Beryl Sutherland, whose narrative is given in this chapter, gives son Graeme an outing in a Homer-type baby carriage.

Weekly News, Bill Beattie photo

with my small son while workmen repaired the approaches to the bridge, till finally we drove up two planks, and off again to Invercargill.

The men told me they thought I was very game to risk driving up those planks. I didn't confess to them, as I will now, that I was much too frightened to risk walking up those planks with such a large audience and with a fierce stream roaring several feet below.

Going back again on that same trip, we had the misfortune to burst a tyre on the Lumsden rail-traffic bridge. As it was then evening, the local garage would not fix it till morning. The parents of one of my Hollyford neighbours gave me hospitality for the night, and the next day we finally made a safe trip home. The most difficult part of the whole excursion was persuading the deaf old grandad in the house where I stayed, that the engineer was *not* my husband and was much happier to go off to the local hotel for the night.

Rearing small children in isolation can bring problems also, but again I was fortunate – healthy children and help given very generously.

Just after the birth of our first child, we moved to the Homer camp, where in fact we lived just on the bushline. Many visitors called because we were the very last house. I was of course glad to see anyone, but soon learned not to be surprised by remarks made. One woman, having asked if she might come inside for a drink of water, turned to her companion and said, "Look, she's even got a cloth on the table!"

One very welcome visitor was Dr Deem of the Plunket Society. She had walked through the partly completed tunnel and, seeing nappies on my line, called in to see if I would like any assistance. From that day, till the time we moved into town, we had correspondence-reared children. I still feel grateful for her care charts worked out so that the babies could be correctly fed on tinned milk, because I was not prepared to use cows' milk carried 100 miles on the NZR bus. I believe that these recipes were later used occasionally at Karitane for babies who did not thrive on fresh milk.

One of the problems in the mountains is, of course, drying clothes. With a very high annual rainfall, with snow lying all winter, this is bad enough – but at the Homer Tunnel, because of the ring of mountains, the sunshine left our house in May and did not reach us again till September. Add to all this the mischievous activities of keas, and you can see how awkward a position develops. Our answer to this was a hut situated near the house. This was the standard type, wooden walls about four feet up and then canvas, with a canvas top, a wooden floor, a door and a large fireplace. Fortunately we had electricity so, by stringing lines across the tent and installing a heater, we managed an effective drying-room. Even the water for washing created a problem. A copper heated the water, but once our tank froze, the copper had to be filled with snow shovelled in through the washhouse window. Anyone who has tried it knows that a copper full of snow produces a very small amount of hot water!

Apart from these difficulties, the winters were better than I had dared hope. Because of the lack of sunshine, everything remained frozen and dry all winter long, and because of the mountains around us, we generally had little wind. Huge fires and heaters kept the house warm.

One of the tunnellers, a Norwegian, built me a wonderful little sledge. On the sledge was bolted a rectangular structure rather like a child's cot, and in this the baby sat, warmly wrapped, on his daily outing. With the top removed, the sledge could be used for tobogganing down the road between the banks of snow.

When I returned recently, and stood on the remains of our house, smashed by an avalanche some time after we left, I still felt the old love of the "high tops", and am glad that our life as a family began in such a place.

Beryl Sutherland refers in her story to a trip across The Wilderness with the bridge overseer, Jack Moore, in his Ford Utility or "tray" as it was referred to in those days. This wilderness was a desolate windswept waste between Mossburn and Te Anau. Thanks to modern farming technology, this area has now been magically converted into fertile farmland.

"The sunshine left our house in May and did not reach it again till September," writes Beryl Sutherland of their Homer camp home. The photo gives an impression of the Homer's sunless, snowbound winter.

George Jones

Overseer Jack Moore and his wife also resided in the married quarters in the Hollyford Valley, and Mrs Moore, while walking along the road one day, was struck by a rockfall and very nearly lost her life.

Beryl also refers to the depredations of keas – those native parrots of the Hollyford. I well remember her telling how they slid down her corrugated iron roof, one at a time, shrieking with joy. They then flew to a heap of bottles "left by our predecessors", as Beryl so carefully explained, and grabbing them in their claws, flew to the ridge of the cottage, releasing the bottles one by one.

Another habit these keas had was to hang upside down on the clothesline and peck the coloured patterns out from the frozen clothes and towels. Husband Jim, however, found an answer. As storekeeper, he had access to a bit of the turkey-red cloth used by surveyors for marking out a survey line. He found that bits of this, strategically placed, would divert the keas to other huts and tents – and leave the Sutherlands in comparative peace.

At one time a German gentleman named Bruno Bayer came to the Valley, and made arrangements for about a dozen keas to be caught and sent to the Berlin Zoo. This did not result in any diminution of the fun and games indulged in by the remaining keas, but it did result in the gift of a couple of pianos for the Hollyford Social Hall. This was in recognition of the gift of the keas.

191

The keas will have a go at anything.

Free Lance Collection, Alexander Turnbull Library

While referring to keas I recollect one occasion when I was talking to the tunnel overseer Jack Dawson at the tunnel mouth. As we stood there three keas flew on to a bench beside us. On this bench was a pile of railway dog spikes coated with ice and frozen into one solid lump. The keas immediately started to peck off the ice and when a dog spike was freed they would nudge it to the edge of the bench and then push it over and spend the next few minutes looking at it with rapt attention. They would then suddenly return to the job of dislodging another spike, and so on. The keas were only a couple of feet away but completely disregarded us. No doubt they knew what they were doing, but we were not sure of this; Jack thought that maybe they were in training for the job of pushing the lids off the rubbish bins at Kurt Suter's cookhouse.

But returning to the "Women of the Road", a famous "first" was achieved by Mrs Ruth Hodge, now residing in Gore. Here is her own version of the incident: "The highlight of my three years at Homer was when the tunnel was pierced and I was invited to be the first woman to go through to the Milford side. The offer just came out of the blue, and I had no time to even think about it. My two daughters and younger son came with me and the overseer. Of course this was not the same as going through today, as the actual

192

opening was reached after climbing a very high ladder flat against the wall and scrambling out to gaze upon the beautiful Cleddau Valley. Going through was fine, but the thought of coming back down that ladder filled me with horror. However, back I had to come as darkness was setting in."

Mrs Tom Cooney who still resides in Invercargill, also achieved a famous first. She was the first woman to fire a round of shots in the Homer Tunnel.

As Jack Dawson explained to me, there were not many "perks" in those days but one little privilege he used to extend was the honour of actually throwing the switch to detonate a round of shots in the tunnel. This was a dramatic moment and the actual firing was quite a coveted privilege on the job.

Other women who helped on the job were those who ran the cookhouses, taught in the school, and the nurses who braved the isolation at Milford Sound.

Finally there were the many wives who looked after their husbands and brought up families in those rigorous conditions. They played their part; they were there to help in times of sickness, accident and sorrow, and they were there to dispense those innumerable cups of boiling tea which enabled the men to keep struggling on when the chips were really down.

25

FAREWELL TO FIORDLAND

THE PROSPECT OF a transfer to another PWD construction job had been mentioned to me, and my wife suggested that we should have a holiday at Te Anau before we said farewell to Sunny Southland and to Fiordland.

Petrol rationing was the first problem, so for a month or two my Austin 7 got very little use and coupons were saved.

My wife discussed the proposed trip with the boss's wife, Enid Maxwell, and as I would be doing quite a lot of fishing, they thought it would be a good idea if my wife had company. What better then if Enid and her small daughter came with us?

We made arrangements to rent a cottage and we set off early in the month. This was important, as the new month's petrol coupons could then be used. My wife Lola is an expert at packing and this has great advantages and equally great disadvantages. If she were a bad packer lots of necessary goods would be left behind, but as she is a good packer all necessary goods can be fitted in and there is still room for a lot of unnecessary goods. As it turned out we weren't badly off for room – or so my wife said.

There was Enid and her daughter Delphine (eighteen months) and Lola and our two Southlander sons – Lester (three years) and Sandy (eighteen months). Finally there was the driver, which was me. The Austin had no boot but it did have a small folding luggage rack at the back. This was piled so high that I couldn't see out of the rear window but I was told that this didn't matter – all I had to do was to look where I was going, not where I had been.

There were no shops at Te Anau in those days so we had to take our food with us, and as two of the kids were still in nappies, there were problems with clothing. Then of course, there was my fishing gear. Space became a bit scarce towards the finish and I had to stow a bag of vegetables on the front bumper and across the radiator.

Finally we were loaded and on our way, and the two women sighed with relief. I sighed also, but it was with apprehension. For the first few miles it wasn't bad going while we were on the bitumen. After we passed through Makarewa and turned north on to the thickly metalled road I found that the car seemed a wee bit sluggish, and I had to drop into third gear and sometimes into second. This really wasn't surprising as there was a stiff head wind and at times we would be running on a long but slow uphill gradient.

On a number of occasions I felt that my trusty steed wasn't just performing as it should have done. Finally things got so bad that I had to stop and survey the position. I shoved up the bonnet and found out the radiator was boiling, and after a bit of an investigation I came to the conclusion that the sugarbag full of vegetables in front of the radiator wasn't helping things, especially as it was a hot day.

I took this bag off the bumper and Lola had to make room for it (and her and Sandy) in the front seat. As I have said before, Lola is a good packer and she managed it all right.

At this point I did a bit of a survey and came to the conclusion that perhaps the Austin wasn't doing so badly after all. When I totted it up there were six people (mixed sizes) plus all our luggage. Added to this was the hot day, the head wind, the deep shingle, the various uphill gradients and the lack of cooling due to the bag of vegetables in front. I was not to know till I got to Te Anau that I also had a slack fanbelt.

At this stage I am going to digress a little to say something about that Austin 7. I bought it new and the price advertised was £239. I had a friend who said that competition was pretty keen and that he thought that he might be able to get the vendor to knock £10 off the price. He did this, and for his trouble I gave him £2, so the car cost me £231. Just as an idea of what things cost those days, I remember that greasing charges were 3s. per service.

I had that Austin for eighteen years and did 92,000 miles and sold it for £135. The only repairs of note that I had done were a set of rings which cost £18 and a rebore costing £65. Over all, major repairs cost me an average of £5 per annum and depreciation was about the same. This is cheap motoring in anybody's language.

My first set of tyres did 24,000 miles. One of the batteries I had lasted me for eleven years — someone had dumped it out in the snow at the Marian camp and I picked it up on spec and had it recharged.

I was living in Wellington when I sold the Austin 7 and no sooner had the purchaser taken delivery than he was transferred to Invercargill and back with him went my old trusty. I saw him some years later and he told me the final story. He had the car for three years and then it was stolen. It was later recovered by the police from a ditch. It had rolled over and was a complete writeoff and the owner collected £100 insurance.

My exploits in that old bus would fill several books – perhaps some day I may even get the urge to write at least one!

But I must return to that holiday trip to Te Anau. The restowing of the vegetables did help but it was a long and laborious trip,

much of which was done in second gear. We were all tired and very thankful when we finally reached that downhill slope taking us to our house in Te Anau.

By the time we got unpacked and everything put away in the cupboards it was getting late in the afternoon, so the women made the tea and in due course put the two younger children to bed. I had promised Enid's husband that I would phone him when we arrived, so after tea I took my elder boy, Lester, to the Te Anau Hotel where there was a phone. Our house was on the main road from Mossburn before the final right angle turn into Te Anau. We had the option of walking down the road and then turning right and walking along to the hotel, or taking the direct route through the manuka scrub. I decided to take the shorter route as there was a bit of a track through the scrub and the light was still good.

When I got to the hotel I booked a call and had to wait quite a while. When the call did come through I left Lester (aged three) just outside the telephone booth and spoke to Enid's husband for a short time. When I got out Lester was nowhere to be seen. I rushed around a bit but could not find him. The light was failing fast and I did not know quite what to do or where to look. I immediately called out for assistance as I was afraid he might have headed back home through the scrub, which was the only way he knew.

The people at the hotel told me that we would have to do some-

196

thing immediately as there were many miles of scrublands back from the road and if he got lost in this it could be very serious. By this time it was dark and the hotel people organised a search while I ran back to the house by way of the road as it was too dark to pick up the track through the scrub. Just as I got to the back door, a little voice said "Hullo, Dad." Lester had headed off through the scrub in the failing light and had fortunately found his way. This was just on top of a full-scale search for him by police and neighbours a few months before, when he decided to do a bit of exploring one Sunday afternoon on the outskirts of Invercargill. I shoved him inside and shot back to the hotel, where I was very pleased to be able to call off the search and shout for the searchers.

Not so long ago Lester's own son Brett (aged three) took off while his mother had him at a supermarket in Auckland, and he was found some time later in a dog kennel down the road, peeping out and carefully avoiding the searchers – like father like son.

The next week or so passed very quickly and I managed to get quite a number of fish by just walking along the shore of Lake Te Anau with a short bait-casting rod. Catching fish up to five and six pounds weight off the beach without getting one's feet wet just sounds too good to be true but that is how it went. There were rainbow trout and Atlantic salmon (*Salmo salar*) and the odd brown trout. My favourite spot was up the road on the beach near the 4-mile peg.

I remember one day casting out my favourite red minnow, and the very second that it hit the water a fish had taken it – and what a fish! It was a rainbow and it was a "slab". I don't know what was wrong with it but its body was just bones and not very much longer than its big head.

One of the overseers at Te Anau at the time was Gus McGregor, and I had his boys as fishing mates. They had casting rods and, like most lads, their gear at times was a bit makeshift, but they caught fish. Their technique was simple but very effective. They cast out the minnow and when they hooked a fish they immediately turned about face, held the rod in a "slope arms" position and ran for dear life up the beach till the fish was on dry land.

I remember one day when they were fishing and I was watching their technique. They had run out of swivels so had adapted the swivel off an old watch chain and it seemed to work all right. They were not having much luck and after a while a prominent Invercargill businessman came down to the lake's edge and started fishing right ahead of them, taking all the good unfished water. He kept on for a while but had no luck, and the boys followed a few yards behind him apparently not at all disturbed by his presence.

197

Author's sons, Lester (*left*) and Sandy – passengers in the Austin Seven through the mob of cattle.

After a while one of the boys did the old about-turn act and ran up the beach and landed a beautiful big Atlantic salmon. I almost expected that businessman to fall in behind the boys to see if that would change his luck.

Next day I had a very interesting time looking over the hatcheries, where they were conducting an experiment in raising American brook trout which it was intended to release in suitable streams.

I also remember talking to one of the local inhabitants and he went on for a long time telling me in detail of the attractions of an area on the other side of the lake. He said that people from overseas who had been in this area had returned to revisit it. So graphic was his description that I thought I might try to get over there, and I started to ask him a few detailed questions. At this point I was to learn that he had never even been there. It is not uncommon to find this sort of thing, even in the most interesting areas.

That evening I got a call to go to the hotel and ring Invercargill and when I did this I was to learn that the Public Works Department had decided to shift me as clerk-in-charge on a big construction job further north. I had a few more days' fishing and, after saying farewell to overseer Tom Plato and his gang, and to Fiordland itself, the faithful Austin 7 was loaded and off we set.

We had eaten all the food and our load was less so we did not anticipate much trouble on the way home – but how wrong we were. Fiordland is a wild and beautiful area and in it I had had many adventures. It was not going to release me without adding to that score.

All went well till we got somewhere round about The Gorge or a bit nearer Mossburn. There was so much action that I just didn't have time to take any bearings. The first sign of anything out of the ordinary was when we came on to a team of stockmen and their dogs. Ahead of them for quite a distance cattle were straggling along and didn't seem very numerous so I just kept on and rounded a corner, but the further I got the more cattle we encountered. By this time we were on a narrow sidling section of road and the cattle were packed tight in one solid mass all around us.

All I could do was to move as they moved. Sometimes I would get a break of perhaps fifteen or twenty feet ahead and, just as I was going to move on, an old bull with great long horns would turn round and put his head down as though he were going to charge. It was a stifling hot day but we had to keep the big side windows shut as we were afraid that an animal would poke its head in. My greatest fear however, was what would happen if the cattle stampeded or surged sideways and took us over the edge and down the steep slope at the side of the road. I tried blowing the horn but this had no effect other than making the beasts in front turn round and lower their heads, and I was afraid that I would be charged or that the radiator would be punctured by the horns.

This was no mob of dairy cattle. It was the annual roundup of wild bush-run cattle from somewhere up the Mararoa River. What I found the worst feature of all was to be sitting there unable to move an inch and to be stared at continuously by enormous beasts about ten inches away from me. The same applied to the womenfolk. I don't know to this day how long we were stuck in that mob of cattle, nor can Enid or Lola hazard a guess. I would say it was over two hours although it seemed like years. How it was that the car was not crushed in, charged, or barged off the road, I just don't know.

We made hardly any progress at all for most of the time, as the road was so narrow that there was just one tight mass, and it was only when the road widened some considerable time later, that we were able to pick our way through. Although we did not realise it at the time, not one word was spoken by the three adults in the car for the full period we were trapped. Fortunately the three young children just took it as a matter of course. I hate to even imagine what would have happened if they had panicked.

This was my farewell to Fiordland, and, on thinking it over afterwards I felt that it was symbolic of this wild but lovely country. It was as if, in waving me farewell, my imaginary and mystic Lady of Fiordland had also gently shaken her fist as a lasting reminder that as well as being a world-class beauty, she could also be a woman of fierce and angry passions. Hers was a land of beauty, of adventures, of lovely bush and rivers and mountains. It was a land of calm, alternated with savage moods – a land I loved.

On returning to Invercargill we began our preparations for a new and exciting life in the last of the big PWD railway construction jobs. It was the linking up of the final section of the South Island Main Trunk railway from Hundalee through Oaro and Kaikoura to Clarence Bridge.

This was also a job of excitement and adventures on a lovely coastal strip stretching north and south of Kaikoura – but that is another story . . .

26

MEN OF THE ROAD

I HAVE REFERRED frequently to the "Men of the Road" and many of these have been given names. Reference to others has been made oblique, for a variety of reasons. At the end of this chapter I have listed quite a large number of names from memory and some of my friends who were on the job have added their quota to this list.

If there are minor errors in initials or spelling of names I must apologise. There is now no record of all the people who passed through this job and for this reason the names of quite à number will be omitted, simply because they have passed from memory. Again I apologise, and if any reader of this book finds that his name has been omitted or incorrectly recorded, I would be pleased to hear from that person.

I have added a few comments on some of the "Men of the Road", that I have listed and if these are predominently about clerical and engineering staff it is only because my association with these departmental officers continued over many years, whereas I lost touch with many who did not remain with the Department – now called the Ministry of Works and Development.

I must also apologise for scanty reference to men on the Milford Sound end of the job. I knew these men well – but for the most part only as names on a sheet of paper. They were New Zealand's "Lost Tribe" but nevertheless they did a great job in their isolation.

There can be no order of preference or seniority in referring to the "Men of the Road" so I will simply take them in alphabetical order.

Austin, Frank Clearwater, J.B. (Bryan) O'Connor, E.M. (Ted) Springford, J.R. (John)	These were some of the "lads" in the office and it is good to know that all of them now hold senior administrative positions in the Public Service. They were great workmates.
Beattie, W.B. (Bill)	Although not a member of the Department, Bill must be included with the "Men of the Road". He was a *Weekly News* and *NZ Herald* photographer for over forty years and visited the Valley almost yearly after 1930, taking thousands of photos – some of which appear in this book. He is the author of *Bill Beattie's New Zealand*.

Boord, Frank M. (Mossy)	Was canteen officer at the Hollyford Valley. He was a brother of Ray Boord, MP for Rotorua. "Mossy" was accidently killed on 29 March 1940 while on final leave prior to going overseas.
Butler, B.W. (Bert)	Another one of the lads in the office Enlisted in the Air Force and was killed in an air crash on 18 April 1941.
Caird, W.A. (Bill)	Was killed by a falling tree in the Lower Hollyford Valley. He called to others to run but was himself pinned down.
Campbell, Dan	Referred to right through the book. Dan died in his hut in the latter stages of the job. This is just as he would have wished it.
Christie, J.H. (John)	Was engineer-in-charge at Marian and later he became asst. chief design engineer at Head Office. He was a keen mountaineer and photographer, and in 1941 with Mr G.P. Rayward made the third ascent of Mitre Peak. (*NZ Alpine Journal*, June 1941).
Clissold, T.C. (Tom)	Was transport officer at the Invercargill office. Went on Captain Scott's polar expedition, and is mentioned in Apsley Cherry-Garrard's book *The Worst Journey in the World*. Also served with distinction in the Navy and Air Force in World War I.
Dawson, N.J. (Jack)	Jack retired as inspector of works, Ministry of Works, Palmerston North. He originally came from Riversdale and is as solid a type as I have ever met.
De Vantier, A.A. (Peter)	Was the New Zealand Workers' Union secretary about the time the 1935 Labour Government was in power. Peter was a dedicated and militant fighter for the rights of the worker. He was killed in action in Italy on 15 December 1943. Duncan White visited his grave near Orsogna in Italy.
Don (Bill) and Beveridge (Morry)	These men were lost on the West Coast for a considerable period but lived off the land and finally turned up at Marian camp as thin as scarecrows. They were as versatile at their work as they were on their survival exercise.
Farquhar, F.J. (Finn)	Married Marge Smith, daughter of Tom W. Smith, tunnel overseer. Finn served overseas and was badly wounded in the North African campaign.
Ferris, Paddy	This man was a blacksmith and farrier and was an absolute master of his trade. He came from Riversdale and with a mate named Bill McNarey he went overseas in World War I and was assigned to duties in Egypt as a farrier. The two mates jumped ship and were landed on Gallipoli. Paddy used to say this was the worst bit of work he ever did. He was under the command of Brigadier Hargest and was one of a party to make the first discovery of water for troops on the Peninsula.
Gawith, H.J. (Joe)	Can tell a really good story. He was in the artillery in Crete as a bombardier. His capture in Crete was recorded in the press as "Brigadier" Gawith. Someone suggested Joe must have put a good story over those Germans – or written the press notice himself. Joe succeeded me as paymaster

202

Gough, H.J. (Hector)   Engineering cadet at Milford Sound. Went overseas and served in Navy under "B" Scheme (Lieut).

Hannan, R.A. (Ray)   Also joined Navy under "B" Scheme (Lieut.).

Henderson, J.F. (Jack)   Was engineer-in-charge at Milford Sound and Hollyford in latter stages. Retired from the Department as district commissioner of works, Dunedin.

Hobbs, E.W. (Ernie)   Went overseas, serving in Crete and Palestine as warrant officer. Died of wounds in Palestine 31 August 1942 – Awarded DCM. Was union president at Hollyford. A genial type.

Hulse, D.F. (Don)   Engineer-in-charge. Killed at Homer Tunnel by avalanche on 4 May 1937.

Hunter, R.H. (Roy)   The life of the party at the Headquarters camp in the Hollyford. Went overseas and died of wounds, Western Desert 25 October 1942.

Jones, G.J. (George)   George was on the engineering staff. A good photographer. Later went as leader of the coast-watching "Cape Expedition" to the Auckland and Campbell Islands.

Keppel, M.A. (Mat)   On survey staff at Invercargill. Went overseas to Middle East with artillery. Awarded an immediate Military Medal on 29 September 1943.

Lloyd, J.T. (Joe)   Was injured in the second fatal avalanche. He retired from the Department as superintendent of works (mechanical), Dunedin.

McKinnon, I.W. (Ian)   Was engineer-in-charge at Milford Sound in the earlier stages. Retired as district commissioner of works, Auckland.

Mullins, G.J. (Jim)   President of New Zealand Workers' Union at Hollyford Valley. Later prominent in Public Service Association affairs in Wellington.

Overton P.L. (Leigh)   Killed in first fatal avalanche on 6 July 1936. His name and those of Don Hulse and Tom Smith are commemorated by a plaque at the Homer Tunnel.

Pearce, W.G.   Mr Pearce was resident engineer, Public Works Department, Invercargill. A capable and kindly man and a good friend to me. He was a great advocate of "The Road". Growing flowers was an integral part of his life.

Plato, T. (Tom)   A genial overseer at Te Anau. Very highly regarded by the Department and residents around Te Anau. Plato Creek near the 46 mile peg is named after Tom.

Rawle, R.E. (Russell)   In the accounts office at Invercargill. Was district accountant at Ministry of Works, Wellington, when he retired.

Smith, Harold Welton   The "Smithy" of Smithy Creek at the 41-mile peg. He was a man with a touch of genius in everything. He succeeded Mr W.G. Pearce as resident engineer, Ministry of Works, Invercargill. Everybody liked Smithy and he was a dedicated supporter of Southland.

Smith, T.W. (Tom)   A giant of a man. Was tunnel overseer at Homer Tunnel and killed in an avalanche on 4 May 1937.

Stewart D.R. (Doug)

An experienced overseer and a veteran of the Tawa Flat tunnel.
Another engineering stalwart and, like George Jones, was a second-generation PWD Employee.

Sutherland, Jim

Came on to the job in the very early stages and carried his pack up the Valley. He was in charge of the stores at the Homer and was one of the last to leave the job when it closed down.

Toomey A.K. (Kevin)

Was in the Invercargill office. Served in the Navy and was one of the 150 New Zealanders lost when the cruiser NEPTUNE struck a mine in the Mediterranean on 19 December 1941.

Uttley, L.M. ("Buster")

As a captain in the Middle East he was taken prisoner of war and transported to Italy by submarine, spent $3\frac{1}{2}$ years in POW camps in Italy and Germany.

White, D.U. (Duncan)

Was engineer-in-charge at Hollyford Valley after Don Hulse. He was wounded at Cassino and invalided home from Italy with rank of major. Awarded DSO. Retired as district commissioner of works, Napier. A long-time friend of mine.

Wyeth, C. (Campbell)

In stores office, Invercargill. Went overseas in Navy, gained rank of lieutenant.

Abernethy, J., Tunneller
Aitcheson, Bill (& wife Melita), Cascade Creek accommodation house
Alcock, Alf (& wife), Surfaceman, Eglinton
Alsweiler, V., Co-op
Anderson, Alf, Storeman
Anderson, (mining student), Tunneller
Anderson, Harold J., Paymaster, Invercargill
Andrewartha, Bill, Tunnel headman, (Downer & Co)
Annesley, George, Tunnel headman
Armstrong, H.L. (Lofty), Draughtsman, Invercargill
Ashwell, W. & T., Co-op
Aspray, J.G. (Jim), Homer
Auld, Frank, Hollyford
Auld, George (& wife Jean), Overseer
Azariti, Nick, Tunneller

Bain, Doug, Labourer, Marian
Ballantyne, Bill, Union president
Banks, Wally, Manager, Downer & Co
Barnett, Tom (& wife), Fitter, Homer
Barwood, Bill, Milford Sound
Baxter, Jim, Hollyford
Beaton, W.R. (Bill), Canteen officer
Beattie, A.J., Co-op
Beck, Alex, Tunnel winchman
Belesky, Joe, Tunneller
Bell, Alf, Tunneller
Bell, Bert, Homer
Bell, Logan, Labourer, Te Anau

Bell, Tom, Eglinton
Bell, (Dr), Lumsden
Beuth, H.R. (Harry & wife), Carpenter
Bevan, Frank, Co-op
Bigwood, Alf, Cabinetmaker
Birsland, Frank, P & T wireless operator
Bissett, J.C., Milford Sound
Black, Tom, (& wife Effie), Baker, Marian
Boatwood, S.A., Milford Sound
Bocock, Max, Hollyford
Boivin, L., Milford Sound
Botting, Jim, Butcher
Bowers, Mick, Co-op
Brazier, Harry, (& wife Ann), Hollyford
Broadfoot, Morry, Tunneller
Bromby, J.W., Milford Sound
Broom, Fred, P & T wireless operator
Broome, Hec, Co-op
Brotherston, A. (Lex) (& wife Mary), Mechanic
Brown, A. (Sandy), Ganger
Brown, Colin, Hollyford
Brown, Jim, Tunneller
Brown, Mervyn G., Bushman
Browning, A. (Fred), Hollyford
Buddle, Ossie, Milford Sound
Burns, Roly, Homer Portal
Burford, Jim, Tunneller
Butcher, Stan, Tunneller
Butler, Matty, Tunnel headman
Buttolph, A.D., Co-op
Byron, W., Milford Sound

Cameron, Jack (& wife Ella), Truck driver
Cameron, L., Homer
Cameron, Tom, Homer guide
Campbell, A.E. (Jack), Stores
Canning, R.W., Milford Sound
Cannon, Jim, Truckman
Cantrick, Herb, Homer
Carter, Bob, Tunnel shift boss
Cavanagh, S.B., Co-op
Cattaruzo, Oscar, Tunneller & stonewaller
Cheyne, W., Milford Sound
Chibba Daya, Co-op
Chisholm, Donald, Carpenter
Christie, ("Brick"), Driver for "Barney" Gilligan
Clark, Leslie, Cookshop
Clarke, Arthur, Surfaceman
Clarke, George, Tunneller
Cockburn, J., Hollyford
Cockroft, L.N. (Lloyd), Electrician
Coats, Bill, Eglinton
Coffey, Jack, Stores officer, Homer
Concannon, Tom, Bushman
Connolly, Paddy, Tunneller
Cook, S. ("Just Testin"), Telephones
Corbin, Charlie, Bushman
Corson, J.S. (Jim), Surfaceman
Cosgrove, Paddy, Marian
Coutts, Jock, Tunneller
Craig, J.H., Manager, Downer & Co
Craig, W. (Bill), Telephone man
Crawshaw, R.C. (Bob), Surfaceman
Cromie, Jack, Downer & Co
Crozier, Bill, Tunneller
Cunliffe, F.P. (Fred), Storekeeper, Invercargill
Curran, Jack, Draughtsman, Invercargill

Daubney, Tom, Bridge carpenter
Davey, Gerald, Bridge gang
Davies, John, Homer Tunnel survey
Davis, George (& wife Myra), Driver
Davis, R., Bridge gang, Milford
Dawson, Brian, Hollyford
Dawson, N.J. (Jack) (& wife Nell), Tunnel overseer
Dawson, Peter, Co-op party
Dean, Frank, Tunneller
Dean, Morrie, Tunneller
De Latour, Harry, Foreman, Downer & Co
De Lambert, J.R., Engineer
Del Favero, Peter, Stonewaller
Denniston, Gordon, Administration, Invercargill
Derrick, Owen, Compressor attendant
De Vantier, Laurie, Tunneller
Devereaux, Lou, Homer

Diamond, Jack (& two brothers), Homer
Dick, Bob, Tunneller
Dickson (or Dixon), Turk, Homer
Dimmock, A.A., Milford Sound
Dimond, S. Milford Sound
Dixon, A.C., Milford Sound
Dixon, ("Soccer"), Co-op
Doley, E.F. (Eddie), Hollyford & "Cape Expedition"
Donaldson, Dick, Surfaceman
Donaldson, Jack, Surfaceman
Donovan, Jack, Marian camp
Donovan, Paddy, Co-op
Double, H.D. (Harry), Administration, Hollyford Valley
Downer, Arnold F., Tunnel contractor
Drinkrow, S.C. (Syd.), Bridge gang, Milford
Driver, Jack A., Foreman, Invercargill
Druskovich, Bosko, Tunneller
Duff, A.R. (Archie), Co-op headman
Duffin, H.R. (Harry), Surfaceman
Duffy, M.P., Homer
Duncan, A.P. (Alec), Tunneller & overseer
Duncombe, Fred (& wife), Electrician
Duskie, Dave, Hollyford
Duston, Tom, Fitter
Duthie, A.L. (Alistair), Guide, Homer
Dwyer, Jack, Bushman
Dyer, Fred, Surfaceman

Eade, Garnett M., Eglinton Valley
Eady, Mrs., Marian cookshop
Eady, J.R., Marian
Eathorne, Jack, Hollyford
Edgar F.G. (Frank), Stores, Invercargill
Edmonds, W. (Bill), Hollyford
Edwards, J.C.C., Transport officer, Invercargill
Egan, Jim, Compressor attendant
Egan Matt, Co-op
Egan Mick, Co-op party
Elms, Charlie, Bus driver
Erskine, J., Labourer, Marian

Fackender, Norman, Labourer, Milford Sound
Fahey, Jim, Tunneller
Fahey, Mick, Tunneller
Fairbank, Allen A., Tunneller
Faithful, J., Milford Sound
Farrington, M.A. (Mick), Tunneller
Fearn, G., Milford Sound
Fennimore, Arthur, YMCA & Post Office
Finn, ("Digger"), Driver
Finnerty, A.J., Milford Sound
Fisher, Len, D6 Dozer driver
Fisher, Norman, Co-op
Fisher, Stan, Survey

205

Fitzgerald, Ted & Jack, Tunnellers
Flanagan, Bill, Camp attendant
Flaws, Bob, Buildings section, Invercargill
Fletcher, Jim, Co-op
Fletcher, Owen, Homer drill shop
Floyd, Teri, Admin., Invercargill
Flynn, Dave, Tunnel shift boss
Flynn, Frank, Camp attendant
Fogarty, Ted, Packman
Ford, Dan, Co-op
Ford, Eddy, Bathhouse attendant
Ford, Martin, Eglinton
Ford, Watty, Drapery salesman
Forsyth D., Co-op & Survey
Fox, Henry F., Admin., Invercargill
Frame, Alan, Radio man
Francis, John M., Homer
Fraser, Bill, Bridge foreman, Invercargill
Fraser, Bill, Cookshop
Fretwell, R., Milford Sound
Froude, Dave (& wife), Homer fitting shop
Froude, W.J.A. (Wattie), Fitter, Homer

Gaffaney, H., Milford Sound
Galvin, J., Milford Sound
Garvie, Sandy (A.W.) (& wife Maisie), Homer cookhouse
Gaskin, Eric, Homer cookhouse
Gaudion, E.J. (Eric), Eglinton
Geange, A., Milford Sound
Gerken, I., Milford Sound
Gibb, Roger B., Architect, Invercargill
Gilchrist, Ray, Tunneller
Giles, Ambrose, Co-op
Gilligan, Barney, Truck operator
Girvan, W., Milford Sound
Glancefield, Ben, Timekeeper
Glass, H., Hollyford
Glasson, S.H. (Steve), Homer Tunnel survey
Glasson, W., Milford Sound
Going, J. & T., Milford Sound
Goldstone, Jack, F., Stores, Invercargill
Goodall, Reg, Shoe salesman
Goodley, Milford canteen
Gorton, E., Milford Sound
Govan, Ernie, Te Anau Hotel
Graham, D., Driver for Barney Gilligan
Grant, Milton, Truck driver
Gray, W. ("Dolly"), Homer
Grigor, Chris, YMCA & Post Office
Grindley, John, Survey
Gwynne, Jim, Admin., Invercargill

Haines, Tom, Labourer, Te Anau
Hall, S.W. (Bill), Homer Tunnel survey
Halliday, Bill, Co-op
Hallimore, Sam, Co-op, Marian
Halpin, T., Milford Sound
Hanna, J.R. (Joe), Surfaceman

Harris, Bill, Homer Tunnel survey
Harris, Doug, Survey
Harrison, J.R. (Jock), Co-op
Harvey, Dick (& wife), Homer
Harvey, Jack, Survey
Hatton, R.J. (Bert) (& wife), Homer
Head, N.G., Co-op, Marian
Heads, Bill, Drapery salesman
Hefford, W. (Bill), Stores, Invercargill
Hellyer, Mrs., Nurse, Milford Sound
Helm, L., Milford Sound
Henderson, Bill, Blacksmith, Homer
Henderson, Charlie, Co-op
Henderson, George, Packman, Marian
Henderson, J.F. (wife Rene), Engineer-in-charge
Henderson, Tiny, Marian
Henery, A.J., Milford Sound
Henry, N.L.G. (Norman), Homer
Herratt, H.A. ("Son"), Co-op
Herring, R., Hollyford
Herriott, Charlie, Surfaceman
Herron, Cliff G. (& wife Marge), Eglinton Valley
Hesselyn, G.A. (George), Buildings, Invercargill office
Hill, Andy, Tunneller
Hill, Fred, Electrician
Hillyer, Ernie, Homer
Hoare, George, Homer
Hodge, Jack (& wife Ruth), Tractor driver and tool sharpener, Homer
Hodgens, Iris (later Mrs A. Ireland), Homer cookhouse
Hogan, J., Surfaceman and bushman
Holmes, Harry, Film projectionist
Hopewell, Doug, Labourer
Horgan, D.G. (Des), Tunneller
Horgan, Geddes A., D7 Tractor driver
Horrell, Miss, Schoolteacher
Horton, J.P. (Jack), Pumpman
Howe, Doug, Tunneller
Howell, E.A. (Ernie), Tunneller
Humphries, Jack, Co-op, Marian
Humphries, R.H., Milford Sound
Hunt, Denny, Co-op
Hunt, E., Mining student, Homer
Hunter, M.D. (Max), Storekeeper, Milford Sound
Hussey, Pat, Milford Sound
Hussey, Tom, Milford Sound
Hutchings, Ernie, Hollyford
Hynes, Jack, Hollyford

Ireland, Arthur, Homer fitting shop
Isaacs, Tony, 1st Driver D7 tractor

James, L.S. (Sam), Engineer
Jenkins, Charlie, Survey, Invercargill

Jenkins, J. (Jack) (& wife Ivy), Time-
keeper, Hollyford
Jensen, C.G. (Snowy), Hollyford
Jerome, T., Co-op
Johns, Ben, Carpenter
Johnson, Lester, Tunneller
Johnson, Adam, Winchman
Johnston, Harry, Labourer, Marian
Jolly, D.C., Co-op, Marian
Jones, Alf, Labourer, Te Anau
Jones, Bill, Marian
Jones, Bob, Sawmill & Homer
Jones, Jack, Fitting shop
Jones, Melton D., Tunneller
Jones, Tommy, Butcher
Jordan, W.B., Milford Sound

Kay, Gordon ("Apples"), Hollyford
Keady, Bartholomew ("Bot"), Bushman
Keady, Paddy, Bushman
Kelly, Ivan, Eglinton
Kelly, Dennis ("Denny"), Tunneller
Kemp, Charlie (& wife Florrie), Homer
Kennedy, Dave, Homer Survey party
Kerr, Tom, Co-op gang
Kett, J.G. & W.G., Milford Sound
Kilkerr, A.F. (Andy), Mechanic
Kingston-Smith, E., YMCA secretary
Kissell, H.J. (Dick), Milford Sound
Knights, Arthur, Homer Survey party
Knipe, A.L. & C., Homer
Knox Bill, Bushman
Krause, J. "Ginger", Tunneller

Laing, Bob & Archie, Co-op
Lamond, J.W., Milford Sound
Larking, Jock, Truckman
Latham, Ivan, Carpenter
Lawrie, Jean, Staff cook
Lawson, E., Hollyford
Leask, Lloyd S., Storekeeper, Invercargill
Lee, Andrew, Labourer, Marian
Lee, Henry, Marian survey
Lee, Rafe, Invercargill office
Leonard, Jack, Co-op
Leen, M.J. (Mick), Tool sharpener
Liddell, E., Milford Sound
Liddy, J.J., Co-op
Lipscombe, C.M. (Carty), Engineer,
Invercargill
Little, Harry, NZR bus driver
Littlejohn, "Scotty", Packer, Marian
Long, C.H. (Charlie), Manager Tourist
Hostel, Milford Sound
Long, Les (& wife Ethel), Head bushman
Lorimer, J.R. (Jimmy), Co-op

Lowe, Charlie, Surfaceman
Lusher, H.W. ("Buck"), Carpenter
Lynch, Jim (father & son), Co-op

Macaskill, Jack, Survey, Invercargill
Macaskill, R. (Bob), Blacksmith, Homer
McAlpine, J., Hollyford
McAuliffe, B., Co-op
McAuslin, Bill, Marian
McBride, Stuart (& wife Vera),
Electrician
McBride, Jack, Stores, Invercargill
McCallum, Bill, Survey
McCann, Hugh, Co-op
McCarthy, Eddie, Bridge carpenter
McCarthy, Paddy, Trucks & survey
McCash, Frank, Tunneller
McConnachie, W.J. Bill), Downer & Co
manager
McCreath, Bert & Les, Marian
McCubbin, F.B. (Brown), Milford Sound
McCullogh, "Mac", Tunneller
McCullum, Bill, Plumber
McCutcheon, W. (Bill), Tunneller
McDermott, J., Tunnel pumpman
McDiarmid, D.C., Milford Sound
McDonald, Euan, Tunneller
McDonald, Percy, Engineer, Invercargill
McDonald, Miss Thea, Schoolteacher,
Homer
McDonough, W.M. (Watty), Tunneller
McDowall, Frank, Homer
McFadyen, J.A., Milford Sound
McFadzien, "Wick", Truck driver
MacGillivray, Miss Rene, Nurse, Milford
Sound
McGregor, G.A. (Gus), (& wife Eve), Te
Anau maintenance
McGuinness, T.J. (Tim), Tunneller
MacKay, Gib, Carpenter
MacKay, J.M. (Jack), Head chainman
Mackie, Bruce, Packer
McKay, Jim, Co-op gang, Cascade Creek
McKenzie, K.J. (Ken), Homer
McKinnon, Hugh, Co-op
McKissock, G.F. (Garnett), Homer
McKnight, Bert, Homer
McKnight, Len (& wife Ruby),
Electrician
McKnight, Noel, Homer
McKnight, Linton, Homer
McKnight, R.P., Invercargill survey
McLachlan, I.A. (Ian), Invercargill plant
overseer

McLaren, Archie, Stonemason (built stonework over tunnel portal)

McLaren, D.P.H. (Danny), Tunneller & overseer

McLaughlan, Jim, Overseer, Milford Sound

McLeay, Jim, Homer & Milford

McLeod, Bill, Downer & Co

McLeod, Jock, Co-op party

McManus, Frank, Lower Hollyford

McMillan Bros, Horse scoop contract

McNaughton, G.Y. (Garnett), Co-op party

McPherson, E.M., Invercargill survey

McPherson, Miss, Nurse, Milford Sound

McPherson, Eddie, Co-op

McQuarrie, W., Milford Sound

McQueen, W., Milford Sound

Maher, Jack, Foreman, Invercargill

Maher, Tom, Carpenter

Manderson, Bill, Labourer, Marian

Mann, Sid, Survey party

Manson, Bob, Homer fitting shop

Manson, Harry, Milford Sound

Manson, W., Milford Sound

Marriott, Joe, Storekeeper, Invercargill

Matheson, H.C. (Harry), Compressor attendant

Matthews, Cleve, Canteen, Hollyford

Mattingly, J., Homer portal

Maxwell, E.A.S. Clerk-in-charge, Invercargill

Meikle, Duncan, Milford Sound

Melrose, Dave, Hollyford

Melvin, Bill, Handyman

Mercer, J.M. (Jimmy), Tunneller

Messent, Dave, Homer Tunnel survey

Michael, Bill, Co-op headman

Middlemass, R., Milford Sound

Miller, A. "Dusty", Packman, Marian

Miller, Gordon, Homer Tunnel Survey

Milne, J.T., Loco driver, Homer Tunnel

Mitchell, Dave, Tunneller

Mitchell, R.S. (Bob), Drill sharpener

Moffatt, Joe, Compressor attendant

Moir, Jack, Blacksmith

Molloy, J.T. (Joe), Surfaceman

Monk, Jack, Plumber

Montagu, Tom M., Tunnneller

Moog, F. ("Dutch"), Milford Sound

Moore, J.R. (Jack) (& wife Eileen), Bridge overseer, Hollyford

Moran, C.J. (Cyril), Stores officer, Homer

Moran, Jerry, Timekeeper

Morgan, Bernie, YMCA secretary

Morgan, Harry (& wife Bertha), Plant overseer, Homer Tunnel

Morgan, Ken, Fitting shop, Homer

Morgan, Watty, Homer. Enlisted at 53 years of age and went overseas.

Mori, F.J. (Jack), Clerk-in-charge, Invercargill

Morrison, Jock & Colin, Tunnellers

Morrison, Stan, Tunneller

Moynihan, T., Co-op

Mullins, J.T. (Joe), Lorry owner-driver

Munro, J.B., Labourer, Marian

Murphy, Bill, Tunneller

Murphy, Jack, Labourer, Milford Sound

Murphy, Mick, Packman & tunneller

Murray, Mr, Schoolteacher, Homer

Murtagh, Alan, Homer

Naylor, Chris (snr), Tunneller

Naylor, Chris (jnr), Tunneller

Nally, J.A. (Jack), Co-op, Hollyford

Neely, Hugh, Tunneller & overseer

Neilson, Andy (& wife), Building foreman for Downer & Co

Nelson, H.M. ("Hec"), Co-op, Hollyford

Newton, Bill, Milford Sound

Newton, Geoff, Labourer, Marian

Nicholson. C.M., Admin. Invercargill

Nicholson, Don, Tunneller

Nisbett, Norman (& wife Ilma), Homer Stores

Oats, George, Eglinton Valley

O'Brien, Bill, Homer

O'Carroll, Tonga, Tunnel shift boss

O'Connell, Tom F. (snr), Timekeeper, Milford Sound

O'Connell, Tom (jnr), Timekeeper, Milford Sound

O'Conner, W. (Bill), Tunnel steelman

O'Dowd, Mick, Co-op

O'Dowd, Tom, Co-op

O'Kane, Bill, Labourer, Marian

O'Keefe, W. (Bill), Milford Sound

O'Neill (2 brothers X Waimate), Marian

O'Neill, Jack, Bushman

Osborne, Nip, Tunneller

Osmond, Val, Homer

O'Sullivan, P. & T., Bush gang

O'Toole, Thomas, Co-op

Paget, Frank, Travelling draper

Paisley, Jim, Overseer, Milford Sound
Palmer, A., Electrician
Palmer, Les ("Ambrose"), Truck driver
Palmer, Ted, Carpenter
Parker, J., Homer
Parsons, Tom, Co-op
Pasalic (Paisley), Joe, Explosives man
Patel, Jim, Vegetable salesman
Patterson, M.O. (Mick), Hollyford
Pearce, Owen H. ("Lofty"), Downer & Co
Peattie, W. (Bill), Co-op
Percival, Jack, Fitting shop
Perry, Jack, Shot-firer
Phelan, Bob, Tunneller
Phethean, Harold, Fitting shop (Homer)
Phillips, Bill, Labourer, Milford Sound
Philp, W. G. (Bill), Surfaceman
Pope, W.R. (Bill) & Jim, Co-op
Popplewell, H,M, (Harold), Stores, Milford Sound
Porter, Claude, Tunneller
Porter, Max, Co-op party
Price, Frank, J., Timekeeper, Hollyford
Pumpa, Ben, Carpenter
Putnik, Ben, Tunneller

Quinn, Jack ("Shorty"), Tunneller

Ramsay, Jim, Homer portal
Ramsay, Joffre ("Jopher"), Tunneller
Rask, Frank, YMCA man
Rask, Lovell P., Bridge carpenter
Rask, Ted, Co-op
Reid, Alan F., Architectural draughtsman, Invercargill
Reid, Charlie, Co-op gang
Reinheimer, Fred C., Rigger
Rendall, Charlie, Truck owner
Rewcastle, M., Milford Sound
Rhind, J.F., Milford Sound
Ricketts, Darcy (& wife May), Fitter
Roake, A.W. (Sandy), Plant overseer, Homer
Robb, R. ("Robbie"), Road engineer, Invercargill
Roberts, J., Winch driver
Robinson, A.B. (Alf), Tutoko, Gulliver Bridges, Milford Sound
Roe, Charlie T., Hollyford
Rohan, Bill (& wife Iris), Homer
Ross, Angus, WEA tutor
Rountree, Charlie, Homer
Rountree, John B., Engineer, Invercargill

Rowan, Bill (& wife Freda), Homer
Rutherford, Mr., WEA tutor
Ryan, Bill, Compressor attendant
Ryan, Bill, Ex Ryal Bush
Ryan, Dave, Labourer, Marian
Ryan, Jimmy ("Red"), Bushman
Ryder, Harry (& wife Annie), Homer cookshop & tool sharpener

Savage, Len, Homer fitting shop
Schroeder, C., Co-op
Scott, Bruce, Hollyford
Scott, Charlie, Co-op party
Scott, Clive (Paddy), Trucks
Scott, Hugh, Co-op
Scott, Ralph, Hollyford
Scully, Bill, Co-op
Scully, Martin ("Digger"), Surfaceman
Searle, Charlie ("Smiler"), Packman
Seidelin, A.G. (Alf), Marian camp
Seyb, Lou, Truck contractor
Shaw, "Curly", Admin., Invercargill
Sheehan, "Hop", Tractor driver
Shirrefs, N., Milford Sound
Shore, S.N. (Stan) (& wife Molly), 1st aid attendant
Shortcliffe, C.J. (Cyril), Hollyford
Sievwright, Jack, Labourer, Homer
Sims, Brian, NZR bus driver
Simmons, Ron, Tunneller
Skelt, P.D., Admin., Invercargill
Skeoch, Stewart, Marian
Smith, George, Bush gang
Smith, Marge, Homer cake shop. Daughter of T.W. (Tom) Smith, now Mrs F.J. Farquhar
Smith, Miss, Schoolteacher, Homer
Smith, Roley, Co-op, Marian
Smith, W.L., Stores, Milford Sound
Smith, Wally, Co-op, Marian
Soper, Ernie, NZR bus driver
Southworth, Jack, Headman Co-op
Spillane, J.M. (Jim), Admin., Invercargill
Spillane, Joe, Tunneller
Stables, George, H., Milford canteen & stores officer
Staunton, Frank J., Homer
Staunton, Tom, (T.J.), Tunneller. Killed in action Sangro River, Italy, 28 November 1943.
Steel, Jim, Tunneller
Stentiford, E.C. ("Bunny"), Tunneller
Stewart, Dick, Co-op
Stringer, Sid, Tunneller

Sturgeon, Frank, Labourer,
Milford Sound
Sullivan, Tim, Bush gang
Suter, Kurt, Guide & cookshop
proprietor, Homer camp
Sutherland, Jim (& wife Beryl), Stores
officer, Homer
Sutherland, Maisie (now Knox), Marian
post office
Sutton, G.D. (George), Buildings,
Invercargill office
Swain, W.D., Co-op
Switalla, F.P. (Frank), Tool sharpener
Symons, Jack, Tunneller
Symons, Samuel Stewart, Tunneller
Symons, S.H.B., Clerk-in-charge,
Invercargill office

Talbot, R. (Dick), Downer & Co
Tangney, M.J. (Mick), Homer
Tattersfield, W.J. (Watty), Marian survey
Tayler, Bill, Trucks
Tayler, G.K., Truck owner driver
Tayler, Jim, Trucks
Tayler, Russell, Trucks
Tayler, Miss ("Topsy"), Staff cook
Taylor, Bill, Downer & Co, manager
Taylor, Bob, Pumpman
Te Raki, Dick, Co-op, Cascade Creek
Thomas, Roy, Stores, Milford Sound
Thompson, Addie, Grocer
Thompson, W.G. (Bill), Co-op
Tierney, J., Milford Sound
Todd, R.H., Co-op
Topping, A.J. (Fred), Eglington Valley
Topping, Ron, Snow plough driver
Torrie, Jim, Hollyford
Tosh, Alex, Co-op
Trebilcock, J., Homer
Tressler, Bill, Grocery salesman
Tretheway, H., Homer
Troon, W.E. (Watty), Carpenter

Tuffrey, Jim, Co-op
Turner, Miss, Nurse, Milford Sound
Tyler, George, Co-op

Vient, W., Milford Sound
Veitch, Bob (& wife), Powerhouse
attendant

Waldron, W.J., Carpenter
Walker, Fred, Lorry owner
Walker, W. ("Grappler"), Hollyford
Walker, Stanley G., Engineer-in-charge
Ward, J.N. (Nick), Head sawyer at mill
Wassell, Bob (R.E.), Tunneller
Watts, H.R. (Bob), Engineer, Milford
Sound & Invercargill
Webb, Roy, Eglinton Valley
Wedderspoon, Andy, Homer cookhouse
Wellman, Bill, NZR bus driver
Wells, Bill, Tunneller
Wells, R. (Dick), Foreman, Milford
Sound
West, ("Walla"), Homer Tunnel survey
Whatson, Bert, Tool sharpener
Whitmore, G.E. (Ted), Clerk-in-charge,
Invercargill
Whitmore, J.H. (Jack), Truck driver,
Hollyford
Williams, Pat (later Mrs Tom Te Au),
Homer cookhouse
Williamson, Bill, NZR bus driver
Williamson, Jack, Truck & NZR bus
driver
Wilson, Alex, Homer
Wilson, Bruce, Engineering asst., Marian
Winn, Reg., Truck driver
Worthington, Mr, First aid man, Marian
Wylie, J., Portal and Co-op

Yarker, Vic, Co-op, Hollyford
Yeo, Eric, Hollyford
Young, W.H. ("Deffy"), Tunneller

1985 APPENDIX

HOLLYFORD VALLEY HEADQUARTERS CAMP 1935/36

This small camp was sited adjacent to the north end of the Marian Camp, and was situated in the narrowest part of the Hollyford Valley, being right at the base of Mt. Christina which towered about 7,000 ft. (2,133 metres) above.

Idyllic in Summer.   *G. J. Jones*

Daunting in Winter.   *G. J. Jones*

[P.W.—5.

WORKMAN'S LEAVING-CERTIFICATE.

PUBLIC WORKS DEPARTMENT,

Holly ford
(Place.)

6 - 10 - , 193 9

This is to certify that Mr. *Edmund Francis Doley*
(Name in full.)

was employed continuously on the *Holly ford — Okuru Road*
(Name of work.)

from 4. 2. 1938, to 6. 10. 1939, and left for the following reason:
(Delete items which do not apply.)

(1) Of own accord.

~~(2) Dispensed with because no further work was available.~~

~~(3) Dismissed for~~
(State reason.)

~~(4) Left to seek further employment with the Department on another work.~~

(5) Any other reason not mentioned above: *Now employed by Messrs Downer & Coy in Homer Tunnel*

D. U. White
Asst Engineer
per ⋈
(Engineer or other Officer-in-Charge.)

ORIGINAL.—Workman's copy.
750 bks./6/37—5245]

In the 1930s jobs were scarce and leaving certificates, references etc. were important.

DAVE GUNN
Dave Gunn whose epic mercy dash is described in Chapter 11.

Courtesy of Murray Gunn

Molly Dwan ("The Maid of the Mountains") visits the Homer Tunnel excavation work in 1935 and wheels a barrow to the tiphead. At the extreme left Tunnel Overseer Tom Smith appears to be critical of the meagre load in the wheelbarrow. Molly's watchdog Roy doesn't appear too happy either.

Jean Auld

Jean Auld with Molly Dwan's dog Roy outside Molly's "East Lodge".   *Molly Dwan*

THE MAID OF THE MOUNTAINS

Recently I travelled by bus from Te Anau to Milford Sound and just before we reached the East Branch Bridge in the Eglinton Valley the driver pointed to the right side of the road to indicate a flat area below a terrace. He told the passengers that for a number of years in the early 1930s a young lady lived on her own at that very isolated spot and that she came to be known as "The Maid of the Mountains". In answer to a question the driver said that beyond this he had no further information.

This story took me back to 1935 when my driver and I would be speeding up the Eglinton Valley on a pay trip and would receive a friendly wave from this lovely young lady, so aptly called "The Maid of the Mountains".

Her name was Molly Dwan and she was invariably accompanied by her dog Roy which I judged to be a collie. Molly lived in a wooden framed tent and ran a small tearoom — also in a framed tent — when the road construction was at its peak in the area. As time went on she planted a beautiful vegetable garden and flower garden, complete with paths and pergolas and a fence to keep out the wild pigs and deer.

This place, which Molly called "East Lodge", became something of a show piece, situated as it was in an extremely isolated area, subject to great climatic variations.

Like the fairy tales of old, this story has a happy ending. Molly left her little home in the mid 1930s to marry Stan Shore, the Medical Attendant at the Homer Tunnel and "they lived happily ever after".

The photos accompanying this little story were loaned to me by Molly's lifetime friend, Mrs Jean Auld, wife of former Hollyford Valley Overseer, George Auld.

THE CENTENARY OF TE ANAU – OCTOBER 1983

These celebrations were attended by many former residents and the local people turned out in a variety of old-fashioned garments appropriate to the occasion. The procession contained a large variety of floats illustrating all stages of development in the area. Of particular interest to visitors was an exhibition of early photos which will be housed in the museum. Former Homer Tunnel Overseer, Jack Dawson, and the author represented the Ministry of Works & Development at this historic function.

Te Anau Centenary Procession — October 1983.   *P. Gregory*

While visiting the Te Anau Centenary Jack Dawson and the author enjoyed a trip around their old haunts and are here seen beside the "sixteen mile peg". These pegs were placed on the Milford Road in the 1930s and in this age of "kilometres" they remain as a feature of interest to tourists.

Author

Well known in Te Anau is Gus McGregor who worked on the Milford Road from 1930 to 1968 when he retired as Overseer. Gus and his wife have worked tirelessly to help improve facilities in the Te Anau district and Gus was recently honoured when he received the Queen's Service Medal "For Public Service".

Gus McGregor Q.S.M. — one of the first "Men of the Milford Road".

Photonews, Wainuiomata

THE HOMER HUT

On page 87 reference is made to this hut which was built to accommodate trampers crossing the Grave-Talbot Pass. On the front of the hut was a noticeboard which read:

GRAVE-TALBOT PASS
WARNING
THIS PASS SHOULD ON NO ACCOUNT BE
ATTEMPTED EXCEPT IN PROPERLY EQUIPPED
PARTIES LED BY EXPERIENCED GUIDES.

The Homer Hut on the right, with former Mt. Cook guide Kurt Suter's hut on the left. Kurt "poses" for his photo while guide Alistair Duthie sits and smiles.   *J. Sutherland*

HOLLYFORD POST OFFICE

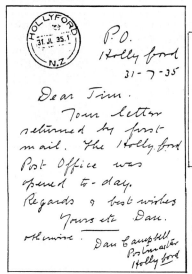

A first day cover sent by Hollyford Postmaster Dan Campbell. (A photo of Dan's Post Office appears on page 23.)

216

1990 APPENDIX No. 1

THE WILLIAM QUILL MEMORIAL

On pages 88 and 91 reference is made to explorer William Quill who fell to his death from the Gertrude Saddle on 15 January 1891.

On 2 May 1932 the PWD at Milford Sound, on behalf of Quill's relatives, concreted a bronze memorial plaque on to a large glacial boulder in the Gulliver Valley below the Gertude Saddle, but some years ago a nephew of William Quill advised me that he had searched the Gulliver Valley but failed to find the plaque. Subsequently extensive enquiries were made without tracing anybody who had seen the plaque on the boulder.

However, I was recently advised by a member of the Southland Tramping Club that a search was to be made for the plaque, and I was able to supply photos of the plaque on the boulder, together with a sketch plan of the Upper Gulliver area given to me by the late John Christie.

Southland Tramping Club members, accompanied by a member of the Quill family

The glacial boulder with the plaque concreted in place and the men who did the job.

Alexander Turnbull Library
D. B. Dallas Photo

A close-up photo of the Quill Memorial Plaque.

Alexander Turnbull Library
D. B. Dallas Photo

visited the Upper Gulliver and positively identified the boulder, but the plaque was missing. However, experienced members of the Club reported that the boulder was subject to avalanches, heavy rock falls and icy conditions. From the state of the growths on the boulder and its situation, it was their opinion that the concrete could well have been loosened by frosts and swept, with the plaque, into the Gulliver River soon after the concreting was done.

Thus ends the saga of the missing plaque, but for the Club members there was more to come. During the afternoon of the search it started to rain and the party camped for the night. Next morning the river was a raging torrent, the party was cut off from the track, and to quote the words of a party member "We had to bush bash our way for four hours to reach the road".

1990 APPENDIX No. 2
(Revised and Enlarged)

JOHN HELLARD CHRISTIE F.I.P.N.Z., M.I.C.E.
Engineer, Mountaineer and Photographer

I first met John Christie in March 1936 when he was Engineer-in-charge of the Milford Road project and we developed a long term friendship.

John was born in Wellington on 29 March 1897. He started work in the Agriculture Department and on 17 April 1917 he enlisted, serving in France, and at one stage was a despatch runner in the trenches. On his return to New Zealand John transferred to the Public Works Dept Head Office in Wellington. He later worked on survey on the Wairoa to Gisborne and North Island Main Trunk railways. In 1922 he commenced engineering studies at Canterbury University and while there, and later at the Waitaki Power Scheme, he made many sorties into Fiordland and the surrounding high country.

He joined the N.Z. Alpine Club in 1933 and held the office of Vice President. He was a foundation member of the Tararua Tramping Club.

John had many mountaineering achievements to his credit, including the third ascent of Mitre Peak, the first crossing of the Homer Saddle, and with three others he made the first known traverse of the mountains and valleys between Lake Hauroko and Dusky Sound, and the return trip via the McKenzie Pass and down the wild Spey Valley.

It was because of his climbing experience and knowledge of Fiordland that John Christie was chosen to lead the Homer Tunnel survey party. This survey was commenced on 18 October 1933 and took seven gruelling months in all kinds of weather to complete the field work alone.

Left to right: John Christie and Mr W. G. Pearce, Resident Engineer, Invercargill, in Eglinton Valley, March 1936.

Author

John H. Christie's original Homer Tunnel survey party 1933.
Left to right: Dave Messent, Arthur Knights, Bill Hall, Bill Harris, John H. Christie, Walla West, Steve Glasson, Gordon Miller, Doug Stewart, Dave Kennedy, John Davies.   *J. H. Christie—courtesy Arthur Knights*

John Christie was short in stature, and of rather light build, but his strength and endurance was incredible and he was renowned for carrying sixty pound packs over rough terrain.

Some years ago John gave me a photo of his first Homer Tunnel survey party but was unable to remember the name of the second man from the right. *The Southland Times* published this photo on 10 May 1986 but readers were unable to identify the man—however, long is the arm of coincidence. Over Christmas 1988 a friend of mine from Auckland visited our home in Linden and he was accompanied by an Auckland friend of his named Arthur Knights. During our conversation Arthur Knights saw a painting hanging on the wall of our lounge and identified it as the Homer Saddle. He then told us that he had been a member of John Christie's first Homer Tunnel survey party. At this point he said that he was the Arthur Knights second to the left in the photo, and what is more, he readily identified the man second from the right as Dave Kennedy, an engineering cadet. In addition he said that he had a large collection of photos taken by members of the survey party, including John Christie; and a number of these photos have been included in this third edition.

On his retirement in 1955 John held the position of Assistant Designing Engineer in the Head Office of the Ministry of Works. In retirement he devoted his time to his greatest hobby which was researching historical engineering projects in New Zealand, and this enabled him to play a major role in advising, editing and proof reading the Ministry of Works' centenary publication *By Design* written by Rosslyn Noonan.

John Christie was engrossed in this historical research and freely made his knowledge available to others. It is a pity he did not write at length of his own experiences, but like many others he found his pleasure in the hunt rather than in the kill.

John Christie died at Kenepuru Hospital on 1 December 1985. He was survived by his widow, three daughters and two sons.

John Christie's 1933 Homer Tunnel survey party shift camp.
Left to right: John H. Christie, John Davies, Arthur Knights, Gordon Miller, Doug Stewart, Steve Glasson.

J. H. Christie—courtesy Arthur Knights

221

1990 APPENDIX No. 3
(Revised and Enlarged)

WILLIAM HENRY HOMER

PUBLISHER'S NOTE: The author continues to receive considerable correspondence about his book and the Fiordland area, as well as additional photos, some of which have been included in this revised appendix. To date, virtually nothing has been known of W. H. Homer's life story but recent research by the author has enabled him to present readers with the following account of the life history of this now famous explorer.

Recently an article in a New Zealand publication claimed that William Henry Homer, after whom the Homer Tunnel was named, built a certain house in Wellington. This caused considerable confusion and I wish to make it clear that the man who built the house was not named William Henry Homer, nor was he any relation of the William Henry Homer after whom the tunnel was named.

However, this incident highlighted the fact that very little has been published about the life of William Henry Homer prior to his discovery of the Homer Saddle in 1889 and this has prompted me to correct the record and as far as possible give a brief outline of the life of W. H. Homer.

William Henry Homer Snr and his wife Mary lived at 16 Burdett Street in the Lambeth area of London in the 1830s. The 1851 census indicated that they had three sons—George William aged 13, William Henry aged 12 and Charles aged 10. This would indicate that William Henry Homer, of tunnel fame, would probably have been born in 1839 and the younger son Charles in 1841. This latter date is correct as Charles is known to have been born on 28 January 1841. Enquiries are underway in an endeavour to obtain a birth certificate of William Henry Homer.

The mother, Mary, died about 1844. The eldest son, George, was married in England but later went overseas and the family never heard of him again. The second son, William Henry, proved to be an adventurer, and at the age of about 16 he "cleared away from home" according to a letter written by his nephew Harry Homer.

The first news his father had from him was a letter to say that he was with the

Charles Homer of Orepuki, brother of William Henry Homer.
Courtesy Mrs Daphne Stewart

Note: Birth certificate now held shows date of birth as 30 August 1838.

MRS CHARLES (MARY) HOMER AND HER 10 CHILDREN

Left to right, back row: Henry James (Mrs Stewart's Uncle Harry), Alice, John Henry, Arthur Gordon.

Middle row: Edith Eleanor, Charles William, Mrs Charles (Mary) Homer, Edward Francis, Mary Elizabeth.

Front row: Clara Isabel, Percy George.   *Courtesy Mrs Daphne Stewart*

British Forces fighting the Russians in the Crimea. At the end of that campaign the young William Henry Homer served in the Indian Mutiny and was present at the fall of Lucknow.

Already this young man was displaying a roving and adventurous spirit which was to become the predominant feature of his whole life. On his return from India the topic of migration to New Zealand was constantly in the news and romantic tales of gold strikes featured prominently. These were more than this young man could resist and in 1862 he decided to emigrate to New Zealand and booked a passage from London to Port Chalmers on the *Sarah M* a sailing vessel of 1018 tons under the command of Captain Raisbeck.

On the day of departure his young brother Charles decided to accompany W. H. Homer to New Zealand. The *Sarah M* arrived at Port Chalmers on 31 December 1862 and next day the two Homer brothers started a new life, in a new country, in a new year.

Gold mining was their first venture but while Charles was contented to work hard and save his money the older brother William Henry developed a passion for exploration and made trips all over the area. On his return he was generally broke and in rags, and for a while his younger brother Charles set him up again, but could see no future in this, and about 1864 they parted company and apparently lost contact with each other for about 14 years.

By the year 1870 Charles had saved quite a bit of money and he decided to return to London. He went first to Melbourne and while waiting for a ship he visited the Working Men's Club where he met a young man named Jack Melanphy who asked him to deliver a letter to his people in London. On reaching London Charles met the

Melanphy family and in 1873 married their daughter Mary Lovett Melanphy in the Church of St. Mary of Lambeth in London.

While living in London they had three children, Mary Elizabeth, John Henry and Alice. The first named, Mary Elizabeth, was the mother of Daphne Stewart who provided much of the information in this account of the Homer family.

In 1877 Charles and Mary Homer decided that there could be a better life for their family in New Zealand and they set sail on the New Zealand Shipping Company vessel *Piako,* a fully rigged ship of 1075 tons and one of the smartest vessels of its day. On this particular voyage the *Piako* recorded its fastest ever trip to New Zealand. It was under the command of Captain Boyd and left England on 20 November 1877 arriving at Port Chalmers on 5 February 1878 after a voyage of 77 days.

The *Piako* was well known on the New Zealand run and made seventeen trips to this country before being sold to foreign owners. In its career it was fortunate to survive two fires at sea.

Leaving Port Chalmers Homer and his family settled in Balclutha and they were living in that town at the time of the big flood in October 1878.

On hearing from his brother and family in Balclutha William Henry Homer suggested that they should shift to Invercargill and this was duly arranged. On 12 July 1879 Charles and Mary Homer had their fourth child, Henry James Homer who was born in Invercargill. It was this son "Harry" Homer as he was known, who wrote a letter dated 8 March 1953 to his niece Mrs Daphne Stewart setting out the details of the early years of William Henry and Charles Homer. Furthermore it was "Harry" Homer who in 1966 organised the erection of the memorial plaque at the Homer Tunnel which reads:

TO THE MEMORY OF
WILLIAM HENRY HOMER
1835-1894
VETERAN OF THE CRIMEAN WAR AND INDIAN MUTINY,
PROSPECTOR, MARTINS BAY SETTLER,
INVETERATE EXPLORER.
Who explored the Upper Hollyford Valley
and in 1889 proposed the driving of a tunnel
beneath the saddle which he climbed
and which bears his name.

This Memorial was erected
by his nephew Harry Homer
and family. 1966

There are no known family records of the doings of W. H. Homer from the time he and his brother Charles parted on the goldfields about 1863-64 until the early 1870s when he is recorded as purchasing a couple of sections in the Jamestown area of the Lower Hollyford Valley and living there for some years. However, stories have been told of a ten-day trip he made in atrocious weather to obtain essential supplies for the local settlers in 1872, and an incident is recorded when he was nearly drowned while on a sealing trip (John Hall-Jones *Martins Bay*). Alice McKenzie, author of *Pioneers of Martins Bay* who lived near Homer in the Lower Hollyford Valley also says "he explored those wild regions, tracing rivers to their sources and finding passes etc". She also outlined the incredible hardships and primitive conditions he endured on his exploration trips.

This certainly confirmed W. H. Homer's way of life as understood by relatives and as later recorded in historical accounts.

As already recorded, Homer was living in Invercargill in 1878-79 when he met up

A close-up of the small plaque on the grave of William Henry Homer.
                              R. E. Knight

Former Homer Tunneller, Eddie Doley, pays his respects at Homer's grave in the Queenstown Cemetery.   *R. E. Knight*

Readers will note that the dates of birth on this memorial plaque and on the plaque at the Homer Tunnel are both incorrect.

A birth certificate now obtained shows that W. H. Homer was born on 30 August 1838 which makes his life span 1838-1894.

with his brother Charles and family. He later shifted to Orepuki for a while and was followed there by Charles and family. In a letter to Mrs Daphne Stewart, her Uncle "Harry" (the son of Charles Homer) told of this trip to Orepuki. The arrangements were that the party comprising Charles and Mary Homer and their children, then numbering four, due to the recent arrival of "Harry" (Henry James) were to travel on horseback. Because of a slip up along the line the horses failed to arrive and the party set off on foot from Riverton.

They had to cover a distance of about 28 miles through slippery bush tracks and along the beaches. On the first night they stayed at Colac Bay and next day reached their destination. Mary Homer carried her new born son "Harry" safely strapped on her back on both stages of the journey.

In due course W. H. Homer returned to Glenorchy in Central Otago where he is known to have spent many years of his life but his brother Charles and family settled in Orepuki and had six more children. The family remained in Orepuki over the years until Charles died on 16 November 1900 and soon after this the family shifted to Dunedin. A brief family tree showing the children of Charles and Mary Homer is appended.

In the years ahead W. H. Homer continued on as a gold prospector, contractor, miner and, as ever, "an inveterate explorer".

Although the term "explorer" would not be applicable to many people in modern times it certainly applied to many in New Zealand in the 19th century. Author Herries Beattie in *Far Famed Fiordland* defined five types of explorers and W. H. Homer certainly fitted type (1) which was "those who go exploring purely and simply for the lure of finding out things".

Over the years Homer made spasmodic visits to Orepuki to see his brother Charles and family. However, very little appears to have been recorded about him until his discovery of the Homer Saddle at the head of the Hollyford Valley in 1889,

Mrs. Daphne Stewart's Uncle Harry, the son of Charles Homer, was 14 years of age when his Uncle William Henry died and remembered his occasional visits to Orepuki, but despite this he did not learn a great deal about W. H. Homer's lifestyle, nor did he or any other member of the family ever recollect having seen a photo of W. H. Homer.

Above left—
The Homer Hut in 1933. In the background (top left) is the lowest part of the Homer Saddle. To the right of this is Talbot's Ladder (see pages 84 and 88).
An interesting feature of the Homer Saddle is that the debris on the Hollyford Valley side extends, in one spot, right up to the top of the ridge. This can clearly be seen in the above photo and the reason for this was explained by PWD Engineer R. W. Holmes in his report of 27 March 1890 where he said "this saddle has been lowered and rendered accessible by an earthquake capsizing the ridge top into the Hollyford Valley".
J. H. Christie—courtesy Arthur Knights

Above right—
Homer Tunnel survey men packing stores in Cleddau Valley. *Left to right:* Dave Messent, Steve Glasson, Arthur Knights. An extract from Arthur Knights' diary of Wednesday, 6 December 1933 reads: "Dave and I with 60 lb (pound) packs, myself with ropes, Dave with Yukon frame. Rained nearly all day. Built iron shelter and big fire to dry clothes. Had tea—tinned mutton, bread and jam. Side blew off the shelter. Had a weka for company. Feel quite good now. Beds made up in old shed. Drew lots for two old stretchers in shed. I lost and slept on galvanised iron sheet between two sacks of coke, a rare and hard contraption. Lights out 11.45."
Photo and diary—courtesy Arthur Knights

Both Mrs. Daphne Stewart and the writer would be very interested to learn whether any readers, particularly in the Orepuki and Glenorchy areas, have any old family records or photos etc. featuring this now famous discoverer of the Homer Saddle.

Despite the fact that little appears to have been recorded about Homer's early days in New Zealand, his discovery of the Homer Saddle and his subsequent campaign through the press to have a tunnel driven below this saddle brought him into prominence. Herries Beattie in his *Far Famed Fiordland* gives extracts from Homer's own account of the trip he made with George Barber when the Homer Saddle was discovered. The following is a brief quote from this, and one can sense the exultation Homer must have experienced. Here are his words: "all the hard work of exploration is over and there is most certainly no other possible route by which the (Milford) Sound can be reached. . . we have headed the Hollyford River, and it is this Saddle or none."

In this same report Homer indicated that what he had in mind at that time was merely "a short tunnel of 100 feet or so" to enable a packhorse to be led through, thus avoiding the acute steepnesss of both sides just below the razor backed Homer Saddle. This tunnel would have been situated near the centre of the saddle and would have been something like 800 feet or more above the eastern (Hollyford Valley) portal of the tunnel as now constructed, and few would have had the nerve to use it.

Following close on Homer's discovery of the saddle in 1889, E. H. Wilmot, a prominent surveyor, with a party including Homer and George Barber visited the area to report on Homer's proposed tunnel, but Wilmot dismissed this as being "quite useless as a route to Milford Sound".

Homer, however, continued his appeals so forcefully that the Engineer-in-Chief of the Public Works Department requested Mr. R. W. Holmes, the District Engineer of the Public Works Department, Wellington, to "furnish a report as to whether or not a particular route existed for the construction of a road to Milford Sound".

In this report Holmes made the following points:
(1) The construction of a road access to Milford Sound was quite feasible.
(2) The best route (at that time) was via the Greenstone Valley (from Lake Wakatipu) up the Hollyford Valley and down the Cleddau Valley on the western side of the Homer Saddle. (As it transpired the construction of the Milford Road from Te Anau to the Homer Saddle avoided the necessity for roading work from Lake Wakatipu via the Greenstone Valley.)
(3) The Homer Saddle was the only practicable way of passing from the Hollyford Valley to the Cleddau Valley.
(4) The Saddle must be tunnelled through.
(5) The scenery up the Hollyford Valley was not to be surpassed for grandeur by any in New Zealand.
(6) The construction of a dray road down the Cleddau Valley to Milford Sound was a very costly undertaking and far in advance of possible requirements.

This "Holmes Report", as it has come to be known, fully supported the two main claims that Homer had been making, namely
(1) That the Homer Saddle was the only practicable way of passing from the Hollyford Valley to Milford Sound.
(2) That the saddle must be tunnelled through to gain access to Milford Sound.

Despite Holmes' confirmation that a tunnel was the answer in providing road access to Milford Sound it was patently obvious to an engineer of his experience that such a stupendous undertaking was unthinkable at that stage and he stressed this later in his report when he made this comment:

"I believe a track up the Hollyford Valley without connection with the (Milford) Sound would alone suffice."

Holmes' statement that the tunnel was "far in advance of possible requirements" was later confirmed by the fact that work on the Homer Tunnel was not commenced until 45 years had passed and it could well have been much later had not the great depression of the 1930s resulted in a start being made on the Te Anau-Milford Sound road in 1929 to provide work for the unemployed. Furthermore, Holmes' estimate of the magnitude of the job was also confirmed when it took John Christie and his skilled party of ten men 16 months from October 1933 just to complete the survey. Furthermore the driving of the tunnel took an additional 4½ years.

On receipt of the Holmes Report Government decided that it was not prepared to proceed with the project, but Homer continued to campaign for a tunnel for the rest of his life.

Homer died at Frankton on 24 January 1894, a single man aged 55, without issue, and was buried in the Queenstown cemetery on 26 January.

Alice McKenzie in her book *Pioneers of Martins Bay* said "only five people

The title of this photo in Arthur Knights' album is "Cleddau Canyon", and what could be more descriptive of these awe inspiring glacial scars throughout Fiordland? The easy approach to the Homer Saddle from the Hollyford Valley side is in stark contrast to the almost sheer drop of 1800 feet from the Homer Saddle to the western portal of the tunnel on the floor of the "Cleddau Canyon".   *Courtesy Arthur Knights*

The quarters of the 1933-34 Homer Tunnel survey party at Camera Flat.
With a base camp subject to such extreme weather conditions little imagination is
required to visualise the rigours of working in the field.　　*Courtesy Arthur Knights*

followed his remains to his last resting place, so little thought did the people of that
time give to men who valiantly endured cold, hunger and hardship to explore the
country of their adoption". But this was said with hindsight after the Homer Tunnel
had been completed and become a world famous landmark.

Perhaps it was that Homer, in his lifetime of exploration, had become a "loner"
and this is possibly borne out by events during his lifetime, first his taking off for the
Crimea without telling his father, and later his decision to leave for New Zealand as a
young man. Other events were his parting company with his brother Charles when the
pair were goldmining in 1863-64, and perhaps the fact that he remained single.

A puzzling point is that Homer's death certificate indicated "parents unknown".
Homer's brother Charles, who lived in Orepuki in Southland, would have been able to
supply correct information and it would seem that Charles may not have been advised
of his brother's death till some time later.

There are many facets of Homer's life story unknown to the descendants of his
brother Charles, and in an endeavour to give them an idea of the family structure Mrs
Daphne Stewart, the oldest living descendant of Charles Homer, has compiled a brief
family tree, copy of which is appended.

In conclusion it can be said that although Homer's dream of a tunnel in his lifetime
was not fulfilled, a number of his contemporaries lived to see the Homer Tunnel
pierced in 1940, and in particular I refer to Mrs. Stewart's "Uncle Harry", a nephew
of W. H. Homer, and to members of the McKenzie family, who along with W. H.
Homer and others, have come to be known as the "Pioneers of Martins Bay".

W. H. Homer's nephew Harry said that when his uncle left Orepuki he said that
his aim was "to put the family name on the map". Today we have the Homer name
perpetuated in the Homer Tunnel, the Homer Saddle, the little Homer Saddle, the
Homer Falls and the Homer Hut (now demolished). Even his dog Monkey's name has
been bestowed on Monkey Flat and the nearby Monkey Creek. Could any man ask
more?

THE HOMER TUNNEL

A view of the Hollyford Valley portal of the Homer Tunnel, guarded as ever, by an inquisitive Kea.

R. E. Knight

A view down the Cleddau Valley from inside the western portal of the Homer Tunnel.
Author

DESCENDANTS OF CHARLES AND MARY HOMER
(NÉE MELANPHY)
Married in 1873 in the Church of St. Mary of Lambeth, London

Mary Elizabeth married Charles Joseph Evans
    Charles John, George Homer, Daphne Consuelo (Mrs Daphne Stewart).
John Henry married Louisa Popham
    John Charles, Andrew William (sometimes known as "Norman"). Ada,
    Gordon.
Alice married Patrick O'Driscoll
    Charles, Matthew, George.
Henry James ("Harry") married Sarah Murdoch
    Henry Lionel, Melvin Melanphy, Maisie Iris, Gordon Robert, Doris Esmay,
    Norman James, Viola.
Charles William married Mary?
    Charles, Mary.
Edward Francis married Kathleen Holland
    Edward, Sidney, Leslie.
Edith Eleanor married Robert Bankshaw
    Mary, Edith, Colin.
Arthur Gordon married Cissie Gilchrist
    Arthur, Leonard, Ashley, Nancy.
Percy George married Sarah Jeffreys (or Jeffries)
    Jeffrey, Mary, George, Elizabeth, Joyce, Jean.
Clara Isabel married Ernest Mains
    Mary, Ngaire, Ernest, Max,

1994 APPENDIX

FIORDLAND REVISITED

EARLY IN MARCH 1992 I received a phone call from Te Anau advising that a "Southland Bush Party" would be held to celebrate the long awaited completion of the sealing of the 76 mile Milford Road from Te Anau to Milford Sound. I was asked whether I, as the author of "The Book" as it is known in Te Anau, and my wife would like to attend this "Bush Party" as guests of the people of Southland. Both Lola and I were thrilled and I informed the caller from Fiordland Promotions that we would be happy to accept the invitation. We both realized that the completion of the road sealing was of major importance to the people of Fiordland as it would result in a great influx of tourists.

Being former Southlanders we knew that there would be a warm welcome for visitors. I was told that the party would be held

on Saturday, 14 March 1992 at "The Divide", which is a Southern Alps mountain pass on the Milford Road, and a spot well known to me. The reason for choosing this site was that it was the area where the final section of road sealing had been carried out.

In due course we were booked to Christchurch on a regular Air N.Z. flight, and would travel via Queenstown to Te Anau. As on the return flight we would have a wait of about two hours at Christchurch, I immediately wrote to my old fishing friend, George Stuffles (see Chapters 18 and 20) and arranged for him and his wife Phyllis to meet us at Christchurch Airport on our return trip. This alerted us to the prospect of many reunions, as visitors were expected from as far away as Auckland and Australia.

At Christchurch we boarded a Mount Cook Airline, twin engined, propeller driven Hawker Siddeley to Queenstown. We then changed to a similar, but smaller plane, and reached Te Anau about midday, after two most enjoyable "bird like" flights.

We were met at Te Anau by Russell Beer, the local manager for Mount Cook Airline, who later handed us over to the care of his wife Jan at their Anchorage Motel.

The next few days involved visits to features in the Te Anau area which were new to us, and we were invited to sign Te Anau's enormous "Doomsday Book". I also spent some hours at Sutherland's "Paper Plus" bookshop autographing new and earlier editions of "Men of the Milford Road". Many other book owners came to the motel to have their books autographed and a few of these were people who had worked on the job in the 1930s.

The callers were often friends or relatives of the men I had known and I was able to answer many questions relating to my former workmates. This to me was one of the most pleasing features of the visit as I recalled many fond memories.

At last came the day of Southland's special event — the "Bush Party" — and the first hint of action was the arrival of Jan Wilson, Chief Executive of Fiordland Promotions, who advised me that Radio Invercargill would be on the phone before long to discuss the events of the day. When this session was over we began to plan for the trip to The Divide.

Frankly, I had some misgivings about this as The Divide is a Southern Alps pass, 85 kilometres north of Te Anau. It is at an altitude of 530 metres, and from my past experience I knew that sudden weather changes were quite possible. However, the gods smiled on us and the day and evening remained fine.

Before we set off, our hostess, Jan Beer, made sure that we were warmly clad, providing me with an extremely nice padded jacket belonging to her husband Russell. On boarding the bus at 4 p.m. I was delighted to find several men I knew from the 1930s so we had plenty of talking points to keep us occupied on the trip into the mountains.

Arriving at The Divide we pulled into a gravelled clearing at the side of the Milford Road where a large marquee had been erected and a "Homer Tunnel Portal" made of timber framing, with a cloth covering, provided an appropriate entrance.

Inside the marquee was a cake seven feet by three feet, with green icing, depicting the final sealing of the Milford Road. It had appropriate models of road sealing machinery and at one end were the words "Milford Road Bush Party". A large number of bales of hay strewn all over the floor of the marquee were being used as seats, but my guess was that they were intended for spreading on the ground in the event of rain.

Another point of interest was the amount, quality and variety of food and drink which was continuously available. I understand that all this was donated by local firms as a practical demonstration of the well-known "Southland hospitality". There was beer, wine, crayfish, and venison served in a variety of forms, as well as the usual party fare.

However, the highlight of the "Bush Party" was the band. For a start it had a striking name — "The Pog-n-Scroggin Bush Band" and its music was as unique as its name. There were about seven players, but the most outstanding was a gentleman who held a long stick which he thumped on the floor with great gusto, at the same time lustily smiting it in the middle with a shorter stick. To add to the din each stick was festooned with bottletops, attached by strings, giving the effect of about fifty tambourines. Another instrument of note was described to me as an "electric bass" and it was contained in a "tea chest" box. It whoofed up the decibels and received plenty of support from a violin and a medley of stomping, singing and clapping. It was a glorious effort, appropriate to the festivities, and when at one stage it proved too much for the generator another had to be substituted.

Strangely enough I cannot recall eating anything of the sumptuous spread other than a few legs off a monstrous crayfish. This was because I was being approached by so many people I had known in the 1936-42 period, or had met on one of our many later holidays spent in Southland. In addition there were a large number of people wanting me to autograph all three editions of The Milford Road which indicated to me that there had been a very active publicity campaign prior to the "Bush Party".

There were also many people present whose parents, grandparents, or friends had worked on the road or the tunnel. They had numerous matters to discuss, and questions to ask. I met a daughter of the well-known Tom Plato, who was the overseer in charge of the highway for many years. We had an interesting chat and

The Scroggin Band and cutting the cake.   *Courtesy Fiordland Photography*

I was brought up to date with events concerning other members of the Plato family. I also met Darrel McGregor who was one of Gus McGregor's sons who had taught me a few points on catching Atlantic salmon and rainbow trout in Lake Te Anau (see page 197).

Another friend of the 1930s was Bob Watts, a civil engineer who was the only former PWD staff employee that I met on this latest trip to Fiordland. We both appreciated that the Milford Road and the surrounding bush had remained virtually unchanged, but Bob pointed to one exception which was the large fleet of parked cars. In our early days very few families owned a motor car, whereas in this modern society car ownership is virtually a necessity.

Another pleasant surprise was to meet a son of Mr Son Tall, a former well-known restaurant owner in Dee Street, Invercargill. Mr Tall Junior mentioned my reference to his father's excellent cusine (see page 70) and asked whether I would like a copy of the 1936 restaurant menu. I welcomed this offer on such a nostalgic occasion. The quality of the cooking had been superb and when one reads such things as "Fried groper and oysters 1/6d (15 cents) occasional references to "the good old days" can be excused.

TALL'S Fish, Luncheon and Supper Rooms.

Phone 1727

MENU

Soup:
(Soup 3d. Extra with 1/- and 1/3 Orders.)

Fish:

FRIED GROPER and CHIPS	-	1/6
FRIED GROPER and EGGS	-	1/9
FRIED BLUE COD	- -	1/6
FRIED FLOUNDER	- -	1/6
FRIED FILLETED SOLE -	-	1/6
FRIED GROPER and OYSTERS	-	1/6
STEAMED FISH (10 Minutes)	-	1/6
SMOKED BLUE COD	- -	1/6
BACON and EGGS	- -	1/9
EGGS and CHIPS	- -	1/6

RETURNS EXTRA.

BOILED EGGS	- - -	1/-
POACHED EGGS on TOAST	-	1/6
SCRAMBLED EGGS on TOAST	-	1/6
TEA and TOAST	- - -	9d.

In Season:

WHITEBAIT and CHIPS	- -	1/6
WHITEBAIT and EGGS	- -	2/3
MUTTON BIRD	- - -	1/9

OYSTERS -	ON SHELL	-	1/3
	FRIED	-	1/6
	STEWED	-	1/6
	CURRIED	-	1/6

OYSTERS and BACON	- -	1/6
OYSTERS and EGGS	- -	2/-

Tea - Coffee - Cocoa

W. SMITH PRINTER, INVERCARGILL

A recent photo of Harold and Lola Anderson.

In due course there was a break in the music and those present were addressed by the Minister of Transport, officials from Transit N.Z., the sealing contractors, the Te Anau Community Board and Fiordland Promotions. All expressed pleasure at the completion of the road sealing which will do so much to boost tourist traffic to Milford Sound.

Then followed the unveiling of a plaque to commemorate the final sealing of the Milford Road, and several "old timers", including the author, took part. The plaque will be affixed to a large rock in the area and reads as follows:

> This plaque
> commemorates the
> completion of sealing
> The Milford Road
> February 1992

The weather remained calm on this eventful evening and festivities continued until quite a late hour.

The next morning we received a fax message of welcome from the directors of Craig Printing Company, Invercargill who are my loyal publishers, and later in the day we had lunch with Colin Smith, Managing Director of the company, and his wife Deidre.

To Lola and me this trip south was a totally unexpected walk down memory lane. We trod familiar ground and once again breathed the clear mountain air. Furthermore, we met people who were young with us in the 1936-42 years. For one whole weekend the clock was turned back. What more could we ask? Our thanks go out to the people of Southland who made it possible.

DISTANCES
(PROCEEDING NORTH FROM TE ANAU)
OF PLACES REFERRED TO IN THIS BOOK

Approximate Mile Peg.	Km	Name of Place
—	—	Te Anau
15	24	Henry Creek
18	29	Te Anau Downs
21	34	Retford Stream (at the lower reaches of the Eglinton Valley)
30	48	Walker Creek (named after engineer Stanley Gordon Walker)
31	50	The Bluffs
33	53	MacKay Creek
36.5	58	Avenue of Disappearing Mountain (seen going north)
40	64.5	Knobs Flat
41	65	Smithy Creek (named after resident engineer Harold Welton Smith)
45	72	Plato Creek (named after overseer Tom Plato of Te Anau)
47	76	Cascade Creek
49	79	Lake Gunn (named after explorer George Gunn)
51	82	Lake Fergus
52	84	Lake Lochie
53	84.5	The Divide (1735 ft, 526m) – head of the Eglinton Valley. The track to Howden Hut leaves here.
54	85	View of Lower Hollyford Valley
55	88	Marian Corner in Hollyford Valley. The site of the old Marian camp and David Gunn plaque. Junction of Lower Hollyford Road.
56	90	Falls Creek – on which are Christie Falls.
59	95	Monkey Flat begins. Straight ahead is Mt Talbot – "New Zealand's most beautiful mountain".
61.75	99	The Forks
62.5	100.5	Hollyford portal of Homer Tunnel (3023 ft, 917m). This is the head of the Hollyford Valley. Site of memorials to those lost in avalanches. Above the portal to the right is the Homer Saddle.
63.25	101	Milford Portal (2620 ft, 789 m). This is the head of the Cleddau Valley.
68	109.5	The Chasm – an awe-inspiring sight.
73.75	118	Milford Hotel with a view of Mitre Peak and Milford Sound.

INDEX

BIBLIOGRAPHY

Herries Beattie: *Far Famed Fiordland.*
                    The Pioneers Explore Otago.
J.H. Christie: *Pioneering the Milford Sound Road.*
Alice McKenzie: *Pioneers of Martins Bay.*

KEY TO LOCATIONS
1   Chasm
2   Grave – Talbot Pass
3   Gertrude Saddle
4   Gulliver Valley
5   Mt Talbot 6945'
6   Grosscut Range
7   Homer Saddle
8   Mt Belle 6850'
9   Mt Christina 8210'
10 Monkey Flat
11 Divide
12 Key Summit 3013'
H   Homer Tunnel
    Old Homer Camp
M   Old Marian Camp
a   Cleddau River
b   Black Lake
c   Forks
d   Falls Creek
e   Christie Falls

Awarua Bay
(Big Bay)

Hollyford R.

Martins Bay

McKenzies

Lake
McKerrow

L Alabaster

MILFORD SOUND

Mt Tutoko 9042'

Mitre
5560 Pk

Milford   Hotel

L Ada   a
                    4
Arthur   1   2 3
R.   7.5. b
               8 .6
Sutherland Falls   Mackinnon   10
L Quill   Pass   Upper Hollyford   12
                   Valley   9 M
MILFORD   d e f
TRACK   L Fergus

Glade House   Dore
              Pass

Route
Burn

L Howden
Howden Hut
L Lochie
L McKellar

L Gunn
Cascade Creek
Plato
Ck
Smithy
Ck
Knobs
Flat

Disappearing
Mountain

MacKay Ck

The Bluffs

Walker Ck

Te Anau Downs
Str

Retford Str

Henry Ck

North
Fiord

Middle
Fiord

LAKE TE ANAU

South
Fiord

Te Anau

Mt
Eglinton
6085'

Nth
Mavora
Lake

Dart
R.

Rees R.

Route
Burn

Kinloch   Glenorchy

Greenstone R.

QUEENSTOWN

Shotover R.

Arro

Kingston

The Wilderness

Mararoa

The
Gorge

Gorge Hill Summit

AKE
MANAPOURI   Manapouri

Oreti

Mossburn

Mataura